ABERDEEN
A JEWISH HISTORY

*105 Years of Congregation B'nai Isaac and
the Community it Brought Together*

SECOND EDITION

ROBIN J. DOROSHOW

JEWISH HISTORICAL SOCIETY OF THE UPPER MIDWEST
MINNEAPOLIS, MINNESOTA
VOLUME 9 FALL 2022
EDITED BY LESLIE MARTIN

ISBNs: 978-0-9993106-3-2 (pbk)

Book cover and interior design by Jess LaGreca, Mayfly Design

Library of Congress Control Number: 2022909670

First Printing: 2022

Printed in the United States of America

This book is dedicated to Bea and Herschel Premack, pillars of Aberdeen's Jewish community and the city of Aberdeen. Their commitment to Congregation B'nai Isaac cannot be overstated. And for all Jewish Aberdonians, past and present.

Bea Wintroub and Herschel Premack Engagement, March 14, 1953 Courtesy of Premack family

Herschel and Bea Premack in front of the Alonzo Ward Hotel building, 104 South Main Street, Downtown Aberdeen, June 26, 2021 Courtesy of author

PREFACE

IF NOT FOR A TRIP that my family took to South Dakota, this book would not exist. I traveled there for the first time in the summer of 2017 with my husband and our two children for two reasons: to visit and speak at the two synagogues I was aware of, and to make the quintessential family trip through the state. Our first Friday night we attended services at Mount Zion Congregation in Sioux Falls. We then visited the Black Hills and the Badlands and spent the next Friday evening at Synagogue of the Hills in Rapid City.

I wrote about my experience at these two synagogues in "Generations," the newsletter of the Jewish Historical Society of the Upper Midwest, where I have been the executive director since December 2016. After it was published, I received a call from Bea Premack of Aberdeen, who informed me that there was a third synagogue in South Dakota: Congregation B'nai Isaac. She said it had been in existence since 1917 and was the only one of the three that was affiliated with the Conservative movement. We had just missed their centennial. Clearly, I had to learn more.

In May 2018, before traveling to Aberdeen, I stopped in Sioux Falls to interview a few community elders, then on to Mitchell an hour away, bound and determined to find the former land of Jewish homesteaders from the 1800s. Two Jewish homesteading colonies arose on farmland southwest of Mitchell in Davison County in what was then Dakota Territory. The first colony, Cremieux, was established in 1882 by Herman Rosenthal, a Jewish immigrant from Kiev. Rosenthal had been the president of a homesteading community in Louisiana, but after devastating floods there, he led a group of 20 Russian families north, to Dakota Territory. They became the core of the Cremieux colony. In their first year, the colonists had success growing rye, oats, barley, flax, and wheat. Subsequent years were not as successful.

The second colony, established just a few miles away, was called Bethlehem Yehuda, and was settled as a commune. It, too, failed and the experiment was over in just a year and a half.[1]

Both colonies were established under the auspices of the Am Olam movement, a movement of "well-educated, secularized, Russian Jewish youth, who emigrated to the United States with the express intent of setting up utopian agricultural communities."[2]

To my dismay, there was absolutely nothing there–not a sign of those adventurous Jews who settled far from home to work the land, with hopes of prospering and living in peace. Not a sign, just farmland. This is the moment I discovered that you can't imagine the distances between places in South Dakota until you're there. You can spend hours on the back roads and still feel as though you've made no progress. Even with a posted speed limit of 80 mph, the trip from the old settlements near Mitchell to Aberdeen takes three hours. I can only imagine the challenges that the early settlers faced traveling in their horse-drawn wagons from town to town for supplies and to sell their crops. I headed for my next destination, Aberdeen.

Aberdeen is the third largest city in South Dakota. With fewer than a million residents in the entire state, Aberdeen, located in Brown County near the northeast corner of the state, counts fewer than 30,000 residents and is exceeded in size only by Sioux Falls and Rapid City.[3]

Courtesy of Dale Bluestein

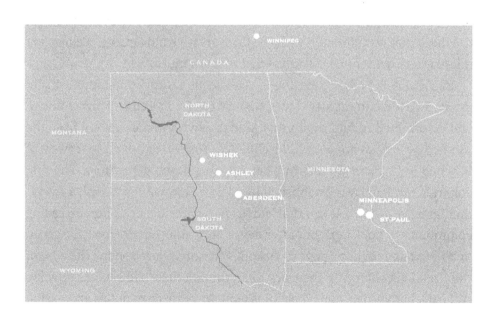

ABERDEEN: A JEWISH HISTORY

I arrived at the home of Herschel and Bea Premack around three o'clock in the afternoon on a Friday, honored that they had invited me to stay with them. Two hours later, we headed for the synagogue. They informed me of the loose rules followed these days, when they never know how many people will show up. If there are simply a couple of people in attendance, they just make *kiddush* (the blessing over wine). But if a few more show up, they hold a *Kabbalat Shabbat* service (Friday evening service welcoming the Sabbath).

We were eight that evening. Herschel Premack has been leading services for many years. He had been taught by the rabbis in Aberdeen and it has served the Jewish community well. He doesn't give a sermon or a formal *d'var Torah* (discussion of the current week's Torah portion) but has a little something to say that's meaningful, a story that relates in some way to Jewish values and tradition. At the conclusion of the service, everyone comes up to the *bima* (pulpit), where small glasses of wine await for kiddush.

After services, the Premacks and I, along with the other five people who had been at services, met for dinner at The Flame, a local restaurant. One of those five was Gail Pickus, who was still living in the Aberdeen home where she and her husband had raised their family. That night, I interviewed Pickus and the Premacks, and continued interviewing the Premacks at breakfast the next morning. Those oral histories, which provided a wealth of information for this book, will be housed in the Nathan and Theresa Berman Upper Midwest Jewish Archives at the University of Minnesota.

It has been my great fortune to be in touch with the Premacks ever since. They came to the Twin Cities in September 2019 on my invitation for the event celebrating the 35th anniversary of JHSUM, at which NPR's Ari Shapiro spoke. Then came the pandemic, which halted our plans to visit for some time.

In the fall of 2020, Bea and Herschel contacted me with a request that JHSUM help document the nearly 105-year history of Congregation B'nai Isaac. They are the last of the once large family of Premacks living in Aberdeen. An arrangement was made to work together, with the synagogue funding the publishing of this book.

My family returned to Aberdeen for Shabbat in June 2021, and in November of that year I returned with Juliana Sellers, JHSUM's development director, and videographer Dale Bluestein, with whom we had been work-ing on video projects for nearly three years. Herschel led us on a tour of downtown, showing us where all the Jewish businesses had been, and took us to a concert at the local college, wanting us to have the total Aberdeen experience.

This project started as a book and is now part of an event scheduled for June 2022, to which Jewish Aberdonians and their descendants have been invited to honor the legacy of the synagogue and Aberdeen's Jewish community. The stories of the Jews who settled in Aberdeen are rich and varied, colorful and meaningful, and will now be preserved as a distinctive part of the fabric of Jewish life in the United States.

INTRODUCTION

THE JEWS WHO SETTLED in what would become South Dakota mostly arrived in the United States in the Third Wave of Jewish immigration. The First Wave were Sephardic (Spanish) Jews, who began arriving in the mid-17th century. The Second Wave, approximately 250,000 German Jews, arrived between the mid-19th century and the beginning of the First World War, overlapping in time with the much larger Third Wave.[4]

More than 2 million Eastern European Jews immigrated in the Third Wave, from the early 1880s to the early 1920s. Most of them were desperate to flee life in the *shtetl* (poor Eastern European Jewish town or village), where they lived under constant threat of pogroms–violent mob attacks against Jews, often with the cooperation of authorities. This New World promised economic opportunity and religious tolerance.[5]

A majority of Third Wave Jewish immigrants remained in New York City and other large cities, many working in the garment industry or as peddlers. Some established stores or other businesses. Jewish organizations on the East Coast wanted to integrate immigrant Jews into other areas of the country to encourage assimilation and reduce anti-Semitism. Some took that route, enticed by an opportunity most had never known: the opportunity to own land, widely denied to Jews in the Old Country.[6]

That opportunity came with the Homestead Act, which was enacted in 1862, bringing hundreds of thousands to the Great Plains to settle and develop the American West, including Jews who eventually came to Aberdeen. While providing unimaginable opportunities for many, the Homestead Act, along with other official U.S. policies, had disastrous consequences for Native American tribes who had lived on these lands for thousands of years.

This book records the stories of Jewish people who came as pioneers to the Upper Midwest, homesteaded, established businesses, and raised their families, the Jews who came later, and the generations that followed.

NAMES, DATES AND OTHER INCONSISTENCIES

Research for this book turned up a few surprises: Jewish-sounding names of people who may or may not have been Jewish; individuals who used a variety of first names; a considerable number of marriages between Jewish men and non-Jewish women; and even a last name spelled one way in the family's newspapers ads for their store but another way on the founder's gravestone.

It was entirely possible to come across siblings having different last names because of differences in spellings, shortened names, Americanized names, and parents' second marriages.

Census records can be quite useful in projects such as this, but they are replete with errors and inconsistencies in names, dates, places of origin, and other details. Information found in census records was checked against as many other records as available, including birth, marriage and death records, newspaper articles, synagogue records, and others.

A final word about names. This book generally refers to married women by their own first and last name when known, except when directly quoting source materials, in which they often were identified as "Mrs." followed by the husband's name.

CHAPTER 1

IN THE BEGINNING

FOR THOUSANDS OF YEARS, the land where Aberdeen would be settled had been home to Oceti Sakowin,[7] known also as Sioux but more commonly called Lakota today, the preferred name of the people.[8]

The first White settlement in Brown County dates to August 1877, and the county grew swiftly thereafter. With about 350 people in 1880, the county mushroomed to a population exceeding 12,000 by the middle of the decade, with about 2,000 residing in Aberdeen.[9]

Dakota Territory became the states of North Dakota and South Dakota on November 2, 1889.[10] Aberdeen has been the county seat of Brown County since 1890.[11]

Aberdeen owes its name to Charles Prior, a railroad pioneer who supervised railroad construction as it expanded into the Dakotas. Prior often named newly established towns and cities after the people with whom he worked and their places of origin. He chose the name Aberdeen in the early 1880s in honor of his boss, Alexander Mitchell, the president of the Milwaukee Railroad, who hailed from Aberdeen, Scotland.[12] The first train came through the town in July 1881 carrying lumber and supplies, followed by the first passenger train, which arrived the next month.[13]

At one time, nine separate rail lines run by four different companies converged at Aberdeen. The tracks came together like spokes on a wheel, meeting at the hub, giving the city its moniker as the Hub City.[14]

The railroad was crucial to the emergence of Aberdeen as an important regional commercial center. At its peak, the Milwaukee Railroad (today Burlington Northern Santa Fe) had 26 passenger trains arriving daily. During World War II, more than 500,000 soldiers were served at the depot's canteen.[15]

Aberdeen was an early center of innovation in telephone communications due to the inventiveness of John L.W. Zietlow, a German immigrant who organized the Aberdeen Telephone Company using his own technology. By the mid-1890s, the city had become the world leader in the number of telephones per person, with one phone for every 6.5 people, compared with 14.5 people in New York City, and 22 nationally.[16] In 1905, Aberdeen became the first city in the nation with an automatic dialing system that allowed callers to make calls without operator assistance. By 1917, the country's first commercial long-distance service became available to customers in Aberdeen, Huron and Watertown, South Dakota.[17] At one time the second largest employer in the city, the company was eventually sold to Northwestern Bell Telephone Co.

Another early Aberdonian of note, albeit for a brief time, was L. Frank Baum. Baum is best known for writing *The Wonderful Wizard of Oz* in 1900, the first of 14 volumes about the Land of Oz. Baum came from upstate New York to Aberdeen, Dakota Territory, in 1888.[18] During his three years

The Land of Oz, Photograph. http://www.aberdeen.sd.us (accessed March 12, 2022)

ABERDEEN: A JEWISH HISTORY

there, he operated Baum's Bazaar, a gift emporium on Main Street, and purchased the weekly newspaper, the *Aberdeen Saturday Pioneer*.[19]

It is widely believed that Baum's writing was influenced by his time in Aberdeen. Notably, the town experienced a big tornado while he lived there.[20] According to local Aberdeen historian, Troy McQuillan, if one digs into Brown County soil, a golden clay is uncovered, which is known as yellow brick.

Try as I might, I did not uncover Jewish connections to booming Aberdeen in the growth of railroads or telecommunications. I held out hope of finding a secret Jewish Baum ancestor, but again, no luck. Although Baum remains legendary in Aberdeen, the only connection between Baum and the city's Jewish community is the Wizard of Oz section of Wylie Park and Storybook Land, for which Bea Premack helped raise funds decades later.

CHAPTER 2
THE EARLIEST JEWS

A MAN NAMED DAN EISENBERG is believed to be the first Jew to have settled in what was then Dakota Territory. Eisenberg operated a trading post on the Missouri River south of what is now Bismarck, North Dakota, around 1869.[21] He later established a dry goods store with advertisements showing up in newspapers as early as 1885.[22] Little else is known of this first Jew to reach the territory.

Settlers with Jewish-sounding names arrived in the region in the 1880s. Haskell, Max, Morris, and Julius Fischbein were merchants in Aberdeen, but extensive research turned up no conclusive evidence that they were Jewish. The same is true for Charles, Isaac, and Louis Appel, who owned a clothing store at that time.

The next verifiably Jewish settlers in the region were David and Anna Strauss and their daughter Carola. David and Anna, both German Jews, immigrated to the United States as part of the Second Wave of Jewish immigration. Before they met and married in Chicago, Anna Graf had served as a private live-in tutor of languages to the children of the famed Rothschild family. Earlier, she had taught German and French at Miss Pinckney's, a private school in Milwaukee, Wisconsin.

The Strausses established their first home and their first clothing business in Vinton, Iowa. A traveling salesman mentioned to David Strauss that Pierre and Aberdeen, South Dakota, and Crookston, Minnesota, were potentially fertile territories for new businesses. He visited and ultimately preferred Aberdeen.[23] He described the town to Anna as small and primitive, and expressed hesitation about bringing her and their child to such a place. In an oft-related story, it is said that Anna Strauss regarded this information as unimportant and wanted only to know whether the people in Aberdeen were nice. With David replying in the affirmative, the decision was made, and off they went to Aberdeen, most likely the first Jews to settle there.[24]

David Strauss opened the Golden Eagle Clothing House to great fanfare.

Strauss, "The Golden Eagle Clothing Man," advertisement, *Aberdeen Weekly News*, September 17, 1896

Strauss, The Golden Eagle Clothing Man
Red Front Corner, Aberdeen S.D.

Has bought for fall and winter wear the finest and best line of Men's and Boy's Suits and Overcoats ever shown under one roof. Strauss has taken special care to bring back to Aberdeen, such bargains that no other reliable clothing house is able to undersell him.

One look into our mammoth establishment will convince the most skeptical buyer that Strauss is master of the situation as to reliability of goods and lowness of price. $6.50, $8 and $10 will now buy a grand suit of clothes or overcoat. You must see our $10 Black Sack or Cutaway Frock Suits, as good as any $15 suit in the market. Strauss has also been able to buy lots of bargains in Underwear, Caps, Gloves and Mittens.

Strauss is going to sell you your Fur Coat; there never was a finer line of Fur Coats shown in Aberdeen, and you'll have the benefit of our low prices, which means a good overcoat for little money.

"The Golden Eagle Clothing House Opens Wide Its Doors to the Public" read the headline of an article in the Aberdeen Weekly News on October 7, 1887. It sounded more like 4th of July than a store opening. The Hub City band, wearing beautiful uniforms, led a procession as they played, and were followed by banner bearers and finally by David Strauss himself behind a "high spirited team" of horses. Inside the store, Anna Strauss presented a souvenir of the occasion to each guest.[25]

The store offered all manner of men's and boys' furnishings, from neckwear to overcoats.

During their decades in Aberdeen, the Strauss family was involved in the general community and appeared regularly in the local newspapers, often in the society pages but also in news about their businesses and land purchases. Advertisements for the store appeared often.

An April 1893 newspaper item reported on the arrival in Aberdeen of Mrs. S. Guggenheim to visit her sister, Anna Strauss.[26] A society page article in August 1906 reported on a "chafing dish" party hosted by Carola Strauss, David and Anna's young daughter.[27]

Anna Strauss was a charter member of the Tourist Club, Aberdeen's second study group, and volunteered in the community throughout her life. David Strauss was a member of the Chamber of Commerce and the Commercial Club, vice president of the Citizens Trust and Savings Bank, and a leader in the Aberdeen business community.[28]

The store operated in various downtown locations over the years and, in 1916, Strauss changed the business name to Strauss Clothing

Strauss, "NOTICE," *Aberdeen Daily News*, November 27, 1932

House and built his own building next to the Alonzo Ward Hotel on South Main Street.[29]

The business thrived for 30 years until David Strauss's death in 1932.[30]

Although the family was not involved in Aberdeen's organized Jewish community,[31] of five charitable organizations receiving gifts via David Strauss' will, three were Jewish organizations.[32]

While no photos of David or Anna Strauss could be located for this book, the entire family rests for eternity at the Lakewood Cemetery in Minneapolis, Minnesota.

Courtesy of author

Courtesy of author

ABERDEEN: A JEWISH HISTORY

HELEN GRAF STRAUSS

Helen Strauss was born to David and Anna Graf Strauss in Aberdeen in 1899, twelve years after her parents and older sister, Carola, had arrived. She remembered her parents speaking of Aberdeen's wooden sidewalks and muddy streets at the time of their arrival and recalled a happy childhood in Aberdeen: Halloween fun, playing games, and watching for the iceman to arrive with a chunk of ice for the icebox.[33]

She said her parents never encountered any anti-German sentiment during World War I (although she said that others may have), nor was she aware of any animosity toward her parents because they were Jewish.[34]

Asked whether her father was a religious man, she said yes but "not by church attendance." Her parents were not involved in the establishment of the synagogue. Nevertheless, she noted, her father was raised quite religious and each of his business ledgers started with the words, "With God." [35]

Like her parents, Helen Strauss was involved in many organizations and clubs during her lifetime. Quoted in an article at the age of age 93 she recalled being the only Jewish student at Central High School in 1914.[36]

Neither Helen nor her younger sister, Elinor, married or had children, and they lived the remainder of their lives in Aberdeen. Carola married a businessman from Chicago by the name Hiram Jacobs in 1913.[37] They settled in Mitchell, South Dakota, and had two daughters. Carola died in 1928 and was buried at Lakewood Cemetery in Minneapolis.

When Helen died in 1998, her memorial service was held at Congregation B'nai Isaac.[38] She and Elinor were also buried at Lakewood Cemetery.

A SHORT MEMORIAL SERVICE WILL BE HELD IN
TRIBUTE TO
HELEN GRAF STRAUSS
AT CONGREGATION B'NAI ISAAC SYNAGOGUE
202 NORTH KLINE. ABERDEEN. SD
MONDAY. JUNE 22. 1998
1:00 IN THE AFTERNOON

"A Short Memorial Service," *Aberdeen Daily News*, June 14, 1998

Charles Goodman and Morris Kastriner also arrived in Aberdeen in the 1880s and were in the clothing business together. According to Aberdeen's city directory from 1887-88, their store was located at 206-½ Main Street, and Goodman boarded with Kastriner.[39]

The business was called New York One Price Clothing House.[40] Between March 1888[41] and the dissolution of their partnership in 1890,[42] Goodman and Kastriner ran hundreds of advertisements in the local newspapers.[43]

A Dollar Saved Is a Dollar Made !

And This is the Place to save it.

Yes, you can save many a dollar by buying your Men's, Boys and Children's Clothing, Underwear, white, percale and flannel Shirts, Hats and Caps, Gloves, Trunks and Valises at the

Sole agents in South Dakota for the

The Best Hat in the World, the

New York One Price Clothing House,

GOODMAN & KASTRINER. Props.

Three doors north of P. O.   ABERDEEN, S. D

New York One Price Clothing House, "A Dollar Saved is a Dollar Made!" advertisement, *Aberdeen Daily News*, August 18, 1889

Grand Spring Opening !

Clothing! Clothing!

JUST RECEIVED

500 Men's Sack & Frock Suits

NOBBY CHEVIOTS,
CASHMERES,
WORSTEDS,
SATINETS

FROM $5 TO $25.

Immense Line of

NOBBY SPRING PANTS !

From one to eight dollars.

Dunlap and Stetson Hats !

Prices Guaranteed to be Rock Bottom.

NEW YORK

One Price Clothing House,

Goodman & Kastriner, Props.

Branch at Groton.   ABERDEEN, DAKOTA, North of P. O.

New York One Price Clothing House, "Grand Spring Opening," advertisement, *Aberdeen Daily News*, March 14, 1888

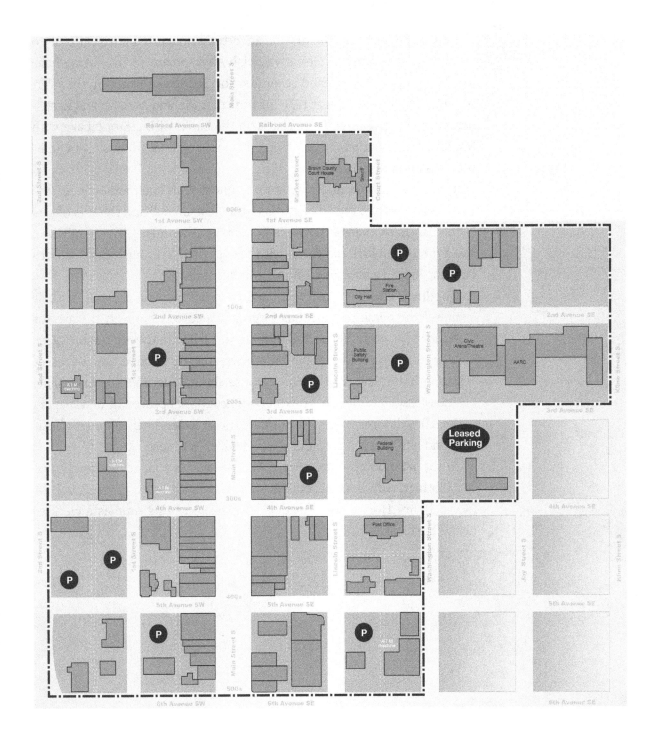

Courtesy of Troy McQuillan

Newspaper announcements and advertisements provide a glimpse into the lives of these and other early Jewish Aberdonians for whom we have no photographs or first-hand accounts. For example, an entry in the "Personal" section from August 1889 informs that Mr. and Mrs. Morris Kastriner would be spending the Sabbath on the banks of Big Stone Lake with Mr. Charles Goodman,[44] shedding light on a personal friendship in addition to a business partnership.

The personal joys and sorrows documented in such announcements include the birth of twin daughters to the Kastriners,[45] and the loss of one of the babies in infancy during their years in Aberdeen.[46] The family also had a run of bad luck thereafter with fires in their later businesses in both Groton, South Dakota, and Duluth, Minnesota.[47]

Goodman and Kastriner remained friends following the end of their business partnership,[48] and Kastriner returned to Aberdeen to care for Goodman during an illness.[49] Goodman was living in the Sherman House, located on the east side of South Main Street at 3rd Avenue, and was associated with the New York Clothing House almost a decade after ending his business association with Kastriner.[50] The store appeared in newspapers under a few different names over the years until Goodman closed his business and left Aberdeen around 1900. He died in Chicago in 1907.[51]

In the 1889-90 city directory, a Michael G. Levy made an appearance as a clothier, with both his business and residence listed as the Excelsior Block. Henry Horwitz also made his entrance at this time as a clerk at Levy's business.[52]

CHAPTER 3

GROWTH IN THE GENERAL AND JEWISH COMMUNITIES

THE MID-1880s to the early years of the new century were a period of rapid growth and transition in Aberdeen. It was incorporated as a town in 1882 and as a city the following year[53] with a population of just under 3,200 that grew to more than 4,000 by 1900. The population swelled to nearly 11,000 in 1910, and more than 15,000 by 1920.

As the general population grew, so too did the Jewish population. Many Jews who came to Aberdeen established businesses and settled in to raise their families, although some stayed for only a few years.

Charles Goodman's business activity in the early 1900s was mentioned in the late-in-life memories of a Jewish woman of Aberdeen, Goldie Smilowitz Krystal, who was born to a homesteading family in McIntosh County, North Dakota. Her family moved to Ipswich and then Aberdeen, where she spent her early years. Her sister, Frances "Fan" Smilowitz, married Julius "Udell" Premack. They were the parents of Herschel, who still lives in Aberdeen.[54]

Krystal recalled that Isadore and Hannah Kraywetz had come to Aberdeen by 1909 and established Metropolitan Tailors.[55] My research turned up sad story after sad story of the Kraywetz family.

THE KRAYWETZ FAMILY

News accounts tell us that I. Krawetz was known at different times as Isadore,[56] Isaac,[57] Israel,[58] but most often, simply I. Krawetz.[59]

Born in 1876, he immigrated before the turn of the century and became a naturalized citizen while living in Stearns County, Minnesota, in the early 1900s. Oddly, his naturalization record lists his first name as Eke,[60] the only record in which that name appears.

Newspaper accounts indicate that young Kraywetz had a reputation as a frequent litigator. An article in the *St. Paul Globe* from 1895 reported on a case in Ramsey County District Court in which Kraywetz, not yet 20, was strongly rebuked by the judge for repeatedly lying under oath. This article reveals not only a misunderstanding of the Jews who came from Russia (referring to them as "Cossacks"), but a strong prejudice against them on the part of the judge as well as the newspaper.[61]

By the early 1900s, Kraywetz was the Stearns County representative for the Leo Zekman Company, a furrier in Minneapolis.[62] In 1900, he became engaged to Fanny Deutsch of Minneapolis[63] and they married in February 1901 in Minneapolis.[64] Their daughter, Beatrice, was born in November that year.[65] Tragically, Fanny died a few months later.[66]

Just days after Fanny's death, the *St. Paul Globe* reported more heartbreaking details of their lives. When Isadore Kraywetz emigrated from Russia to the United States, he left Fanny Deutsch behind. They had been close since childhood. After working for some years, he finally had enough money to send for her to join him in St. Cloud, Minnesota. (By the time of

"Jews of City Perfect Organization of Synagogue at Meeting Sunday." *Aberdeen Weekly News*, January 25, 1917

Jews of City Perfect Organization of Synagogue at Meeting Sunday

Aberdeen members of the Jewish faith perfected the organization of a synagogue to be known as the Congregation of the Sons of Isaac at a meeting in Maccebee hall Sunday afternoon and on Monday made application to Pierre for a charter granting incorporation as a religious body.

Plans for the proposed temple to be erected in this city were discussed and a committee appointed to find temporary quarters for the holding of religious services.

The following are the officers of the congregation: President, Ben Brussel; vice president, Isador Predmesky; secretary, I. Kraywetz; treasurer, Sam Calmenson. Members of the board of directors are: William Riunick, Harry Abramson, N. Becker, Max Anton.

their engagement, her family had also immigrated and were living in North Minneapolis.) On her transatlantic voyage, Fanny developed a severe cold, which eventually turned into consumption, of which she eventually died.[67]

Isadore Kraywetz then married Hannah Jacobson, a Swedish immigrant, in 1908.[68] Perhaps seeking a fresh start, they moved to Aberdeen in 1909. Their son, Rudolph, was born there in 1909, and eight-year-old Beatrice, sometimes known as Bertha, was also living with the family at that time.[69]

Isadore Kraywetz was instrumental in the founding of Congregation B'nai Isaac. In 1917, he led the campaign for the relief of "Jewish war sufferers" in Europe,[70] and served as secretary of the congregation.[71] Interestingly, I did not find records of any involvement in the Jewish communities where he had lived before. Hannah Kraywetz became involved in the Aberdeen community through an organization called Prairie Flower Camp[72] and served as secretary for the Jewish Ladies Aid, of note because she was a recent immigrant from Sweden and there is no indication that she was Jewish.[73]

Metropolitan Tailors, "Easter Greeting," advertisement, *Aberdeen American*, April 11, 1909

The Kraywetzes' business, Metropolitan Tailors, appeared frequently in the newspaper with both news and advertisements, and seems to have thrived for many years.

Kraywetz published ads entitled "Talks on Tailoring" in 1910, in which he addressed readers in a personal, conversational manner.[74]

Later, however, the Kraywetzes' business interests–Metropolitan Cleaners and Consumers Clothing Co., which operated a store called Economy Clothes Shop–ended in bankruptcy.[75]

Troubles seemed to follow this family. They moved to Omaha, Nebraska, where they again met with tragedy. Their son Rudolph died at age nine after being hit by an automobile.[76] During his brief life, Rudolph had been involved in music and was mascot of Aberdeen's Modern Woodmen of America camp in 1916.[77]

Whether going by Isadore, Isaac, Israel, Eke, or I., the years he spent in Aberdeen, when he was active in the fledgling Jewish community[78] and running what appeared to be a successful business with Hannah,[79] seem to have been the happiest.

"Rudolph Harold Kraywetz, mascot of Camp 2094, Aberdeen, S.D." *Modern Woodman*, August 1916, Vol. 33, No. 8

Rudolph Harold Kraywetz, mascot of Camp 2094, Aberdeen, S. D. He was 7 years old August 6, and his father writes that he intends to have him grow up and become a staunch and loyal Modern Woodman. His father has been a Modern Woodman for twenty years, and he is almost as proud of the Society as he is of his boy. His young son is something of a musician and is taking lessons on the violin. We wonder how many foresters teams have mascots, and just suggest that if one hundred of them would send in the photograph of their mascot, we might publish a page of halftones of those boys who are to make future Modern Woodmen.

A 1920 U.S. Census report gives Hannah's occupation as seamstress.[80] Mr. Kraywetz, then using the name Isaac, died in Omaha just before his 52nd birthday.[81] After marrying Charles Diehl in 1926,[82] Hannah lived the remainder of her life in the Omaha area, meeting her death in the same manner as her son, Rudolph, after being hit by an automobile in 1959.[83]

THE EARLY PIONEERS MOVE ON, AND NEW FAMILIES ARRIVE

As indicated in the 1903-04 city directory, many of those who had settled in Aberdeen, established businesses, and become part of the city's pioneering Jews had already left the city. Goodman and Kastriner were nowhere to be seen, and neither was the New York One Price Clothing House.[84] Of those who remained, David and Anna Strauss were still active in business and the general community.[85]

About 15 Jewish families lived in Aberdeen around 1910,[86] many of whom were merchants. These families included the Calmensons, Holtzes, Sudows, Sonofskys, Machovs, Salinskys, Amdurs, and Strausses.

In 1910, Isaac Salinsky married Leona Gold of Brooklyn, New York.[87] Salinsky, who had owned the New York Store in both Deadwood and Rapid City, moved with his wife to open Aberdeen's branch,[88] offering women's ready-to-wear clothing.[89] Despite the name, there is no evidence connecting this store to Goodman and Kastriner's New York One Price Clothing Co.

By 1911, Sidney Abrams and Sam Calmenson each had clothing stores in Aberdeen, and in the next two years, a small boom brought even more Jewish merchants: Harry Abramson, who had Sherman Dry Goods; Benjamin Brussel, who was in the men's apparel business; William Ribnick, one of the owners of Western Hide and Fur; and Sam Salinsky at the New York Store with Isaac Salinsky. In addition, John Salinsky worked for the railroad and Nathan Calmenson worked as a clerk. Many of these names would later be prominent among the founders of Congregation B'nai Isaac.[90]

More Jewish families arrived and established themselves in Aberdeen in the late teens and in the decades that followed.[91]

The Sunday edition of the *Aberdeen American* newspaper on April 20, 1919, provided an overview of various Aberdeen businesses, including

Western Hide and Fur, established in 1909 by W. and J. Ribnick, F.M. Stein, and J.M. Ribnick. The business was described as one dealing in hides, furs, wool, pelts, and tallow, shipping exclusively to tanners and brokers around the country. Described as "progressive businessmen," they also had a location in Devils Lake, North Dakota, run by F.I. Ribnick.

THE CALMENSON FAMILY

Ben Calmenson was born in Aberdeen on May 25, 1918. His mother, Rose Beaver Calmenson, was born to Russian Jewish immigrants in Wisconsin, and his father, Sam Calmenson, to Russian Jewish immigrants in St. Paul.[92]

In a written history, Ben reported that his father came to Aberdeen alone in 1911 and purchased Palace Clothier,[93] which then became Calmenson Clothing Co. at 22 South Main Street.[94] Newspaper articles, however, indicate that Calmenson already had a presence in Aberdeen as early as 1907: he attended a funeral[95] and was a groomsman in a wedding that year. Of note, the wedding was held in Aberdeen's Episcopal Church,[96] indicating that Calmenson was well integrated into the general community very early on.

Rose and Sam Calmenson, undated photo, Courtesy of Margie Calmenson Howell

A 1913 newspaper article[97] reported on Sam's marriage to Rose as well as their honeymoon, during which he rather unfortunately contracted poison ivy.[98]

Another sign that Sam Calmenson was integrated into Aberdeen's general community is news of his golf games at the Country Club in 1913,[99] with Rose joining in soon thereafter.[100]

The Calmenson Clothing Co. did well and in 1916 the size of the store was doubled.[101] The following year, it became the exclusive carrier of the Aberdeen Country Club collar, made by Arrow and named by Calmenson himself.[102]

Max Rosen worked at the Calmenson's store for 31 years. For a few years just prior to his death, he owned the Shamrock Bar, which was located behind the Calmenson store.[103] Originally from New York City, he married native Aberdonian Irma Hirsch. They were members of

Exterior, Calmenson Clothiers, Hatz Block,
Courtesy of Susan Calmenson.

Interior, Calmenson
Clothiers, Courtesy of
Susan Calmenson

the synagogue, and both were involved in many of the city's civic organizations. Irma was particularly active in the Delphian Society, a national organization that promoted the education of women.[104]

In 1916, the Calmenson Clothing Co. sponsored a local baseball team, Calmenson's Colts, which enjoyed many seasons of play.[105]

By the summer of 1917, Calmenson's Clothing had branch locations in Watertown, South Dakota, and Montevideo, Minnesota[106]

Sam Calmenson was a committee member of the Commercial Club as early as 1909.[107] By 1920, he was serving on its board of directors. The next year, a fourth Calmenson Clothing Co. location opened in Milbank, South Dakota.[108]

A November 1921 edition of the *Aberdeen American* carried an article titled, "Calmenson the Style Center of Good Clothes," with the subtitle, "A Successful Man Always Known By the Condition of His Wearing Apparel." This glowing article, with its over-the-top praise, may well have been promotional material provided by the company.[109] "There is not an institution in the Great Northwest," it read, "better equipped to tender satisfactory service from the standpoint of providing the necessities for the well-dressed man than the Calmenson Clothing company,"[110] which "commands one of the top-most positions in the commercial world."[111]

Catering not only to the businessman, the store carried attire for the working man, young man, boys, and children, in addition to trunks, bags and suitcases.[112] The store even had on display for a short time a hat worn by Tom Mix,[113] the then popular star of cowboy movies who was said to be half Jewish.[114]

Ben Calmenson remembered that his father was involved in many social clubs. He was a Shriner and the vice president of the Tri-State Fair.[115]

Rose Calmenson was active in Order of the Eastern Star (OES), a women's organization affiliated with the Masons.[116] Her obituary from 1944 in the *Aberdeen American* mentioned her volunteer work with the American Red Cross, the Women's Club, Hadassah, Ladies Aid, and Congregation B'nai Isaac.

Sam Calmenson played a large role in the acquisition of the synagogue building which will be described in Chapter 5.

Calmenson home, 902 S. Jay Street, Aberdeen, undated photo, Photo courtesy of Margie Calmenson Howell

THE PREDMESTKY FAMILY

The Predmestky family had a number of clothing stores in Aberdeen. Different spellings of their name appear in articles[117] and ads and also as "Pred's" Popular Price Store.[118]

That store was founded in 1916 by Isaac Predmestky, who was also known as Isadore. He had emigrated from his native Russia by way of France, where he met the French-born Rebecca Jacobson, whom he married. Records indicate that some of their children were born in Russia, some in France, and some in the United States. Abraham "Abe," the fifth of their seven children, was born in Nebraska. Abe shortened his last name, married Sonia Bloom Pred, served in the Army in World War I, and ran the family store with his son Jack. Abe Pred will also be seen in later chapters. Their other children were Esther, Eva, Israel, and Dan.

At first, the store offered women's and men's attire, but a 1917 article announced that the men's department had closed. Located at 312 South Main Street, the store claimed to have the basics and "a hundred and one other things for the gentler sex," and was described in an article as one of the "most liberally patronized establishments in our city."[119]

Referring to the Predmestky sons as "chips off the old block," the article said that I. Predmestky, Jr., A.D., and B. Predmestky were in business with their father at the Aberdeen store, and that A.D. and B. ran the family's newly established location in Wakefield, Nebraska.[120]

Jews who settled elsewhere in the region became part of the extended Aberdeen Jewish community. In towns such as Bowdle, Ipswich, Hosmer, and many others, they were often the only Jews in town.[121]

"Formal Spring Announcement," advertisement, *Aberdeen American*, March 18, 1917

"Buy Liberty Bonds Today," advertisement, *Aberdeen American*, September 28, 1918

CHAPTER 4

THE JEWISH
HOMESTEADERS

WHILE JEWISH IMMIGRANTS were establishing businesses in Aberdeen and nearby towns, and seeding its organized Jewish community, another group of Jewish immigrants was undertaking an entirely different type of settlement to the northwest in McIntosh County, North Dakota.[122]

What drew them was the prospect of owning land, made possible by a federal policy enacted 40 years earlier: the Homestead Act of 1862. This appealed to some Jewish immigrants because, by law, most Jews in Eastern Europe were forbidden to own real property, one of many limitations on their economic and personal opportunities.[123]

The Homestead Act provided 160 acres to any citizen or future citizen who filed an application, paid a small fee, and agreed to "improve" the land in some way, whether farming or establishing a residence or other building.[124] The term of "improvement" was for five years uninterrupted, although a much costlier early buyout was available for those who didn't want to remain on the land.[125]

Beginning in the early 1900s, about 400 mainly Third Wave Jewish immigrants settled on 85 farms in McIntosh County near the towns of Ashley and Wishek, in the southeastern part of North Dakota. These two towns, 80 and 100 miles northwest of Aberdeen respectively, became home to two Jewish communities.[126] Many traveled to the untamed prairie shortly after arriving in the United States, but others were said to be land seekers who had immigrated earlier to Minneapolis and New York.[127]

As homesteaders, the Jewish immigrants came late in the game, arriving in the early part of the 20th century. By that time, their gentile neighbors had already claimed the best farming lands, leaving the worst parcels in hilly sections.

Known as Volga Germans, their neighbors referred to these areas as "Judenberg" or the Jewish Hills.[128] South Dakota had a significant population of these ethnic Germans, whose ancestors had been invited to farm the land in Russia. Due to increasing ethnic hostility they, too, had fled for many areas in the Upper Midwest.[129]

Around the same time, in 1900, the Baron de Hirsch Fund, formed in New York by members of the already established German-Jewish community, created the Jewish Agricultural and Industrial Aid Society and the Industrial Removal Office to resettle Third Wave Eastern European immigrants to areas outside of large, crowded cities. A similar organization was established in Chicago called the Jewish Agriculturists Aid Society of America. These aid organizations were created at least in part out of fear that anti-Semitism could be stoked by large concentrations of Jews in big cities. There was also a fear that such large communities might not acculturate to American life.[130]

These organized efforts contributed to a large influx of Jews to the Dakotas in 1903-1908. The areas around Ashley and Wishek became home to perhaps the largest concentration of Jewish homesteaders in the Dakotas.[131] With an estimated 1200 Jewish individuals on 250 farms in 1910, North Dakota had the fourth largest number of Jewish farmers in the United States.[132] Their experiment in farming was relatively short-lived with only traces remaining by 1920.

Jewish homesteader, Ida Parkansky, stakes a claim. "At the Land Office," *Bismarck Daily Tribune*, August 2, 1907

At the Land Office.

The following entries were made at the land office yesterday: Edward R. Lueck of Zumbrota, Minn.; Warren McMullen of Henry, S. D.; Edwin Hermanson of Bowdon; Lillie Kory of Coldwater; Ida Parkansky of Ashley; John Stewart of Stewartsdale.

ABERDEEN: A JEWISH HISTORY

KEEPING KOSHER ON THE PRAIRIE

Life wasn't easy for the homesteaders. For observant Jews, keeping kosher (following Jewish dietary laws) and observing the Sabbath and holidays were of utmost importance. Jewish farm families had to be enterprising to keep the religious commandments. This often meant having kosher meat only when a *schochet* (Jewish ritual slaughterer) was in the area. Jewish farm families sometimes traveled great distances to gather with other Jews for religious services.[133]

Despite the many challenges, these homesteading Jews maintained their traditions and became active members of their communities. In addition, and remarkably, they were very quickly accepted into both the business and social spheres of the area. The marriage of Jewish immigrant Louis Rubin was announced in local society pages just a few years after his arrival. As president of Ashley's board of trustees, Rubin was, in effect, the town's mayor.[134] Nathaniel Auerbach was described as one of Wishek's progressive businessmen, and his bride, Helen Hess, as the daughter of the "venerable" Rabbi Julius Hess, who would become Aberdeen's first rabbi.[135]

The hardships of farm life coupled with the additional requirements of an observant Jewish life ultimately led to the rapid depopulation of rural areas after 1910 and the decline of Jewish homesteading activity in the region. By selling their homestead property, many Jewish families were able to parlay the proceeds into businesses such as general stores, which allowed them a chance to earn a living in a more familiar way.[136]

In addition to the Jewish homesteaders who lived in McIntosh County, several Jewish merchants owned and operated stores of various types in Ashley, Wishek, and other small towns in the vicinity. For many years before they had resident rabbis, area Jews gathered informally for holidays with community members serving as lay rabbis, and socialized on farms and in homes in town.

"Jews Take To The Farm," *Wahpeton Times*, March 21, 1907

The State DAY BY DAY

JEWS TAKE TO THE FARM.

Colony in Ashley, N. D., Prospering at Beginning of Third Year.

The Jewish problem is beginning to solve itself. The practicality of Zionism is to all indications still far distant, but those who treat the Jewish problem as an economic one are already seeing results.

The Jewish colony which was started near Ashley, N. D., in September, 1905, is prospering wonderfully. At that time twelve families moved to the colony, and since then it has grown rapidly. There are now thirty-two Minneapolis families there who have taken homesteads. They are proving daily that the Jews make as good farmers as students, vindicating that they are willing workers, and many of them would have long been "tillers of the soil" had they but had the opportunity.

Louis Wolfson and Isidor Auerbach were sent to New York city as delegates from this colony in order to obtain aid from the Jewish and Industrial Aid society, whose headquarters are there.

They remained there three weeks negotiating with the business committee, and are to be congratulated on their success. They obtained $27,000 to help the colony and the settlers.

Last spring they found it difficult to break in the land, for they were hampered, not having sufficient machinery and horses. But next spring they will be fully equipped.

They have a shochet there, and services were held during the holidays last fall

HOMESTEADERS' SYNAGOGUES

By 1911, the Jews of Ashley had organized a congregation, and by 1914, the Jewish Chautauqua Society of America had dispatched Rabbi Julius Hess to serve the Jewish communities of Ashley in McIntosh County and Wing in Burleigh County, North Dakota.[137]

In Ashley, Louis Rubin purchased a building that had previously been used as a Baptist church and moved it to the north side of town. The Jewish community converted it to a synagogue in 1917, calling it Beth Itzchock (House of Isaac).[138]

The McIntosh County Jewish community was substantial enough in the second decade of the 20th century to employ two resident rabbis. Rabbi M. Ostrowsky arrived shortly after Rabbi Hess to serve Wishek's Jewish community. By 1916, the two rabbis had exchanged pulpits, with Rabbi Hess in Wishek and Rabbi Ostrowsky in Ashley.[139]

Although the Ashley synagogue was maintained for two decades, few Jews remained in the area, and in 1938 the building was sold, and has been used as a private residence ever since.

Wishek's Congregation Beth Joseph (House of Joseph) was dedicated in 1916 and at its height had around 40 families.[140] After most Jews had migrated elsewhere and the congregation numbered far fewer, Beth Joseph officially closed in 1935, when its Torah scroll was presented to Gemilus Chesed Congregation, which merged with what is today Sharei Chesed in Minneapolis.[141]

These Jewish communities have long been lost to time but the Beth Itzchock Jewish cemetery, just a few miles north of Ashley, remains as a permanent memorial to a once vibrant Jewish community. The cemetery has been on the National Register of Historic Places in North Dakota since 2015.[142]

Wishek Jewish congregation, circa 1908, Courtesy of the Nathan and Theresa Berman Upper Midwest Jewish Archives, University of Minnesota

THE JEWISH HOMESTEADERS' CEMETERY

The Jewish homesteaders' cemetery was established in 1913 just north of Ashley. One of the graves at the Beth Itzchock cemetery is that of Isador Smilowitz, the original name of the Smilo family from which today's Premack family descends. When Smilowitz died around 1913 at age 17, his family had already moved from their Ashley area homestead to Aberdeen, which has never had a Jewish cemetery. His body was transported by freight train from Aberdeen to be buried at the homesteaders' cemetery. His parents, Sam and Sabina (Herschel Premack's maternal grandparents) and younger sister, Goldie, rode in the caboose. The cold made digging the grave difficult. Nevertheless, Ashley cattle dealer Noah Dorfman conducted the graveside funeral service.[143]

These markers were erected in 2017 by the Jewish American Society for Historic Preservation.

Interpretive markers help identify and tell the story of the Jewish homesteaders buried in the cemetery located just north of Ashley, ND. Courtesy of Dale Bluestein

ABERDEEN: A JEWISH HISTORY

As recently as 1987, non-Jewish Ashley residents remembered some of the Jews who count homesteaders as their forebears, including cattle buyers Noah Dorfman and Hank Greenberg, and Dr. Leo Cohen, a dentist who died in 1983.[144]

Dorfman Lake near Ashley is likely named for the Jewish pioneers, including Dr. Leo Cohen's mother, Rose Dorfman Cohen[145] and Noah Dorfman.[146]

Other than the Jewish cemetery, not much remains of what was once a substantial Jewish presence in McIntosh County. In 1917, after just a few years serving these homesteader communities, Rabbi Hess of McIntosh County went on to become the first rabbi of Congregation B'nai Isaac in Aberdeen.

Following the relatively brief experiment in farming, some of the homesteader families came south to Aberdeen and small towns in the area. Among the homesteaders who came to Aberdeen were the Smilowitzes and Parkanskys.

Dorfman Lake in McIntosh County— a remnant of the county's Jewish past, https://gf.nd.gov/ gnf/maps/fishing/ lakecontours/ dorfmanlake2013.pdf (accessed November 10, 2021)

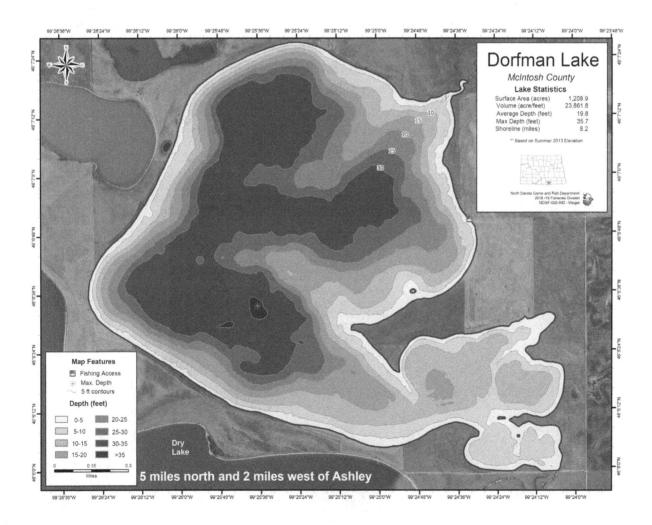

THE SMILOWITZ/PREMACK FAMILY

Herschel Premack, lifelong Aberdonian and the last living link to the very early years of Jewish life there, recalled in detail how his Jewish homesteader forebears in McIntosh County became an integral part of Aberdeen's Jewish community.

Herschel's father, Udell Premack–who sometimes went by the name Julius–was born in Russia in the late 19th century and came to the United States with his family when he was about five years old. As a teenager, Udell traveled from his home in Minneapolis by horse and wagon to visit his two sisters, Ida Premack Levy and Helen Premack Ribnick, both of whom had married Jewish men who had businesses in Aberdeen.[147]

Herschel's mother, Fan Smilowitz Premack, was born to Jewish immigrants in New York City. Her father, Sam Smilowitz, immigrated to the United States in his late teens. He met and married his wife, Sabina, a German Jewish immigrant, in New York City. In the early 1900s, making an abrupt change to their lives, Sam brought Sabina and their children from New York to Ashley, North Dakota, to become homesteaders. The Smilowitz family stayed on the farm for a relatively short time, "proving up" on the land as required, moving to Ipswich, South Dakota, for a few years and then on to Aberdeen by World War I. Sam went into the fresh produce business, trucking goods from Minneapolis. From his store in Aberdeen he distributed to small grocery stores within 30-40 miles. As

Sam Smilo, later in life, Courtesy of Premack family

Herschel recalled many years later, his grandfather used charcoal heaters in the winter to keep the produce from freezing and ice in the summertime to keep it cool. They had old trucks that sometimes got stuck in snowstorms. It wasn't an easy life.[148]

Although Sam and Sabina later retired to Los Angeles, their daughter Fan remained in Aberdeen, where she married Udell Premack, who started the family business, Aberdeen Wrecking Company. It was a scrap and auto parts enterprise that would remain in the family with their son Herschel at the helm until he sold the business in 1988.[149]

Aside from his years in the service at a naval air station near San Diego in 1945-46, Herschel Premack has spent his entire life in Aberdeen. About growing up Jewish there, he said, "It was good and there was very little anti-Semitism."[150]

Herschel's older sister, Sybil Premack Balasco, attended the University of Texas, where she met her husband, Ralph. Both became attorneys, with Sybil eventually elevated to the bench as an associate judge in the Houston Domestic Relations Courts. She passed away in 2021.[151]

Herschel married Bernice "Bea" Wintroub in her hometown of Omaha, Nebraska, in 1953. They settled in Aberdeen and raised their three children there. While Ellen, Judy, and Paul attended college elsewhere and settled in larger cities, Bea and Herschel continue to reside in Aberdeen to this day.[152]

HUGE NEW BUILDING TO HOUSE AUTO WRECKING CONCERN ON WEST SIDE

Will Be Biggest Station of Its Kind in This Part of Northwest When Done.

The new home of the Aberdeen Wrecking company which is being built on the corner of First avenue north and Second street will be ready on next Saturday, October 30, it was announced today. The former home of the wrecking company was next to the Milwaukee tracks in the old Equity Creamery building. The Aberdeen Glass and Roofing Co., has leased the old creamery building and will move in as soon as the wrecking concern vacates.

The new building is of one-story structure and measures 100x145 feet. The main building has been built at a cost of $5000, and when completed will be one of the largest automobile wrecking companies in the northwest. The building is divided into three rooms, the front will be reserved for the offices, the stock department will occupy part of the rear and the repair department will take the rest of the building. A smaller addition will be built on the rear of the building later, this will hold the complete stock. The addition will extend back 85 feet farther than the main building, making the entire building 230 feet in length.

More than 38,000,000 pounds of butterfat sold by South Dakota dairymen, during fiscal year ended June 30.

New Home for Aberdeen Wrecking Co. *Aberdeen Daily News*, October 22, 1926

Fan and Udell Premack, undated photo, Courtesy of Premack family

CHAPTER 5

A SYNAGOGUE IS BORN:
THE RABBI JULIUS
HESS YEARS: 1917 - 1922

INFORMATION ON ABERDEEN'S early Jewish community is known only because of a history project undertaken by Bea Premack in the 1980s. Without synagogue records, Bea gathered information by taking oral histories of Jewish elders with Aberdeen roots. Bea's research revealed the beginnings of an organized Jewish community dating to 1908-09, when a small group of Jews met and held services in a rented space on the second floor of the Northwestern Public Service building, located downtown at the southwest corner of Main Street and Fourth Avenue.[153] Sam Salinsky recalled the need to build a coal fire to heat the large room.[154]

Dr. Sigmond Rosenthal, undated photo, Ancestry.com

Around this time, Dr. Sigmond Rosenthal, a physician living in Java, South Dakota, about 75 miles west of Aberdeen, traveled regularly between his home and medical practice in Java, to Aberdeen to conduct Hebrew school classes.[155] This would have been no small feat given the lack of modern transportation and roadways at the time, to say nothing of the weather conditions during many months of the year.

It is amusing that this communal space, which also housed the Elks, was later known as Maccabee Hall. The name referred to the Knights of Maccabees, a fraternal organization founded in London, Ontario in 1878,[156] which held its meetings there. What a coincidence, that Jews had met in a space by that name and that it had nothing to do with the Jewish Maccabees, rebel warriors known for their revolt against the ruler Antiochus in the second century BCE.

This was the foundation of Aberdeen's organized Jewish community that became Congregation B'nai Isaac.[157]

THE AMERICAN JEWISH WORLD

ABERDEEN ORGANIZES CONGREGATION.

Aberdeen, South Dakota, whose Jewish Community has been growing proportionately, with the rapidly increasing population of the entire city, is about to become the center of Jewish activities in that state. With about twenty-five Jewish families now residing in the city, the community has found it necessary to organize a congregation. An English speaking rabbi has been engaged who will look after the religious and educational interests of the community.

Interestingly, Aberdeen's newspapers regularly published articles about Jewish holidays even before the meetings of the downtown Jews in 1908-09. As early as 1901, an article about Rosh Hashanah (the Jewish New Year) appeared in the *Aberdeen Daily News*.[158]

Courtesy of Congregation B'nai Isaac

> ARTICLES OF INCORPORATION OF CONGREGATION B'NAI ISAAC
>
> Be it REMEMBERED, that by the incorporators, Ben Brussel, Isadore Predmestky, Samuel Calmenson, Isadore Kraywetz, and William Ribnick, all of the city of Aberdeen, county of Brown and state of South Dakota in order to form a corporation for religious purposes, under and by virtue of §762 of the Civil Code of the State of South Dakota and amendments thereto, it is hereby declared that:
>
> 1. The name of this corporation, and the synagogue, society, or association constituting the same, shall be "Congregation B'nai Isaac".
>
> 2. The location and domicile of this corporation, congregation B'nai Isaac, shall be at Aberdeen, Brown County, South Dakota.
>
> 3. The purpose and plan of this corporation is, and shall be, to promote conduct and maintain religious worship according to the general usage, customs, and teachings of the Hebrew faith as promulgated by Moses and the prophets and recorded in the books of the Old Testament scriptures, and as declared by the laws and decrees of the Talmud, with such reformed interpretation thereof as me be adopted my this congregation.
>
> 4. All persons believing and accepting the Hebrew faith as above set forth shall be qualified to become members and may be admitted to full membership upon conforming to the rules and regulations of this congregation.

Congregation B'nai Isaac received its charter of incorporation from the State of South Dakota on March 5, 1917. Signers from the congregation included President Ben Brussel, Vice President Isadore Predmestky, Treasurer Sam Calmenson, Secretary Isadore Kraywetz, and Director William Ribnick.[159]

Soon thereafter, Rabbi Julius Hess and his wife, Francesca, arrived to serve the growing Jewish community.[160]

A FAMOUS RELATIVE

The Hess family name appears to have been shortened from Hesselson.[161] In other documents it appears as Yoelson.[162] A variation of this name would later be made famous by a member of the rabbi's extended family. Rabbi Hess's older brother, Rabbi Moses Rubin Yoelson, settled in Washington, D.C., married, and had several children, including Asa Yoelson, who became vaudevillian Al Jolson. Jolsen starred in the first talking movie, "The Jazz Singer" in 1927 and became the highest paid entertainer of his day. he was one of the first openly Jewish Americans to achieve stardom. [163]

Rabbi Hess was recognized by an acquaintance at a Chautauqua performance in Bismarck, North Dakota, in 1915. Asked what brought him to the show, he said he had come to see his nephew perform.[164]

Rabbi Hess came to Congregation B'nai Isaac in the spring of 1917.[165] The Jewish community held a gathering on March 11 at Maccabee Hall with Rabbi Hess as the guest of honor. Something called a "parcel post sale," likely an auction of unclaimed parcels sent through the U.S. mail, was held in conjunction with the event honoring Rabbi and Mrs. Hess. The sale raised a substantial sum of money for Jewish victims of World War I.[166]

The raising of funds for victims of war and others in need became a hallmark of Aberdeen's Jewish community. For decades, practically every event included a fundraising component.

The *Aberdeen Daily News* reported on the festivities welcoming the Hesses. The rabbi was referred to as "the new pastor" in the headline, and the honorific "Reverend," was used in the article, something fairly common at the time. The rabbi was further described as having held "a pastorate" in Wishek, North Dakota, immediately before coming to Aberdeen.[167]

In the summer of 1917, Sam Calmenson, the synagogue's treasurer, purchased the property at 202 North Kline Street from the Missionary Society of the Wesleyan Methodist Connection of America.[168] On it stood a building that had housed the First Wesleyan Methodist Church, which was built in 1886. Today it is one of the ten oldest non-residential buildings still standing in Aberdeen.[169] A month after purchasing this property, Calmenson sold it to Congregation B'nai Isaac. [170]

Aberdeen Daily News,
August 18, 1917

HEBREWS PURCHASE LOCAL CHURCH

HEBREW CONGREGATION BUYS WESLEYAN METHODIST CHURCH

The synagogue building was formally dedicated on September 9, 1917, shortly before the High Holy Days. To mark the milestone, the congregation first gathered at Maccabee Hall.[171] While there are no news accounts to confirm it, the congregation likely walked the short distance from Maccabee Hall to the new synagogue carrying the Torah scroll. The tradition of *Hachnasat Sefer Torah* (welcoming a Torah scroll into its new home) is accompanied by singing and dancing, a festive occasion akin to a wedding.[172] The newspaper reported that Leona Premack and Goldie Smilowitz marched through the street carrying a banner, which certainly sounds like it could have been part of such a procession.[173]

Aberdeen Jews to Dedicate New Synagogue Next Sunday

Aberdeen Daily News, September 6, 1917

Courtesy of Congregation B'nai Isaac

Original Ten
Commandments,
Congregation B'nai
Isaac, Photo courtesy
of *Aberdeen News*,
October 4, 2017

Original *Yahrzeit*
board, Photo courtesy
of *Aberdeen News*,
October 4, 2017

Ten Commandments,
Photo courtesy
of *Aberdeen News*,
October 4, 2017

One of the ways the congregation had raised money for the synagogue was by "selling" certain privileges. For this occasion, Paul Savatsky had purchased the privilege of being the first to open the doors. Sam Calmenson presented him with the key, Savatsky opened the doors, and the congregation marched in. Max Vinegar bought the privilege of carrying the Torah scroll into the new synagogue. W. Ribnick bought the rights to turn on the lights and fulfilled his duty with dramatic flair. During the dedication ceremony, as Rabbi Hess read from Genesis 1:3. "And God said, 'Let there be light,'" on came the lights.[174] Sam Calmenson had purchased the honor of igniting the *ner tamid* (also called the eternal flame, a lamp that burns perpetually as a reminder of God's abiding presence[175]).

The choir sang, with Eva Pred as soloist, and Gertrude "Goodie" Hess accompanying on the organ.[176]

According to retired architect, Louis Davidson, who along with his wife, Ronnie, have traveled the world photographing synagogues, the B'nai Isaac building was built in the vernacular style.[177] Defined as "a type of local or regional construction, using traditional materials and resources from the area where the building is located. Consequently, this architecture is closely related to its context and is aware of the specific geographic features and cultural aspects of its surroundings, being strongly influenced by them."[178] Congregation B'nai Isaac is one of fourteen synagogues featured in Davidson's wooden synagogues collection on his website.[179]

Once the congregation moved into this building, it never left. While a renovation in the early 1950s removed the steeple, revised the entrance, and added a basement with a kitchen and social hall, much of the structure remains unchanged. Original windows as well as wooden pews remain in the sanctuary, where today's members and guests experience the space in much the same way community members have for more than one hundred years.

In the four years that Rabbi Hess led the congregation, news from the synagogue appeared often in the *Aberdeen Daily News*, the *Aberdeen American*, the *Aberdeen Weekly News*, and the *Aberdeen Journal*. The articles highlighted holidays including, in 1917, Sukkot (the Festival of Booths celebrating the fall harvest), which was referred to as "the Jewish Thanksgiving."[180] The newspaper gave detailed explanations of the holidays' customs, practices, and history. A 1919 article described Purim as a "season of great merrymaking and the exchanging of gifts, dating to the time of the fair Esther and loyal Mordecai, who defied the mighty king of Persia to save their people from destruction." The article goes on to say that all proceeds from the Purim party, held at the Odd Fellows' Hall, would go to the poor, with a large part going to the Jewish relief fund in war-stricken Europe.[181]

Courtesy of Dale Bluestein

ABERDEEN: A JEWISH HISTORY

A NOTE ON TZEDAKAH

Charitable giving, called *tzedakah* in Hebrew, is a central tenet of Judaism. While frequently translated as charity, tzedakah is a commandment to care for the poor.[182]

Less than a year after Rabbi Hess arrived in Aberdeen, the community, under his leadership, raised $1,200 in war relief funds,[183] more than $22,000 in today's dollars.[184] Sam Calmenson is said to have spoken "feelingly" to the women of B'nai Isaac to do their part in American Red Cross volunteer work.[185]

Rabbi Hess's leadership extended to Jews and non-Jews outside of Aberdeen. As a representative of Aberdeen's Jewish community, he frequently spoke about Judaism throughout the region.[186]

By 1921, B'nai Isaac was listed in an article about the churches of Aberdeen and their impact on the community. The synagogue was described as the first Jewish house of worship in the community, with forty-two congregants, sixteen Sunday school students, and three Sunday school teachers.[187]

THE SYNAGOGUE BLOSSOMS

Efforts to organize Jewish youth in the community had begun before the building's dedication. In July 1917, a group of twelve Jewish youth pic-

"Perhaps Purim?" Some of the names of those pictured: from left back row: Mrs. Hess, Goldie Smilowitz Krystal, Minnie Salinsky, Sophie Parkans, Bea Kadesky, and from left in front row: Eva Ribnick, Mrs. Rabinowitz, Goodie Hess Becker, Fan Smilowitz Premack, Courtesy of Premack family

nicked at Tacoma Park. Attending the event were Goldie Smilovitz [sic], Minnie Hendelman, Gertrude Hess, Eva Pred, I. Pred, Beatrice Kadesky, Bernard Strauss, Daniel Pred, Ben Zavat, Arthur Rosenthal, Esther Pred, and Minnie Fenshon.[188]

The following month, a meeting was held at the rabbi's home to plan the formation of both "a young men's and a young women's Hebrew association," with Abe Pred being named secretary pro tem.[189]

THE SALINKSY FAMILY

Sam and Lillian Salinsky were two of several children born to Harris and Esther Salinsky in New York. There is no evidence that Lillian, who was nine years younger than Sam, ever lived in Aberdeen, but Sam spent a good portion of his adult life there. *Siddurim* (prayer books) bearing the names of Sam and Lillian remain in the synagogue to this day.[190]

Prayer was undertaken regularly as evidenced by well-worn, century-old, prayer books, Courtesy of Congregation B'nai Isaac

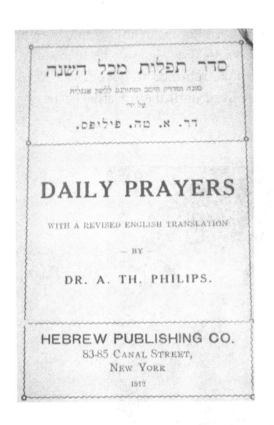

Courtesy of
Congregation B'nai
Isaac

Born to early Third Wave, Eastern European immigrants in 1881, Sam Salinsky arrived in South Dakota in 1906. In 1917, he married Minnie Gluck of Michigan, and the couple returned to his beloved New York Store in Aberdeen, where they lived until their deaths, he in 1951 and Minnie in 1957.[191]

Photo of Sam Salinsky, 1932, Ancestry.com

ABERDEEN: A JEWISH HISTORY

A DEEP SENSE OF PATRIOTISM

Not quite a year after arriving in Aberdeen, Rabbi Hess and his family celebrated the bar mitzvah of their son, Abraham Lincoln Hess. An announcement in the regional edition of the *American Jewish World* noted that Abraham read from the Torah and delivered oration in both Hebrew and English, and that at a dinner following the service, every member of the congregation was present. The occasion resulted in the collection of about $100 for the Jews in Europe.[192]

Naming their son after an American president was but one indication of the family's patriotism. In a letter to the editor in April of that same year, Rabbi Hess wrote that his son-in-law, Herman Braufman, of nearby Ipswich, had been called up for military duty and was then training at Fort Dodge, Iowa. The rabbi added that his daughter, Herman's wife, was investing in Liberty War Bonds from her meager savings to "help lick the kaiser [sic]," as she had "inherited a sense of deep patriotism, peculiar to the Jewish people," and thus wanted to do her part. He signed the letter, "Yours in Patriotism, Rabbi Julius Hess."[193] The rabbi's sentiment is certainly reflective of the feelings of many immigrant Jews of that generation for their adopted country.

Toward the end of his time in Aberdeen, Rabbi Hess had the pleasure of officiating at the double wedding of two of his children—Goodie Hess to David Becker, and Melville Hess to Lillian Altrowitz—at their family home

American Jewish World,
April 19, 1918, Vol. 6,
No. 32.

in Aberdeen. Melville and Lillian were first to stand together under the white satin *chuppah* (wedding canopy). Minnie Salinsky played the Wedding March from Wagner's Lohengrin (something that would hardly be done today because of the composer's antisemitism, which was amplified by Hitler's adoration of the composer). The second couple went next to the *chuppah* and were also accompanied by Minnie Salinsky at the piano. Thirty-five guests were in attendance, some having traveled from Minneapolis, Edgeley, North Dakota, and Roscoe and Bowdle, South Dakota.[194]

A note in a society page column in June 1918 indicated that the women of the congregation had formed a group called the Self Denial Club. While its purpose is not given, even such a whimsically named group had at its core the goal of raising funds to improve the community. The club's first meeting was held

Aberdeen American,
March 22, 1919

ABERDEEN: A JEWISH HISTORY

at the home of Mrs. I. M. Ribnick as a fundraiser for the Young Men's Hebrew Association.[195] This same column informs that the Ladies Aid was hosting a banquet at the Tea Cup Inn honoring four young men from the congregation—Max Rosen, Abraham Pred, David Miller, and Louis Amdur—who were entering the service of the United States.[196] Dinner was served to 55 guests and Rabbi Hess was described as "an eloquent and witty toastmaster."[197]

A society column noted the celebration of Arthur Ribnick, describing it as a "confirmation" held on a Saturday in the synagogue. Based on the wording of the article, it is clear that this event was Arthur's bar mitzvah.[198]

By 1919, B'nai Isaac appears in the church section of the Aberdeen City directory,[199] and the community did not shy away from sharing the plight of their coreligionists overseas[200] and asking for financial assistance.[201]

Aberdeen Daily News,
March 23, 1919

PICKUS GRAVEL, WESTERN HIDE AND FUR, AND THE NEW YORK STORE

Among the newcomers to Aberdeen by this time were Herman Pickus and his wife, Corinne Wetherhorn Pickus, who came from an old established Southern Jewish family. Born in Sioux City, Iowa, Herman Pickus was the eighth child in his family of Russian immigrants and the first to be born in the United States. The Pickus family was in the gravel business. Each of the sons was sent to a different location to expand the enterprise. Herman and Corinne landed in Aberdeen, where he ran the gravel business, and they raised their family.[202]

Also in business in Aberdeen at that time were Max and Lena Anton and Julius and Helen Ribnick, who together ran the Western Hide and Fur business.[203] Sam and Minnie Salinsky of the New York Store started a long tradition of hiring local Jewish young women as clerks until they decided whether they were going to go away to school, get married, or do something different.[204] Among the first hired were Fan and Goldie Smilowitz and Leona Premack.[205]

Courtesy of Premack family

ABERDEEN: A JEWISH HISTORY

Names of some pictured: Mr. Boimel in back (who lived with Sam and Sabina Smilowitz for many years) In front of Mr. Boimel: from left: Goodie Hess, Gretchen Hess, unknown woman; next row forward: from left: Goldie Smilowitz, Pauline Auerbach, Fan Smilowitz, and front Gertrude Rabinowitz, Courtesy of Premack family

Photo of best friends Goodie Hess Becker and Fan Smilowitz Premack, Courtesy of Premack family

"JEWISH WINE GOES TO JAIL"

That was the title of an article describing what was far and away the most unexpected item that turned up in my research. The article described the April 1920 caper that landed Rabbi Hess in court. In preparation for Passover, the rabbi had ordered more than 100 gallons of wine for his congregants' use. Not only did the shipment arrive too late for Passover, which began on March 20 that year, the shipment was seized by state authorities, and Rabbi Hess was charged with violating state law, which limited the import of sacramental wine to eight gallons.

The following day, at the behest of the Jews of Aberdeen, Gov. Peter Norbeck released the seized wine for delivery to Rabbi Hess's home to be allotted to congregational households.[206]

That was hardly the end of the matter. South Dakota's law conflicted with the federal law at the time, which had no fixed maximum limit.[207] The matter was therefore set to be heard in Brown County as a test case on the constitutionality of South Dakota's more prohibitory law.

On Thursday, April 15, Judge McNaughton continued the case until the following Wednesday, and when the rabbi appeared in court, he was released on his own recognizance.[208] No further news reports could be located. According to Brown County court personnel, no court papers regarding this matter could be located.[209] Given the early intervention by the governor, and the lack of any subsequent news reported, it is likely that the case was disposed of in a manner beneficial to Rabbi Hess and the Jewish community, and presumably they had plenty of wine for Passover the following year.

In 1921, with the community flourishing, they placed ads in a national Yiddish newspaper published in New York to recruit someone who could perform specific Jewish rituals. The first ad in *Yiddishe Tagblat* (*Jewish Daily News*), sought a *schochet* (ritual slaughterer) who could also serve the Aberdeen community as a *mohel* (specially trained in circumcision) and a Hebrew teacher.[210]

The ad contained the term "greenhorn," a derogatory word commonly used at that time referring to someone newly arrived in the country. The second ad, published a few months later, dropped the potentially discouraging phrase requiring the applicant to "not be a greenhorn."[211]

ספרי תורה, תפילין, טלתים,
ספרים, ש"ס'ן, משניות'ן, עין
יעקב, כלי קודש און פרכת'ן.
מ. מישקין, 79 קלינטאָן סט.,
ניו יאָרק

M. Mishkin, 79 Clinton St., New York

אבערדין, ס. דאקאטא
סערלאנגט א שו"ב און מוהל, וואָס זאָל
אויך זיין א גוטער לעהרער עברית באנגלית,
ניט קיין גרינער, געהאלט פון 15 ביז 18 הונ־
דערם דאָלאר א יאהר לבד הכנסה. ביטע זיך
וועגדען נור שריפטליך צו:
J. D. Premack, 14 So. Main Street,
21)   Aberdeen, S. D

לינקאָלן, נעבראסקא
קאנגרעגיישאן תפארת ישראל סערלאנגט א
מצדערנעם אָרטאדאקס ראבייא, זאָל זיין א
גוטער דיספוטשלינער, זאָל לערנען א טעגליכע
און סאנדיי סקוהל, פון זיין א גוטער אידישער
און ענגלישער רעדנער. שרייבט סאלערי פער־
24)   לאנגט.
J. Shapiro, 1234 O St., Lincoln, Neb.

התלמוד תורה מסאלט לייק סיטי, יוטאה
סערלאנגט א גוטען טיטשער, לפי רוח הזמן,
אויב מוהל איז מה טוב, זיכער א גוטען לעבען
צו מאכען צום פארמענדען מאן, זיך וועגרען צום
20)   טשערמאן פון דער תלמוד תורה.
Sam Guss, 254 East 7th Street,
                           Salt Lake City, Utah.

This ad, written in Yiddish translates as follows: "Aberdeen, S. Dakota. Seeking a ritual slaughterer and mohel who should also be a good teacher of Hebrew in English, not a greenhorn, salary from $1,500 to $1,800 per year, apart from lodging. Please write to: J. D. Premack, 14 So. Main Street, Aberdeen, South Dakota" *The Jewish Daily News*, 20 November 1921[214]

The 1920s marked the beginning of the growth of Aberdeen's Jewish community that would last through the 1950s. At its height, the city had about 40 Jewish families.[212] The names of some Jewish families who came over these years included Parkansky (later "Parkans"), Fein, Juster, Radin, Holtz, Frankman, Guttman, Schpok, Pikovsky, Ehrlich, Frank, Rich, and Friedman.[213]

CHAPTER 6

1922: TWO RABBIS IN ONE YEAR

RABBI HESS LEFT BIG SHOES to fill when he left for what was then the Orthodox Sons of Israel Congregation, South Dakota's first Jewish house of worship, founded in 1916.[215] Mrs. Hess and their son, Henry, remained in Aberdeen for a time before joining him there, and their adult children remained in Aberdeen.[216]

Two rabbis succeeded Rabbi Hess in 1922. The first, Rabbi S. Segal, sometimes spelled Siegel, came from Austin, Texas, and served from Purim through Passover. His arrival was mentioned in conjunction with a notice about the Purim service, which was described as Orthodox.[217]

The next reference to Rabbi Segal appeared just days later in a newspaper article entitled, "Rabbi Segal Corrects Errors Appearing in the Journal", which did just that. Apparently, the earlier article, which I was unable to locate, stated that Rabbi Kleiman of St. Paul had led the Purim service. This newspaper's correction of the other newspaper also set the record straight as to who was in charge of the congregation. This is the only correction by a rabbi or anyone associated with the Jewish community or synagogue that I found in Aberdeen's newspapers.[218] The final words I found on Rabbi Segal appeared in the *Aberdeen Daily News* on Passover that same year, where it is clearly stated that Rabbi Segal was in charge and would officiate at all services,[219] so there would be no confusion on that matter. His departure from Aberdeen, quite soon thereafter, was not noted in the local press.

Rabbi S. B. Yampolsky became the new spiritual leader about a month later. The *Hebrew Standard*, an English language weekly published in New York, reported that the rabbi would be relocating from Minneapolis after being elected by the Aberdeen Jewish community.[220]

Hadassah minutes report the introduction of Mrs. Yampolsky at a meeting that same month.[221] (Unfortunately, I was unable to locate her first name in any of the reliable resources.) The *Aberdeen American* mentioned Rabbi Yampolsky later in 1922, announcing that he would be delivering a message of special importance to "the men, women and young people of the church" at the synagogue.[222]

SMILOWITZ - PREMACK ENGAGEMENT AND WEDDING

Not much more is known about Rabbi Yampolsky's short stay in Aberdeen, but of note, he was the officiant at the November 1922 wedding of Julius "Udell" Premack and Fan Smilowitz, parents of Herschel Premack.[223] Their engagement notice on the society page, in which Fan was described as "a popular, young bride," had appeared in the *Aberdeen American* in October 1922.[224]

The Smilowitz-Premack wedding was held on a Sunday in the sanctuary of B'nai Isaac synagogue. Theirs was a double wedding, something

Courtesy of Premack family

ABERDEEN: A JEWISH HISTORY

common in those years. Also wed that day were Gale Friedman (a cousin of Fan's,[225]) of Sioux City, and Gertrude Rabinowitz of Jamestown, North Dakota.[226] The Jews of Aberdeen and Sioux City, many of whom were related, celebrated the weddings along with Gertrude's friends and family from Jamestown.[227]

Appearing in the ceremony were twin flower girls, who would have been four years old at the time. They would grow up to be famous.[228] Identical twins Esther Pauline and Pauline Esther Friedman, known as Eppie and Popo, were born in Sioux City to Russian Jewish immigrants, and would achieve fame as advice columnists Ann Landers and Dear Abby, respectively.[229]

ANN LANDERS AND DEAR ABBY

The Ann Landers advice column launched in 1955, with Dear Abby following the next year. This was a half century after the Jewish Daily Forward commenced its advice column, *A Bintel Brief* (a bundle of letters), which addressed concerns of Jewish immigrants as they navigated their individual courses in becoming Americans. Ann and Abby brought that model to the general population.[230]

The twins themselves married in a double wedding on July 2, 1939, when Esther Pauline Friedman (Eppie, Ann Landers) married Jules Lederer, and Pauline Esther Friedman (Popo, Dear Abby) married Morton Phillips.[231]

Ann Landers column, Courtesy of the University of Minnesota

Dear Abby column Courtesy of newspapers.com

Another Aberdonian interviewed in her later years, Leona "Lee" Premack Arnold, remembered some of those who joined the community in the late teens and early 1920s. Adding to the growing Jewish merchant community in the clothing business were the families of J.D. Premack, Louis Amdur, Max Amdur, Nathan, Noah, Sam and Sara Sudow, and Morris and Ida Levy. Aberdeen had its share of Jewish-owned groceries, as well.[232] Other Jews living in the community in the 1920s, she recalled, included the Pickus, Hirsch, Rosen, Holtz, Machov, Sonofsky, Shom, and Ginsberg families.[233]

THE AMDUR FAMILY

Gussie Amdur was Aberdeen's "mikvah lady." The home that she shared with her husband, Louis, at 717 North Lincoln Street, had a *mikvah* (Jewish ritual bath) in its basement. While there are no first-hand accounts of the mikvah, it is believed that the Amdurs maintained it and opened it to anyone who wished to use it for ritual purposes.[234] While the house still stands, the status of the mikvah was unknown until I rang the doorbell in mid-June of 2022. The current owner had no knowledge of the former mikvah, and reported that the entire basement is tiled, with nothing indicating that a ritual bath had once been there.

Louis and Gussie Amdur, undated photo, Courtesy of Barbara Amdur-Hirschberg

Gussie and Louis celebrated their first wedding anniversary in their Aberdeen home in February 1922, with twenty-five guests. Louis's brother, Max, who had been educated in Lithuania as a rabbi,[235] served as toastmaster.[236] Also known as Mottel, Max was in the men's clothing business as was Louis. Herschel remembered their stores being across the street from each other.

Max and Bessie Amdur had been active in Jewish causes in Frederick, South Dakota, before moving to Aberdeen. As members of the Aberdeen District Zionist Society, they raised funds for Palestine.[237]

Max and Bessie raised four children—Saul, Elias, Libby, and Harvey—at 615 North Lincoln Street, down the block from Louis and Gussie, who did not have children. Bessie and Gussie were both involved with Ladies Aid in the early 1920s.[238]

Bessie Amdur in front yard of family home at 615 North Lincoln Street, Courtesy of Barbara Amdur-Hirschberg

AMDUR FAMILY: THE NEXT GENERATION

Barbara Amdur-Hirschberg is the granddaughter of Max and Bessie Amdur. She remembers regular trips to Aberdeen from their St. Louis Park, Minnesota, home throughout her childhood. Her father, Saul, had fond feelings for Aberdeen his entire life. His final trip home was for his 60th high school class reunion in the early 1990s.[239]

Saul was a pharmacist in Minneapolis, where he and his wife, Janet Karol Amdur, raised Barbara.[240]

Saul's sister Libby married Sam Millunchick at Congregation B'nai Isaac in June 1940.[241]

Their brother, Elias, had excelled in debate in high school and was part of the winning team at the district meet in 1934.[242] He earned a bachelor's degree in chemistry from the University of Minnesota in 1938, and later a master's and Ph.D. at the university, where he became a member of the professional staff.

Dr. Amdur's advanced degrees involved the drying of biological materials, which led to the development of a new type of drying machine, developed by the Institute of Research and the Department of Horticulture at the University of Minnesota.

He was part of the Minnesota delegation to the first National Economic Conference for Israel, held in Washington, D.C., in 1951.[243]

Their brother Harvey was seven years younger than his closest sibling. He lived in Minnesota as an adult, married and had a son, Louis, who lives in California. Louis owns a wine shop offering "natural and unusual wines,"[244] and is married to acclaimed *New York Times* film critic Manohla Dargis.[245]

Saul Amdur on bima at Congregation B'nai Isaac on 62nd anniversary of his bar mitzvah, circa 1989, Courtesy of Barbara Amdur-Hirschberg

Libby Amdur at her wedding in June, 1940 at Congregation B'nai Isaac, Courtesy of Barbara Amdur-Hirschberg

Sam and Sara Sudow owned a clothing store that they called "the Savings Bank Store" to emphasize their low prices.[246]

Hyman and Bella Pikovsky owned Hyman's Grocery and Kosher Meat Market.[247] An ad in September 1922 noted that the store would be closed for the weekend for the Jewish High Holy Days.[248] Something called Sioux City bread was advertised as arriving every Thursday.[249] (I wondered if this was perhaps challah for Shabbat but could find no evidence that it was.) Other Jewish grocery store owners included Jake and Sophie Parkans and Ben and Sarah Ribnick.[250] By the mid-1950s, the Pikovsky family owned Hyman Transportation Company.[251]

CHAPTER 7

THE RABBI AARON MICHAEL HARDIN YEARS: 1923-37

RABBI AARON MICHAEL HARDIN arrived in Aberdeen in 1923. Born Avram Gardashnikov in 1891 in a shtetl near Prelukye, Ukraine, he was sent shortly after his bar mitzvah to the Yitzhak Elchonen Yeshiva, one of the finest institutions of Jewish learning in Lithuania. As a Lithuanian-trained rabbi, he felt comfortable embracing modernity while also upholding the Orthodox tradition.[252]

Rabbi Hardin left his *smicha* (rabbinical ordination) papers behind in his haste to flee after receiving his draft orders for the Russian Army, to which Jews were often conscripted for terms three times longer than non-Jews, and in which they were often treated as the enemy.[253] He made his way through Belgium and onto a New York-bound freighter, disembarking at Halifax, Nova Scotia. Trained as a schochet as well as an Orthodox rabbi and cantor, his first job in the New World was as a meat cutter.[254]

Feeling lonely and depressed, he wrote to a cousin in Medicine Hat, Alberta, Canada. She urged him to join her and sent him a one-way train ticket. He worked at her trading post until he had earned enough money to bring two of his siblings from the Old Country, then left Canada intending to go to Chicago or New York. His train stopped in Grand Forks, North Dakota, on a Friday evening and he disembarked for Shabbat. There he met Rabbi Benjamin Papermaster. Rabbi Papermaster and his wife, Chaya, had 10 children at that time, three of whom were young women for whom they wished to find suitable husbands. Their eldest daughter, Rebecca Leah, would become Rabbi Hardin's bride.[255]

They married on June 14, 1918, in Grand Forks. The groom's address at the time of their marriage was listed as Moosejaw, Saskatchewan, Canada.[256]

Marriage License of Rev. Aaron M. Hardin and Rebecca Leah Papermaster. Ancestry.com

On February 28, 1919, at Dickinson, North Dakota, he pledged under oath his Declaration of Intention to become a United States citizen.[257]

Declaration of Intention
Ancestry.com

RABBI BENJAMIN PAPERMASTER

Rabbi Benjamin Papermaster was commonly referred to as "Reverend." Born in 1860 in Analova near Kovno, Lithuania, which was then part of the Russian Empire, he was sent by the Chief Rabbi of the Kovno Yeshiva in 1891 to North Dakota. At the time, Rabbi Papermaster was a married man with four sons.

When his wife died at a young age, his sons journeyed from Lithuania to join him in North Dakota. Eventually, he married again, producing another seven children.[258] Rebecca Leah, who would marry Rabbi Hardin, was one of the children born in the United States.

Rabbi Papermaster (also spelled Papermeister), who spoke multiple languages, traveled on horseback to small communities in North Dakota in the early years, according to his granddaughter, Beryl Hardin Silberg.[259] He served as rabbi in Grand Forks for more than forty years until his death in 1934.[260] Rabbi Papermaster had established himself as a leading figure among Jews and non-Jews. His pallbearers included not only rabbis from the region, but also the mayor of Grand Forks and many church leaders.[261]

Rabbi Benjamin Papermaster, Chabad.org

Rabbi Hardin and Rebecca Leah went on to have six children of their own. They settled in Aberdeen in 1923 after serving a Jewish community in Mississippi. Their Aberdeen years are said to have been the happiest years of their lives.[262] The Hardins, like their predecessors, Rabbi Hess and his family, became well integrated in the Aberdeen community.

Above: Rabbi Aaron Michael Hardin and Rebecca Leah (Papermaster) Hardin, undated photo, Courtesy of Betsy Rosenbaum Scheiner

Left: Hardin children, undated photo, Courtesy of Betsy Rosenbaum Scheiner

Ben Calmenson, who grew up in Aberdeen, remembered Rabbi Hardin well. Ben became bar mitzvah at Congregation B'nai Isaac and remembers that the rabbi was one of his Sunday school teachers along with Harold Feinstein, Malcolm Hardin (the rabbi's son), and Heinie Dervin, sometimes called Heimie or Hymie.[263] Dervin's father, Sam, was a well-known window cleaner in town.[264]

In 1924, Rabbi Hardin officiated at the wedding of Aberdonian Leonard Premack and Sophie Levy, a seamstress from Minneapolis. The affair was held at the Commercial Club and was described as one of the largest attended wedding ceremonies Aberdeen had seen that year.[265]

Leonard was the son of Mrs. A. Premack, who along with a business partner, A. Ginsburg, owned the North Side grocery store.[266] Leonard and Sophie made their home in Aberdeen, where they raised their sons, Franklin and David,[267] and owned and ran the Arcola grocery store.

THE ARCOLA STORE

Leonard Premack was remembered as usually being behind the vegetable bin at their Arcola grocery store because he didn't want to get into trouble with his wife, according to Aberdeen elders. He was known to dump the strawberries out and display only the beautiful ones, and his wife, Sophie, would say, "Leonard!"[268]

Aberdeen Daily News, December 25, 1927

PREMACK THE NEXT 2 GENERATIONS

Franklin and David Premack are remembered as very bright and accomplished. Franklin became a journalist, rising to the position of chief of the *Minneapolis Tribune*'s special reporting team. He married a nurse by the name of Solveig, with whom he would have two children. He died suddenly of a heart attack at age 42 while reporting from the Minnesota State Capitol.[269]

For many years after his death, the Frank Premack Public Affairs Journalism Awards Program was administered by the School of Journalism and Mass Communication at the University of Minnesota.[270]

David Premack attended the University of Minnesota and became a psychologist and a professor at the University of Pennsylvania. He is noted for his research with chimpanzees. His name has been immortalized in the Premack Principle, which refers to reinforcing a target behavior by awarding some privilege to engage in a more desired behavior afterward.[271]

His wife, Ann James Premack was born in 1929 in Shanghai. Her father was a Minnesota native who moved to China after World War I and operated restaurants for expatriates. Her earliest years were lavish and cosmopolitan, aside from her education at a nearby convent.[272]

Her fortunes changed at age 14, when Japanese troops interned her family in a Shanghai-area prison camp for two years. During this time, she, her sisters, and parents lived in a horse stable, but they all survived. [273]

After the war, at age 16, Ann was sent to the United States with her younger, learning-disabled twin sisters.[274]

She met Dave while in college at the University of Minnesota, from which she graduated in 1951 with a degree in occupational therapy. While David would later become something of a celebrity among his fellow psychologists, Ann kept the family fed in their early years with a then-coveted job as a telephone operator.[275]

While raising her children and pushing forward her husband's research, she pursued a master's in linguistics. During the Vietnam War, she was active in the anti-war movement. [276]

Ann and David Premack had three children.[277] They were not only spouses but also did a great deal of academic work together.[278] After a distinguished career, David died in 2015 at age 89.[279]

Aberdeen elders recalled three of Leonard and Sophie Premack's grandchildren. One grandson became a chef. Another grandson's work in the development of charter schools took him to Sacramento, California.[280] A granddaughter, Lisa Premack, married and moved to Israel, where she danced professionally with the Israel Classical Ballet.[281]

Frank Premack Journalism Award, University of Minnesota
http://mjc.umn.edu/assets/doc/2010premackonlineflier.pdf

INVOLVEMENT IN
JEWISH ORGANIZATIONS

Despite its size, the Aberdeen Jewish community was always actively involved in regional, national, and international Jewish organizations.[282] Their contributions, in terms of time, talent, and treasure, as they say in fundraising, far exceeded their numbers a century ago and throughout the years.

   It wasn't only Jewish people who gave to Jewish causes. In April 1922 an article entitled "City Under Canvass for Jewish Funds" listed more unfamiliar surnames than Aberdeen Jewish surnames.[283]

Aberdeen Daily News,
April 5, 1922

CITY UNDER
CANVASS FOR
JEWISH FUNDS

People Throughout Town Will Be Asked to Help Save Starving People.

Dr. Louis Holtz, who is listed on the letterhead of the American Jewish Relief Committee as secretary of the Brown County division, also served as Aberdeen's city health official during the Spanish Flu pandemic.[284] He was quoted as saying that he believed that fewer than half of all cases were being reported.[285]

EXECUTIVE COMMITTEE
LOUIS MARSHALL, Chairman
J. L. MAGNES, Vice-Chairman
CYRUS L. SULZBERGER, Secretary
A. E. ROTHSTEIN, Associate Secretary
ARTHUR LEHMAN, Treasurer
PAUL BAERWALD, Associate Treasurer
20 Exchange Pl., New York
EDWIN C. VOGEL, Associate Treasurer

National Director
HENRY H. ROSENFELT

STATE COMMITTEE
JOE LIVINGSTON, Chairman
SAM FANTLE, Vice-Chairman
JOE HENKEN, Vice-Chairman
BEN KATZ, Vice-Chairman
DAVID FINNEGAN, Treasurer
MISS FLORENCE LIVINGSTON,
Executive Secretary
GEORGE BURNSIDE
T. W. DWIGHT
W. Z. SHARP
JOHN WADDEN
SAM CALMENSON
DR. LOUIS HOLTZ
S. D. SLOAN
HARRY BRODKEY
MRS. SYLVIA JACOBS

APPEAL ENDORSED BY
WARREN G. HARDING,
President of United States
W. H. McMASTER,
Governor of South Dakota
HERBERT HOOVER,
Secretary of Commerce

AMERICAN JEWISH RELIEF COMMITTEE
FOR SUFFERERS FROM THE WAR
CO-OPERATING WITH
CENTRAL AND PEOPLE'S RELIEF COMMITTEES

Suppose
You
Were Starving

ABERDEEN, S. D.

NATIONAL ADVISORY COUNCIL
DAVID A. BROWN, Chairman
JAMES H. BECKER
JACOB BILLIKOFF
JULES E. MASTBAUM
PAUL L. FEISS
FRED LEVY
CHARLES RUBENS
ALBERT M. ROSENTHAL
HENRY H. ROSENFELT
S. C. LAMPORT
FELIX M. WARBURG
LOUIS E. KIRSTEIN
IRVIN F. LEHMAN

BROWN COUNTY DIVISION
G. M. L. ERWIN, Chairman
Ex-Governor C. N. HERRIED, Treasurer
DR. LOUIS HOLTZ, Secretary

Letterhead, American Jewish Relief Committee, Brown County Division
Courtesy of the Nathan and Theresa Berman
Upper Midwest Jewish Archives, University of Minnesota

"Spanish Flu epidemic," Aberdeen, Courtesy of *Aberdeen Magazine*

An eerily familiar image in 2022, but from another health crisis more than a century earlier.

Holtz's wife, Fannie, was also quite involved in the community, and the local Hadassah chapter would later be named after her.[286]

Examples of how Aberdeen Jews participated regularly in major events include the local Hadassah chapter's participation in an international Hadassah event in 1925,[287] and representation at a regional conference of the United Jewish Campaign for overseas refugee relief held in Sioux Falls in early 1926.[288]

Jews from Aberdeen, Sioux Falls, Yankton, Watertown, and other communities attended the UJA conference. The national chairman of the $15 million campaign ($220 million in today's dollars[289]) made a flying tour of the Midwest to acquaint himself with conditions in the region. Aberdeen was represented by Sam Calmenson, Sam Sudow, William Ribnick, David Strauss, Sam Salinsky, and Rabbi Hardin, among others.[290] This is the one mention I found of David Strauss being involved with a strictly Jewish organization.

In May of that year, a local committee, including the oft-noted volunteers Sam Calmenson, Sam Sudow, William Ribnick, Sam Salinsky, A. Ginsberg, M. Amdur, William Brussel, and Rabbi Hardin, began a drive to raise $5,000 from Aberdeen Jews as part of the national effort. Nearly one-third of this goal was donated by the volunteer committee itself at its planning lunch held at the Sherman Hotel.[291] That amount is equivalent to just under $79,000 in today's dollars.[292]

Second of four buildings named the Sherman at the same location at South Main Street and 3rd Avenue, Courtesy of Northern State University Beulah Williams Library Archives and Special Collections

In interviews I conducted and and in research on the Aberdeen community, I have been told many times that the Jewish community of Aberdeen was philanthropic well beyond what their numbers would suggest. This certainly seems to be the case, based on the amounts of money raised that were recorded, to say nothing of funds that likely were raised but not recorded.

Support for Israel is another example. The Aberdeen community strongly supported the Zionist dream. Around the High Holy Days of 1926, Max Shapiro of Minneapolis (not the Minneapolis rabbi of the same name) spoke at B'nai Isaac about a $5 million drive for the "reclamation and redemption of the beautiful country of Palestine." Aberdeen Jews raised $1,400 at that meeting alone,[293] the equivalent of $20,000 in 2022.[294]

At this time, the major Jewish organizations in the United States were run by men,

Courtesy of Congregation B'nai Isaac

and Jewish women were denied leadership roles. Jewish women were, of course, equally committed and organized: they ran the synagogues, raised money, and were very involved in Jewish and other community organizations. A new organization brought a new opportunity. Hadassah, The Women's Zionist Organization of America, was founded in 1912 by Henrietta Szold, and the women of Aberdeen soon formed a local chapter.

First organized in 1919, the chapter reorganized at a meeting in 1921 at the home of Sara Sudow.[295] Hadassah happenings appeared in local news as early as 1921, when it was reported that the women of the chapter were meeting to sew for Jewish orphans in Palestine. Their process was described in great detail. The cut pieces of material were sent from Hadassah to the Aberdeen chapter and the women sewed them and returned them to New York for distribution in Palestine.

Courtesy of
Congregation B'nai
Isaac

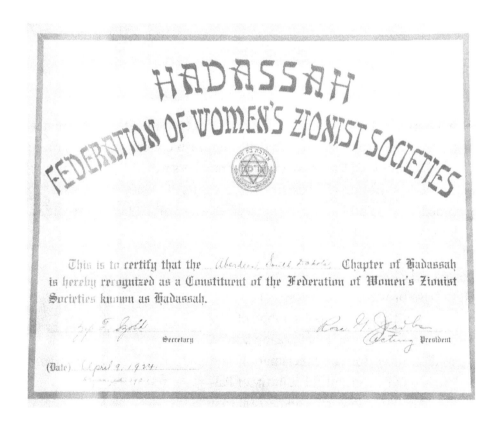

This was not a casual sewing circle; the women met at the YMCA each Tuesday and sewed during one of two shifts: the afternoon shift from 2-5

p.m. under the direction of chapter president Sara Sudow, or the evening shift from 8-10 p.m. under the direction of chapter secretary Fannie Holtz. Each session drew about 15 participants. In addition to completing the work, the Aberdeen chapter paid for the materials and made additional financial contributions to support Hadassah's nascent medical establishment in Palestine.[296]

Additionally, these industrious women devoted their social and business meetings to charitable ends, and hosted showers to collect linens for hospitals and other organizations to distribute to those in need.[297] The women changed it up regularly, shifting to a different shower theme each week, such as Ivory soap and wash rags, [298] bath towels, [299] and hosiery.[300] *

The Hadassah chapter applied in 1922 for membership in the City Federation of Women's Clubs[301] to which they were welcomed.[302]

Courtesy of the Nathan and Theresa Berman Upper Midwest Jewish Archives, University of Minnesota

A meeting of the Hadassah Circle was held Tuesday, Dec. 13, at the home of Mrs. Salinsky.

Owing to the absence of the chairman, Mrs. Parkins was elected chairman for the meeting.

The minutes of the last meeting were read and approved.

The following report of the committee in charge of the Chanuka affair was read and approved:

The Committee decided that the Chanuka affair should be a dance and card party, to be held on Dec. 26, at the Labor Temple on 3d Ave. S. E. Refreshments will consist of weiners, tongue, potato salad, rolls, cake, and tea. Practically everything needed will be donated. The charge for admission will be $2.00 a couple, which will include the cost of refreshments. We are trying to have as little expense as possible.

Mrs. Willis and Mrs. L. Amdur were appointed to fill the places of Mrs. Sudow and Mrs. N. Mechov on the committee as these will be unable to attend.

This meeting is a soap and wash rag shower and 25 bars of soap and 28 wash rags were donated.

The next meeting will be held at the home of Mrs. L. Amdur, and will be a bath towel shower.

On motion the business session was closed.

After a social game of cards the hostess served dainty refreshments.

Respectfully submitted,
Fannie Holtz,
Secretary.

A discussion of the division of profits between the Zionist Organization and the Hadassah took place, and on motion the chairman was asked to attend the meeting of the executive committee of the Zionist Organization and ask that the entire amount should go to Hadassah as we are in need of funds at this time.

In response to a letter from the secretary the Palestine Supplies Department agreed that it was an expensive procedure to pay express on garments to and from New York, and asked that instead of doing the sewing ourselves that we send the money with which to purchase material to be sent to Palestine.

The matter of the change of relation of the Hadassah Chapters to the Zionist Organization of America was explained at length, and hereafter Hadassah members will pay their dues directly to the local Hadassah Chapter instead of to the local Zionist district. The dues are $4.00 per year, of which $1.00 is kept in the local treasury and $3.00 sent to Hadassah headquarters in New York. Of this amount $2.00 is turned over to the Zionist Organization and $1.00 retained by Hadassah headquarters. The treasurer was supplied with membership cards and members are urged to pay their dues for 1922 soon.

Upon motion it was decided that we apply for membership in the local Federation of Women's Clubs.

The shower at this meeting resulted in the collection of twenty towels.

The next meeting will be at the home of Mrs. Calmenson and will be a tooth brush shower.

After the adjournment of the business session, a social game of cards and light refreshments were enjoyed. Respectfully submitted
Fannie Holtz, Secty

Resoluations of Respect.

Whereas the Almighty has seen fit to remove from our midst a true and noble soul, "Mrs. Fannie S. Holtz," who has passed into an eternal and prolonged sleep.

Be it Resolved-: That in this great loss and afflic- tion that the Aberdeen Chapter of Hadassah extend their most heartfelt sympathy to Dr. Louis Holtz, Baby Harry and Spielberger family.

Therefore be it Resolved-: That in the death of Mrs. Fannie S. Holtz we have lost a highly respected and esteemed friend, who will be missed by us in the daily walks of life.

Be it further Resolved-: That the Aberdeen Chapter of Hadassah has deemed the honour of adopting her name, calling it "Fannie Holtz Chapter of Hadassah Organi- zation" and also a contribution has been made in her memory.

Be it further Resolved-: That a copy of these Resolu- tions be sent to Dr. Louis Holtz, Baby Harry and Spiel- berger family, and also be spread upon the minutes of the Fannie Holtz Chapter of Hadassah Organization.

Mrs Sam Salinsky (Sec)
5-18- 22

Tragedy led to the chapter taking on a new name in May 1922. Chapter Secretary Fannie Holtz[303] died the previous month at age 25. The chapter would thereafter be known as the Fannie Holtz Chapter. Minnie Salinsky, Sam's wife, succeeded Fannie Holtz as chapter secretary.[304]

Seldom would a month pass without a mention of Hadassah in the local news.[305] References to the Aberdeen chapter and its activities appeared in the newspapers hundreds of times between the early 1920s and 1935, with readings and musical presentations being common features of meetings and events. [306]

In 1926, Hadassah brought in a speaker, social worker Charles Cowen, for a special event open to the public at Maccabee Hall.[307] The Sudows hosted a private formal dinner in his honor at their home for a small group that included Rabbi and Mrs. Hardin.[308] The dinner table was decorated in the Zionist colors of blue and white.[309]

Some of the women's meetings and programs appear to have been quite formal. It was noted in the news that Mrs. Sam (Minnie) Salinsky would be giving a paper on the composer Franz Liszt and performing one of his piano compositions. Mrs. J. Silver gave a biography of British financier and philanthropist Moses Montefiore, and Mrs. U. Premack (Fan) presented on the life of Abraham Geiger, a German rabbi and scholar who is considered the founder of Reform Judaism.[310]

When a Jew of some note came to Aberdeen, the community came together to celebrate, as did Hadassah when pianist Rae Bernstein visited the city in 1928.[311]

members. The questions answered ... questions ... educati ... The questions aroused orally by ten different and discussion. Mrs. Brody then introduced ... Mrs. Salinsky who had recently returned from a two-month sojourn in Florida, where she attended several Hadassah functions, notably a donor luncheon where our National President, Mrs. Judith Epstein was guest speaker. She described very minutely the Oneg Shabbot which she attended in Chicago in company with a few former Aberdoni ... Her vivid talk, which was like re-visiting the various places with her on a magic carpet, was very much enjoyed by all. Mrs. B. Cowan then lea ... in the singing of Hatikvah, after whichall prese ... entered the dining room to participate in the candle-lighting ceremony in commemoration of Hadassah's 26th birthday, lead by Mrs. Perrman, who gave a very fitting and timely prayer for th ... welfare of our brethren. The participating of refreshments then began with our President, Mrs. Salinsky cutting Hadassah's birthday cake, and our Vice-President, Mrs. Calmenson, the Purim cake, with Hadassah's emblem and color scn ... of blue and white predominating as a fitting setting for the day.

Respectfully submitted,

Sophie E. Radin

Sophie E. Radin

Courtesy of Nathan and Theresa Berman
Upper Midwest Jewish Archives, University of Minnesota

William Ribnick, a founder of Congregation B'nai Isaac, raised a family and ran a business in Aberdeen, but he still found time to *daven* (pray).

Courtesy of
Congregation B'nai
Isaac

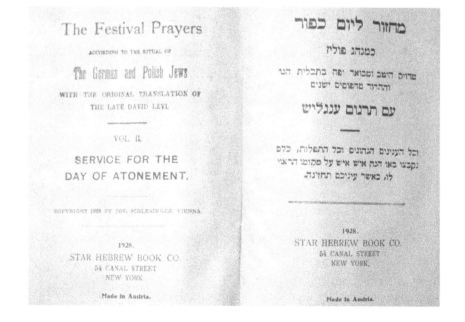

ABERDEEN: A JEWISH HISTORY

MORE JEWISH-OWNED BUSINESSES

Jewish-owned businesses continued to open and thrive in Aberdeen, including the Economy Grocery, opened in 1934 by Sam Levy.[312] The centrality of the railroads to the local economy is highlighted in an Economy Grocery ad that includes the information that "WE CASH F.R.A. CHECKS," referring to the Federal Railroad Administration.[313] Albert and Bess Premack, who raised their three daughters in Aberdeen, owned the Quality Grocery Store.[314]

Economy Grocery, "OPEN For INSPECTION," *Aberdeen Daily News*, January 24, 1934

A SMALL BUT MIGHTY CONGREGATION

The High Holy Days of 1928 were announced in the newspapers, with a note that many of the stores managed by Jewish people would be closed.[315]

Among the many Jewish merchants sponsoring the ad was Ben Brussel, yet another clothing merchant,[316] who, along with his wife, Jennie, was actively involved in the young congregation and Jewish community.[317]

In 1925, Jewish clothing merchant Myer Kadesky sold his store and inventory to Brussel and left for Frederick, South Dakota, where he planned to open another clothing store.[318] It appears that his wife Anna

Courtesy of Congregation B'nai Isaac

Aberdeen Daily News,
September 21, 1928

had passed away just a few years earlier at a fairly young age.[319] Many records, including this plaque memorializing Anna Kadesky, have spelling variations. Most references to this family use the Kadesky spelling. Oddly, the synagogue yahrzeit plaque, employs a different spelling.

Records indicate that Kadesky remarried a woman by the name of Anne or Annie, and they maintained their residence in Aberdeen for many years.[320]

Born in Minsk, Russia in 1884, Ben Brussel arrived in the United States in the first years of the new century. Records indicate that Brussel staked a claim west of the Missouri River in Perkins County, South Dakota,[321] before heading east to Brown County where he married Jennie Levine in 1912.[322] In addition to raising his family with Jennie in Aberdeen, Ben Brussel's one of the premiere men's clothiers in town. Along with fellow businessmen, he was one of the five original incorporators of Congregation B'nai Isaac in 1917. (See Chapter 5).

Ben Brussel's Men's Clothier, *Aberdeen Daily News*, November 15, 1928

MORE JEWISH-OWNED STORES

The Golden Rule store in Aberdeen was part of a chain founded by James Cash Penney–of JC Penney fame–in the early 1900s.[323] The Aberdeen store was owned by a member of the Feinstein family.[324]

The Paris, a women's clothing store, was owned by Irving Light, a member of the Pred extended family.[325] We will learn more about the Feinstein and Pred families in later chapters.

Standard Clothing, located at 14 South Main, was the name of the men's store owned by Louis and Gussie Amdur. Gussie, introduced in Chapter 6 as the mikvah lady, had a women's department in the basement of the store.[326]

MORE JEWISH COMMUNITY CELEBRATIONS/EVENTS

The abundance of holidays on the Jewish calendar gave the community endless occasions for gatherings. Presentations of song and drama were made by various groups, including tableaux by the Hadassah Glee Club and a play by the Daughters of Judea and the *Ivre* (Hebrew) Club at a 1928 Purim Party held at the Knights of Columbus Hall.[327]

Aberdeen Daily News,
April 10, 1927

Aberdeen Daily News, April 18, 1928

Aberdeen Daily News, January 16, 1929

In 1930, the annual mother-daughter Hadassah event celebrated the 70th birthday of Hadassah's founder, Henrietta Szold. It appears that Hadassah had various groups under the Aberdeen umbrella, as this event featured "Hadassah Mothers" inviting "Daughters of Judea," and "Junior Judeans" to the festivities. Seventy candles were lit by officers of each of these groups, Rebecca Leah Hardin recited a tribute to Szold, and Miriam Ginsberg gave the opening prayer in Hebrew. Harriet Premack performed a piano rendition of *Kol Nidre*, the prayer that ushers in Yom Kippur, even though it was December. Minnie Salinsky, who hosted the gathering at her home, gave a presentation on Szold's life on behalf of Hadassah Mothers. Renette Schpok (on behalf of Daughters of Judea) and Doris Ribnick (on behalf of Junior Judeans) "gave responses." The event culminated with the serving of tea, which was poured by Minnie Salinsky and Anna Premack.[328]

In 1930, the Jewish Telegraphic Agency reported that Sara Sudow had been elected as one of four vice presidents of the Northwest Region of Hadassah.[329] The Sudows traveled internationally and attended an international Rotary convention,[330] bringing back stories of their travels to share with the local community.[331]

Sunday, November 21, 1926

BNAI BRITH LODGE WILL HOLD DANCE

New Organization to Have First Social Event On Monday; Sam Sudow Is President

The Bnai Brith Lodge No. 289 of Aberdeen will give its first dance at the Maccabee hall Monday night, November 22.

This is a new fraternity organized last April for purely benevolent purposes. Its mission is to foster hospitals, orphan homes, schools for the intellectually unfortunate, and other benevolent institutions. The lodge now has 45 members, both from Aberdeen and surrounding territory and meets twice a month.

The president of the fraternity is Sam Sudow; secretary, Norman Matchoff; treasurer Sam Salinsky; Vice president, Max Amdur; trustees, Sam Calmenson and William Ribnick.

All out of towns members and their ladies are expected to attend this fete Monday night, which is the beginning of a series of entertainments. It is planned also to vary these programs and bring to some of the future gatherings noted out of town speakers.

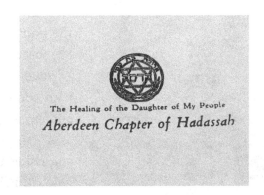

The Healing of the Daughter of My People
Aberdeen Chapter of Hadassah

Left: *Aberdeen Daily News*, November 21, 1926

Right: Courtesy of Premack family

B'nai Brith made its entrance in Aberdeen in November 1926 with a dance at Maccabee Hall.[332]

The men also kept busy with their clubs and had many contacts throughout the region. In 1927, the Aberdeen Lodge of the Independent Order of B'nai Brith hosted Fargo lawyer and officer of the Grand Lodge Harry Lashkovitz, who spoke on behalf of the B'nai Brith Wider Scope Committee.[333] As a young boy, Lashkovitz immigrated from Ukraine with his parents, and the family settled in Fargo, North Dakota. He attended City College in New York and returned to Fargo to practice law. Lashkovitz married Etta Levitz of Devils Lake, North Dakota, in 1917, and they raised their four children in Fargo.[334] The oldest of their children, Herschel Lashkovitz, served as Fargo's mayor from 1954-74, and was a representative in North Dakota's state legislature from 1975-89. A Fargo Central High School classmate of his, Arthur Naftalin, also entered politics, becoming the first Jewish mayor of Minneapolis in 1961.

In 1929, the B'nai Brith Lodge's newly elected officers were President Sam Sudow; Vice President Norman Machov; Secretary J. Cofman; and Treasurer Sam Salinsky. Additionally, Rabbi Hardin was named as "monitor," Ben Brussel as "warden," and D. Becker as "guard."[335]

Under the leadership of Rabbi Hardin, the general community made special accommodations for members of the Jewish community. For example, Jewish junior high boys were given a later time on Saturdays to use the gym facilities to allow for attendance at Shabbat morning services.[336]

Rabbi Hardin served as a leader, along with community church leaders, at a boys' annual camp at Pickerel Lake.[337]

A "surprise wedding"—with the couple surprising their unsuspecting friends—was held at Rabbi Hardin's home in February

Courtesy of Congregation B'nai Isaac

1928. The marriage was that of Josephine "Jo" Hirsch of Aberdeen and Martin Rich of Philadelphia, Penn. A newspaper article noted that the new Mrs. Rich was employed by the New York Store.[338]

In August of that year, a large wedding with many out-of-town guests took place in the ballroom of the Alonzo Ward Hotel. The bride, Celia Ribnick, the only daughter of William and Sarah Ribnick, was married to Bennie Kluner of Winnipeg, Manitoba.[339]

Herman Ehrlich came to Aberdeen from Butte, Montana, around 1928 and worked at a local jewelry store. A few years later he purchased the inventory of the J. H. Parden store, establishing his own jewelry store.[340]

Strangely, no further news of the Hardins appeared in the local newspapers after 1935. A 1937 article in the *American Jewish World*, however, indicated that Rabbi Hardin would be assuming the pulpit at "congregation B'nai Abram"[sic]—B'nai Abraham Congregation—in Minneapolis in June of that year after 14 years in Aberdeen.[341] The Hardins left Minnesota for Oklahoma in 1946 and remained there for decades, serving yet another congregation. Both died in Oklahoma in the mid-1970s. Rabbi Hardin's gravestone in Oklahoma City says, "Rev. Aaron M. Hardin," even though the Hebrew reads *"harav"* (rabbi).[342]

BEA LEVY RECOLLECTIONS

Bea Levy, an Aberdonian from the age of seven, loved veal. Kosher cuts of veal, however, were not readily available in Aberdeen in the 1930s and 40s so she occasionally bought non-kosher veal on the sly. After buying some from the Arcola Grocery, the store owned by her aunt and uncle, Leonard and Sophie Premack, her Aunt Sophie reported to her Bea's father, Sam (Sophie's brother), exactly what she had done.[343]

Sam confronted Bea saying, *"men tor nit,"* Yiddish for "it is not permitted,"[344] explaining to his daughter that eating non-kosher meat would lead to a loss of her Jewish identity. Bea, who was 97 years old when we spoke on the telephone in 2022, did not say whether she took her father's advice in this regard, but she did share a number of stories with me.

Bea was born in Brooklyn, New York, in 1924 to Sam and Leda Levitt Levy. Both parents were born in Russia. Sam owned a grocery store but hated New York. When the stock market crashed in 1929, Sam got in his

Aberdeen Daily News,
January 7, 1951

truck and drove west. He stopped in Minneapolis, where he experienced a health crisis requiring surgery. His siblings, Morris and Sophie, came from Aberdeen to care for him, and after his recuperation he joined them there.

Two years later, Bea and her mother joined him in Aberdeen, where Sam and Leda ran the Economy Grocery store, and became active in the Jewish community.

Morris and Ida Premack Levy owned Pioneer Wrecking in Aberdeen.[345]

Bea remembered how active the Aberdeen Jewish community was in raising money, adding that it was her understanding that they raised the most per capita of any Jewish community at the time.[346]

She recalled that before Passover each year, all the regular dishes (two sets of everything, one for meat and one for dairy) had to be moved from the kitchen to the basement, and the Passover dishes (also two sets of everything) had to be moved from the basement to the kitchen.[347]

"If the girl in the house made a mistake," she said, referring to the maid, "there would be all sorts of things out in the dirt." That was a reference to the practice of burying in soil any kitchen item mistakenly used for the wrong food (i.e., a meat fork used for a milk product) for a period of time

Aberdeen Daily News,
February 14, 1951

ABERDEEN: A JEWISH HISTORY

to make it fit again for its intended purpose. Although a common practice, there is no *halachic* (rooted in Jewish law) basis for it.[348]

Private homes didn't have freezers in those days, she commented, but they could be rented near the railroad station. Leda rented one so they could store the kosher meat that was brought in from Minneapolis. Bea also recalled having kosher poultry on occasion when a schochet would come through town.[349]

Although some children worked in their parents' stores, such was not the case for Bea. In fact, her father paid her $6 a week *not* to come to the store. Her first employer was the Aberdeen Woolworth store, where she worked at the candy counter.[350]

When Bea was in high school, her very close friend was Muriel Calmenson, known as Muggy. The two were in a junior sorority. Once, when her father had a customer who couldn't pay his grocery bill, the customer paid his debt by turning over his car, a fairly new model. This became her car, which she used to pick up Muggy and other sorority friends on the way to school.[351]

Another friend, Jane Feeley, was a cousin to the movie star Spencer Tracy, and they all spent time together when he came to town to visit. Bea was involved in radio in high school, and Tracy secured an interview for her in New York with a show called *Let's Pretend*. She traveled with her mother to New York for the interview. Bea said that after that experience she decided to attend Northwestern University, where she had already been accepted. She pointed out that Northwestern at that time maintained a quota.[352] The university did, in fact, cap the admission of so-called "religiously affiliated" Jewish students per class until 1964.[353] Bea said that, in her day, Jewish students were limited to 0.1% of the student body.

A bit of research uncovered news of Bea's many talents. As an elementary student, she studied piano with Mrs. Louise Fedje and performed at several concerts.[354] At age eight, she studied at Northern State Teachers College music program with other local Jewish youngsters, including Norlie Feinstein and Miriam Ginsberg.[355] As a Central High student, Bea won the 1939 declamation contest along with three of her classmates.[356]

Years later, Bea had two stores in Aberdeen: Skar's and United Clothing. She sold Skar's to Jo Rich, who changed the name of the store.[357]

After Bea's father, Sam, and her Aunt Sophie Levy Premack had both passed away, their spouses married. Bea's mother, Leda Levitt Levy Premack and Leonard Premack were together for fourteen years until Leonard's death. Their family provides an example of how many Aberdeen families were related—and related again—through marriages.

Bea recounted a touching story that her father had told her. Before he left Russia for the United States, he promised his mother that he would always take care of his sister, Sophie. He made good on his promise, even in death. At the foot of his grave in Minneapolis lies Sophie, as though he continues to watch over her.[358]

CHAPTER 8

RABBI PERMAN, 1938-1944 AND RABBI GOTTESMAN 1948

RABBI NORMAN (NOACH) PERMAN and his wife, Tzipporah, sometimes known as Sylvia, came to Aberdeen to serve Congregation B'nai Isaac in 1938.[359] Both were born in Warsaw, Poland, and immigrated to Winnipeg, Canada, where their two older daughters were born.[360] The first reference to Rabbi Perman in regional news was in September 1939, when he officiated at the wedding of Bernise Ribnick of Aberdeen and Hy Pitts of Sioux Falls. The Orthodox wedding ceremony held in Aberdeen was attended by 200.[361]

In early 1943, Rabbi Perman traveled a distance of more than 300 miles to the hospital in New Underwood, South Dakota, upon the birth of a boy to Mr. and Mrs. Louie Sinykin of Wall, South Dakota. Referred to as a "vresse," and described as a christening ceremony, the occasion no doubt was the boy's bris.[362]

The only other information found on Rabbi Noach and Tzipporah Perman is that they are buried in Israel.

ALONZO WARD HOTEL

The Alonzo Ward Hotel was the site of many Jewish community events over the years.

Alonzo LaRue Ward, born in Ohio and raised on a family farm in Iowa, is said to have arrived in Aberdeen in 1883 with only a nickel in his pocket. A true rags-to-riches story, he built his hotel the very next year and it thrived until it was destroyed by fire 42 years later just before Thanksgiving 1926.[363] Undaunted, he built a new one two years later. The structure still stands at 104 South Main Street, now divided into condos and apartments.[364]

Just Marvelous FOOD

ALONZO

Recommended by DUNCAN HINES and Hundreds of Satisfied Patrons

WARD HOTEL

Aberdeen Daily News,
Monday, October 22, 1951

Hebrew Ceremony At Alonzo Ward Is Brilliant Function

At the Alonzo Ward ball room Sunday evening marriage vows were exchanged between Celia, only daughter of Mr. and Mrs. William Ribnick, 614 Kline street south, and Bennie J. Kluner, youngest son of Mr. and Mrs. J. Kluner, of Winnipeg, Canada. Rabbi A. M. Hardin read the Hebrew service at 6 o'clock, in the presence of over 150 guests, as the bridal couple and their attendants stood under the canopy of blue velvet cloth, which was held by four boys, Alfred Ribnick, Joseph Sudow, Marvin Calmenson and William Brussel.

The Klitz orchestra played Lohengrin's wedding march announcing the processional and during felicitations there was also nuptial music by the orchestra.

The bride's maid of honor was her cousin, Miss Hanna Sagal. Her attendants were Miss Mariam Mindell, niece of the groom from Winnipeg, Miss Celia Rosen, the bride's cousin from Minneapolis and the Misses Phyllis and

Announcement

Monday

Yeomen lodge—Eagles hall at 8 o'clock. To make plans for fall entertainment. Program and refreshments.

* * *

Aberdeen lodge, No. 42, I. O. O. F.—Important business meeting in I. O. O. F. hall at 8 o'clock sharp.

* * *

Tuesday

Circle No. 2, Zion Lutheran aid—Picnic at Melgaard park at 2 o'clock.

* * *

Woman's Relief Corps—G. A. R. hall at 3 o'clock for work meeting.

Harmony Camp, R. N. A.—Business meeting in Society hall at 8 o'clock. Program and refreshments.

MISS CHRISTMAN

Aberdeen Daily News, August 6, 1928

Courtesy of South Dakota State Historic Preservation Office

Credit to Alonzo Ward Condos

Front table from left: Louis and Gussie Amdur, Rose and Sam Calmenson, Rabbi and Mrs. Perman, Sophie and Jake Parkans. Others community members pictured include: Albert and Bess Premack, Ira and Bert Feinstein, Corinne and Herman Pickus, Fan and Udell Premack, Julius and Helen Ribnick, Leonard and Sophie Premack, Florence Parkans, Natalie Feinstein, Abe and Mattie Feinstein, Harold Feinstein, Bill and Eva Feinstein, Hyman and Bella Pikovsky, circa 1939-40, Courtesy of Premack family

ARTHUR GREEN

Arthur Green was born on October 9, 1927, in Graceville, Minnesota, and his family moved to Aberdeen around 1934. His father traded in scrap iron, metal, other scrap commodities, animal furs, skins, and bones. After his parents divorced in 1948, he and his siblings remained in Aberdeen with their mother. He counted Harvey Amdur as one of his closest friends.[365]

The family kept kosher and were active members of the synagogue. He remembered Rabbi Perman's wife, Tzipporah, and their children, Chana Rebecca, Florence, and Isaac Wolf. He also recalled that Rabbi Perman was a schochet and prepared kosher meat for the local community.[366]

Green remembered Rabbi Perman as an "outstanding" and "extraordinary" person who had a profound, positive influence on his life. He described him as very spiritual and learned in Torah, and an excellent teacher and *chazan* (cantor).[367]

With so few kids in his age group, Green had the opportunity to study one-on-one with Rabbi Perman. From the rabbi he learned Torah, ritual slaughter, and cantorial and other skills that enabled Green to assist the rabbi in teaching and to serve in various roles in other Jewish communities over the course of his life.[368]

The Jewish community was still somewhat Orthodox and quite viable, Green said, estimating that there were about 120 people in the congregation.[369]

Arthur's brother, Nathan Green, remained a member of Congregation B'nai Isaac well into the 21st century. We'll learn more about Nathan in a later chapter.

RABBI ELI GOTTESMAN: 1948

A rabbi by the name of Eli Gottesman served the congregation for a short time following Rabbi Perman in the 1940s. The Aberdeen city directory lists "Rev. Eli Gottesman" as the clergy at B'nai Isaac as well as his home address but no other information is available about his time in Aberdeen.[370]

CHAPTER 9

RABBI SELIG SIGMUND AUERBACH: 1949-1953

IN RESEARCHING Rabbi Selig Sigmund Auerbach, I came upon a German book on the internet entitled, *Selig Sigmund Auerbach: Ein Deutsches Rabbinerschicksal im 20 Jahrhundert*.[371] Naturally, I wanted to know if this was the same Rabbi Auerbach who served the Aberdeen Jewish community.

After a bit of Googling, I was fairly confident it was the same Rabbi Auerbach, so I ordered the book. A German translator[372] confirmed it, and with her assistance I learned the details of the sad fates of both Rabbi Auerbach's and his wife Hilda's families during the Holocaust.[373]

The book only briefly touches on the family's time in Aberdeen, but details Rabbi Auerbach's flight from the Nazis via the Netherlands to London, his rabbinical ordination, and finally, the couple's entry into the United States. Hilda attended college during their time in Aberdeen and became a teacher.[374]

Selig Sigmund Auerbach, A German Rabbi's Fate in the 20th Century

Church Services

SABBATH services at B'nai Isaac Synagogue will be held Friday at 8 p. m. Rabbi Selig S. Auerbach will dedicate his sermon to the annual Jewish Book month. His topic will be "The Great, but Still Unknown Book." Services Saturday at 9 a. m. During the services the Barmitzvah of Arthur Radin, son of Mrs. Norman Radin, will take place. Rabbi Auerbach's topic at this service will be "Never Give Up." Sunday school Sunday at 10 a. m.

Rabbi Auerbach was introduced as the new rabbi at Congregation B'nai Isaac in June 1949. He had previously been the executive director of the St. Joseph Hebrew School in St. Joseph, Missouri.[375]

News accounts of Rabbi Auerbach and his family flourished beginning in 1951 and continued throughout their years in Aberdeen. Detailed articles about Sabbath services, holidays, youth services, and Sunday school abounded. Special events such as bar mitzvah ceremonies, including that of Arthur Radin in November 1951, were included in local coverage.[376]

A special Shabbat observance in celebration of the 50th anniversary of the Rabbinical Assembly of America was held early that year.[377]

In February 1951 a Boy Scouts Shabbat was held at the Alonzo Ward Hotel. Scouts from B'nai Isaac included Charles Levy, Leland Frankman, Harvey Guttman, Lewis Liszt, and Larry Ribnick.[378]

The synagogue hosted a Girl Scouts Shabbat in November 1951, with Girl Scouts and Brownies from the congregation participating in the service. These girls included Ruth Auerbach, Betty Lou Feinstein, Dottie Premack, Beryl Radin, Sandra Schpok, and Hannah Helen Auerbach.[379]

Involvement in the general community is also evidenced by presentations by the rabbi and his wife, Hilda, at church events[380] and Rotary club meetings.[381] They spent a week during the summer as faculty at a church-sponsored senior leadership camp in North Dakota, teaching courses in "Old Testament" and lecturing about Jewish customs and ceremonies.[382] Hilda Auerbach served as a girls' counselor. Each was also involved in the PTA[383] and YMCA.[384]

Jewish holidays were once again being regularly reported in the local newspapers starting with *Selichot* (the opening service of the High Holy Days season) in September 1951.[385] Services were generally announced according to the specific Torah reading for that Shabbat or holiday. For example, on the Shabbat that occurs during the eight days of Sukkot, the service was announced as "*Shabos Chol ha-Moed Sukkos*".[386]

Young members of the congregation participated regularly in services. For a number of months during Rabbi Auerbach's years in Aberdeen, when the synagogue underwent a remodel, services were often held at the Alonzo Ward Hotel. At one such service in February 1951, the young participants were Herschel Premack, Manny Skar,[387] and Beryl Radin.[388]

City Hall and the Northwestern Public Service Co. became temporary sites for B'nai Isaac's Hebrew School during the remodel. Neither City Hall nor Northwestern accepted the offered payment for the use of their facilities.[389]

Following the remodel, the synagogue no longer had a steeple, and had gained a basement with a full kitchen and room for communal celebrations. The sanctuary remained largely unchanged.

Courtesy of Aberdeen News, March 10, 2017

Remodeled interior of synagogue from newspaper, Courtesy of Congregation B'nai Isaac

THE COMPLETELY REMODELED Congregation B-Nai Isaac synagogue at 202 Kline st. N., is shown above. The present owners acquired the synagogue in 1916. It was then the old Wesleyan Methodist church. Improvements were started on the building in February of this year. An entirely new basement, siding and entrances were added. The steeple was removed and the roof completed with new roofing. Pictured below is the interior which has been enlarged both upstairs and downstairs. The altar can be seen in the lower picture. The altar steps were changed and widened. A large recreation and fully equipped kitchen are now part of the synagogue. The sanctuary ceiling was enlarged to obtain more effective lighting. Rededication services for the remodeled synagogue will be held in the near future, Rabbi Selig Auerbach, announced.

Congregation B'nai Isaac kitchen, Courtesy of author

Westinghouse vintage roaster, Courtesy of Leslie Martin

Talit, Courtesy of Dale Bluestein

Glassware, Courtesy of Leslie Martin

Ashtrays, Courtesy of author

The Aberdeen lodge hosted the spring convention of B'nai Brith's Dakota Council in 1951, with activities at the Sherman and Alonzo Ward Hotels. At that time, Al Goodman of Aberdeen was president of the Dakota Council and Leonard Ribnick was the Aberdeen lodge president.[390]

Israel and Jewish organizations remained a high priority for the community during these years. The Hadassah chapter thrived. In 1951, the Donor dinner was held at the Alonzo Ward Hotel under the leadership of Mrs. Marvin (Jeanne) Schpok, and once again the chapter members performed a skit.[391] The following year, Hadassah's annual dinner was held at the same location and drew 66 members and guests. This dinner coincided with the 40th anniversary of Hadassah and the fourth birthday of the new state of Israel.[392]

Mrs. Samuel (Helen) Ziff of Minneapolis was the speaker, and the cleverly named skit, "Oh Shoshanna," was presented by Sybil Pilch, Jeanne Schpok, Bertha Feinstein, Phyllis Frankman, Dottie Premack and Betty Lou Feinstein. The narrator was Barbara Feinstein, with piano accompaniment by Fay Ribnick. Jeanne Schpok presented the slate of new officers: President Corinne Pickus; Vice President Sophie Radin; Secretary Fay Ribnick; and Treasurer Sybil Pilch.[393]

Hadassah Donor Dinner, from left: Maxine "Bubbles" Pred, Fan Premack, Hariett Premack Soll, Corinne Pickus, Jo Ribnick, undated photo, Courtesy of Premack family

PAUL GUTTMANN SOLOMON

Paul Guttmann Solomon shared memories of growing up in Aberdeen. His father, Michael Guttmann managed the Orpheum theater for many years, and Paul recalled meeting The Mills Brothers and the Lennon Sisters when they were in town performing. Michael passed away when Paul was only 18. He had told Paul that the original family name was Solomon, and that for some unknown reason it was changed to Guttmann when they immigrated from Romania to the United States. Michael was seven years old when the family immigrated. Paul decided to legally change his name back to Solomon when he was 36.[394]

Paul remembered Rabbi Auerbach from his very young years and recalled that Rabbi Kertes was his Hebrew teacher. As a teen, Paul was active in B'nai Brith Youth Organization, and he became involved in its leadership in the Dakota Region.[395]

He felt enormous pressure, particularly from his mother, Edith, to not get serious with anyone who wasn't Jewish, and was told to wait until he got to college, where there would be many Jewish young women. Paul left Aberdeen to attend the University of Minnesota after graduating from high school.[396]

The Guttmann family were among the regulars at the synagogue. Paul said that his father was the main contact person when the synagogue was looking for new rabbis, and helped the new rabbis and their families settle in when they got to Aberdeen. His dad was involved in Rotary and the Chamber of Commerce in addition to his Jewish community involvement.[397]

Aberdeen Daily News, June 28, 1951

A few stores changed hands at this time. Bea Levy sold Skar's to Jo Rich, who changed its name to Jo Rich.[398] Levy also owned a store called United Clothing,[399] which, in 1951, she sold to Norman Pred. It became Norman's Men's Store, located at 12 Main Street.[400]

Aberdeen Daily News,
January 24, 1954

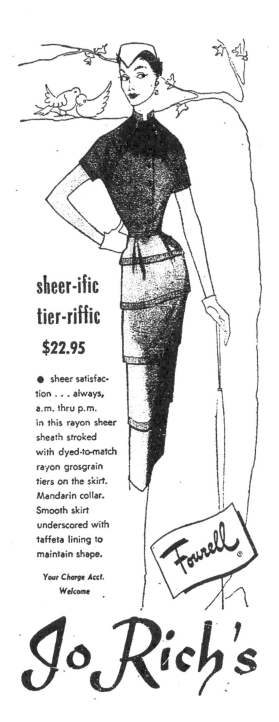

sheer-ific
tier-riffic

$22.95

● sheer satisfac-
tion . . . always,
a.m. thru p.m.
in this rayon sheer
sheath stroked
with dyed-to-match
rayon grosgrain
tiers on the skirt.
Mandarin collar.
Smooth skirt
underscored with
taffeta lining to
maintain shape.

Your Charge Acct.
Welcome

Fowell

Jo Rich's

ABERDEEN: A JEWISH HISTORY

LELAND FRANKMAN

"There's a certain feeling that I get in this little synagogue, this little building, that I don't get in Jerusalem or in Minneapolis . . . or anywhere else," Leland Frankman quoted in Aberdeen American News, September 19, 2004.[401]

Leland Frankman was born and raised in Aberdeen. His parents, both from the East Coast, owned a store downtown called Frankman's.[402]

Leland's mother, born Phyllis Mann, was the youngest of thirteen children and was just twelve years old when her mother died. One of her many older siblings was Gussie Amdur, who was living in Aberdeen at the time. By the time Phyllis was 13, she was living in Aberdeen with Gussie and Louis and attending school.[403]

After graduating from high school in Aberdeen, Phyllis attended Boston University, where she met Harry. They married and came to Aberdeen to start a business and raise a family. According to Leland, his father had always wanted to "go West."[404]

Leland said he had a full and rich Jewish life growing up in Aberdeen, and also did a lot of hunting and fishing. He remains a sportsman to this day. Now retired from the practice of law, although occasionally doing some work with his son, Harry Frankman, in the Twin Cities, Leland and his wife, Marlys spend a lot of time in Florida, where he enjoys fly fishing, a longtime passion.[405]

Aberdeen
Daily News,
March 25, 1951

Rabbi and Hilda Auerbach left Aberdeen in 1953 and he became the rabbi at the Superior Wisconsin Hebrew Congregation.[406]

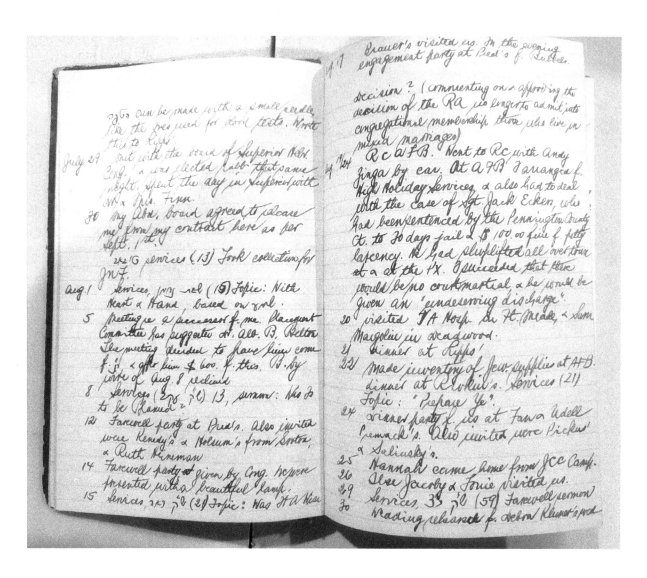

Rabbi Auerbach's daily journal entries from his final days as Congregation B'nai Isaac's rabbi. Courtesy of the Auerbach family

CHAPTER 10

RABBI DR. ABRAHAM KERTES, KERTES I YEARS: 1953-56

RABBI DR. ABRAHAM A. KERTES retains the distinction as the only rabbi to serve Aberdeen at two different times.

Rabbi Kertes was born in Hungary, where he received a Doctor of Laws from Francisco-Josephina University. His doctoral thesis was entitled, "The Rights of the Child Born Out of Wedlock," which covered the laws of European countries and the United States. It was published in Hungarian and Hebrew. It's not clear when and where he received his rabbinical ordination.

He was taken prisoner by the Russians during World War I, and escaped exile to Siberia only because he had befriended the mayor of the town, who came to his aid. After the war, he practiced law until Hitler's rise and, seeing the writing on the wall, moved to Palestine in 1934. He was sent by the rabbinate to Cyprus to minister to Jewish refugees during World War II and continued that work in the Dominican Republic in 1947. He was an expert in family legal matters and the situation of the *agunah* (chained woman)—women unable to get a religious divorce under Jewish law.[407]

The Jewish Bar Association published his paper, "Woman's Position in the Jewish Legal System." Rabbi Kertes believed that seven years' absence of a husband was much too long to prove his death considering all the advances in communications at the time.

During his time in Cyprus, according to Aberdeen's elders in later years, Rabbi Kertes served as a judge in rabbinical court and addressed the agonizing question pertaining to Jews whose spouses presumably had perished in the Holocaust and whether they could remarry without having conclusive evidence.[408] While we do not know when or where Rabbi Kertes married Margaret, who was also a native of Hungary, we do know that the two were married during the time he served as a judge in Cyprus.

After serving congregations on the East Coast, Rabbi Kertes was elected rabbi by B'nai Isaac Congregation in the fall of 1953.[409]

During these first Kertes years, Congregation B'nai Isaac affiliated formally with the Conservative movement.[410] The beginnings of the Conservative movement of Judaism in the United States came in the late 19th century. Conservative Judaism came to represent the middle ground between Orthodoxy (strictest) and Reform (the most liberal). Conservative Judaism is described as having "a dedication to *halakha* (Jewish law) as a guide for Jewish life, a deliberately non-fundamentalist teaching of Jewish principles of faith, a positive attitude toward modern culture, and an acceptance of both traditional rabbinic modes of scholarship and modern critical study of Jewish religious texts." Conservative Judaism has roots in Positive-Historical Judaism, developed in Germany in the middle of the 19th century in reaction to the liberal positions of the Reform movement.[411]

Like many of his predecessors, Rabbi Kertes became involved in the general community. Gov. Sigurd Anderson appointed him to the state's committee on children and youth[412] even before he was officially welcomed to the Jewish community.[413]

Like several of his predecessors, he noted that he and Margaret liked living in Aberdeen more than New York, where "everyone was a stranger."[414]

Shortly after his arrival in Aberdeen, he took part in the community's Memorial Day programming, giving the invocation.[415] The following year did the same at a community Veterans Day program.[416] In fact, he spoke at several Veterans Day programs during his years in Aberdeen.[417]

Just a year into his first residence in Aberdeen, Rabbi Kertes was quoted as saying that he and Margaret had found friendliness and extraordinary lovingkindness–and no signs of anti-Semitism–in Aberdeen.[418]

Becoming naturalized citizens was one of the many highlights of their first residency in Aberdeen.[419]

Margaret Kertes, front row, standing, third from left, takes oath of allegiance to the United States. *Aberdeen Daily News*, April 20, 1955

Rabbi Kertes, front row, seated, far left, becomes a naturalized citizen. *Aberdeen Daily News*, June 16, 1964

An active synagogue youth group flourished during these years, and a large interfaith youth gathering was held at the Congregation B'nai Isaac in 1954.[420]

The rabbi contributed a meditation on brotherhood on the church page of one of the local newspapers in February 1954 [421] and a column on the wisdom of the Talmud in December of that year.[422]

Like his predecessors Rabbis Hardin and Auerbach, Rabbi Dr. Kertes played a role in interfaith activity[423] and education at summer camps[424] and was active in a local group of clergymen.[425]

In addition to her duties as the rabbi's wife and involvement in a variety of organizations and causes, Margaret Kertes taught Hebrew. One of the Feinstein boys who had grown up in Aberdeen before moving to Israel returned to Aberdeen and visited Mrs. Kertes, known to the students as *morah* (teacher). According to community elders in more recent years, when he knocked on her door and spoke to her in Hebrew, she responded, "Speak English. I don't speak Hebrew." The elders relished this story since Morah Kertes was the one who taught all their children to read Hebrew and follow along in the prayerbook.[426]

Gail Pickus recalled that when one of her three sons, Michael, was in kindergarten, he came home from a class with Morah, repeating the lesson she had taught that day, most likely in preparation for *Pesach* (Passover). It took a while to figure out what he was saying because he repeated the lesson with Morah's accent, saying, "I know von, von is to God." Without Morah's accent, the phrase becomes more familiar—"I know one, one is for God"—from the Passover seder.[427]

Rabbi Kertes drew parallels between the circumstances of the Purim story and Communism.[428] This was during the Cold War, and the evils of Communism figured into many articles he wrote and in which he was quoted.[429]

In a year when Passover and Easter fell on the same day, Rabbi Kertes wrote a column that showcased his deep knowledge not only of Judaism but of Christianity.[430]

For the High Holy Days in 1954, the congregation for the first time engaged a cantor, Joseph Miller, to officiate along with the rabbi.[431] A Hebrew school chorus sang at the synagogue in the season of Shavuot, which was referred to as the "Jewish Pentecost."[432]

Aberdeen Daily News,
May 15, 1956

THE "BABY" OF THE Minneapolis Youngdahl family, the Rev. Reuben Youngdahl, pastor of Mt. Olivet Lutheran Church, gave his thoughts on the "Muddle in the Middle East" at a program sponsored by Hadassah Monday evening in the Civic Theater. Dr. Youngdahl chatted before the event with Mrs. Leonard Ribnick, president of the Aberdeen chapter of Hadassah, and the Rabbi A. A. Kertes. (American-News Photo)

GAIL PICKUS

Gail Pickus moved to Aberdeen during the first Kertes years following her marriage to Herman "Buddy" Pickus, whom she had met in college at the University of Iowa in Iowa City. Following his service in the military, they settled in Aberdeen. Gail was born and raised in Chicago in an area with a lot of Jews, a stark contrast to Aberdeen's much smaller Jewish community. This contrast, however, was entirely positive from Gail's point of view.

"Life was very comfortable," she recalled. "It was easy, lots of friends, and we were very active." That activity included Hadassah, B'nai Brith, and Sisterhood. She taught Sunday school and directed student plays at Congregation B'nai Isaac for many years.

Gail's father, Boris, an immigrant from Russia, was a commercial artist, and her mother, Avery Kite Hamilton, was a ballet dancer. Gail followed in their footsteps, studying art and becoming an artist in her own right. While raising their three sons in Aberdeen, Gail taught art classes for her neighbors, sometimes on the front lawns of their homes. This helped her keep her love of art alive during those busy years.[433]

Although her modesty prevented her from sharing this information herself, I learned that Gail was Beta Sigma Phi's First Lady of Aberdeen in 1995.[434] An international sorority, Beta Sigma Phi was founded in 1931 to bring women together for social, educational, and cultural exposure during the Great Depression. Its members raised $22 million in U. S. War Bonds during World War II.[435]

The First Lady of Aberdeen project began in 1948 to honor a local woman who contributed greatly to the community. Nominees were voted upon by Aberdeen's Beta Sigma Phi Council and First Lady committee members, with a new First Lady named each year.[436]

Gail's friends decided to surprise her with news of the award. It was December and a group of Aberdonian snowbirds had gathered at the Texas winter home belonging to one of them. Someone casually popped a videocassette into a player and Gail heard herself being described as a person with a "cheerful personality" as her trademark, and as a model that many wish they could follow. Then came the announcement that she had been named Aberdeen's First Lady for 1995.[437]

Gail's involvement in the community has included serving as one of Aberdeen's first hospice volunteers. She has also volunteered with the Aberdeen Area Arts Council, Aberdeen Community Theater, and Dakota Ballet Association, to name just a few. She has served on many boards including that of the Aberdeen Adjustment Training Center, Aberdeen's School Task Force, and Library Foundation.[438]

In addition to her commitment to the synagogue and Jewish organizations, Gail often appeared in local public school classrooms to talk about Jewish holidays and customs.[439]

Gail accompanied Helen Strauss, daughter of pioneer Jews, David and Anna Strauss, to Aberdeen Community Theater's production of *Arsenic and Old Lace* to celebrate Helen's 95th birthday in 1994.[440]

Although her three adult sons and their families live out of state, Gail continues to live in Aberdeen and serve on Congregation B'nai Isaac's board of directors.

MORE JEWISH ORGANIZATIONAL LIFE IN ABERDEEN

In 1953, the local B'nai Brith held an installation of its new officers at the synagogue. They were President Norman Pred, Vice President Herschel Premack, Recording Secretary Herb Goldberg, Financial Secretary Harry Frankman, and Treasurer Herman Ehrlich.[441]

Hadassah teas drew hundreds to the synagogue for a presentation by a Mrs. Arthur Greenwald of New York on her multiple trips to Israel.[442] The 11th Hadassah Donor dinner attracted 65 guests and included a skit called *The Case of the Wily Weapons*, presented by many of the women of the Hadassah chapter.[443]

Courtesy of
Congregation B'nai
Isaac

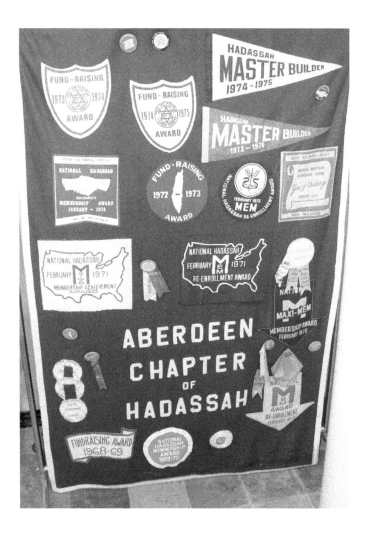

![ALEXANDER GOODMAN plaque with Hebrew text: זעליג ב"ר יוסף לייב — JUNE 7, 1956 — כ'ח סיון תש'ט"ז](inscription)

FUNERALS AND BURIALS

As mentioned earlier, there has never been a Jewish cemetery in Aberdeen. Many Aberdeen Jews have been buried in Jewish cemeteries in other towns and cities, including Minneapolis. Some have had services in both Aberdeen and the burial location.[444]

In 1944, Rabbi Perman consecrated a plot at the city's cemetery for the burial of Martin Rich. Eleanor Frank recalled that in 1951 when her father, Max Rosen, died, the congregation took a $100 option on a portion of the cemetery to create a Jewish section. Abe Feinstein, a leader in the congregation, was superstitious about the practice, and blocked the purchase. Rabbi Auerbach consecrated a separate area for Mr. Rosen's burial.[445]

When community leader William Ribnick passed away in 1954, a funeral service at a local mortuary honored his life in Aberdeen. In attendance were his fellow Rotary and Elks members, with Rabbi Kertes officiating. His burial in Minneapolis followed a second service at a Jewish funeral home there.[446]

Similarly, when Alexander Goodman passed in 1956, the burial in Minneapolis followed a local service attended by members of the American Legion and the Last Man Club of World War I.[447] When Sam Levy passed in 1971, a local service was held followed by burial at a Minneapolis Jewish cemetery.[448]

IN LOVING MEMORY OF זאב אליהו ב"ר אברהם WILLIAM RIBNICK 1881-1954 5641-5714 FOUNDER OF CONGREGATION B'NAI ISAAC

MORE ON JEWISH-OWNED BUSINESSES

Long associated with the Salinsky family, the New York Store was owned later by the Schpok family. Marvin and Jeanne ran the store from about 1950 to its closing in early 1979, as noted in the synagogue's cleverly named newsletter, *Practically the Whole Megillah*.[449]

Owned by the Frank family, The Main and Mister's were also downtown institutions. Burt and Eleanor Frank established their first store in the 1950s, which remained in operation, in various locations, for decades. Their son Steve was with the family business until its closing day, January 20, 2003.[450]

The Jewish community honored the Kerteses on their 25th anniversary with a celebration at the synagogue.[451]

Rabbi Kertes wrote a newspaper article about Hanukkah and the story of the Maccabees.[452]

The synagogue's mortgage was paid off in 1956 and the congregation held a mortgage-burning. A few months later, Rabbi and Margaret Kertes would end their first tenure in Aberdeen,[453] after the rabbi accepted a pulpit in Chatham, Ontario, Canada.[454]

Courtesy of Dacotah
Prairie Museum

Courtesy of *Aberdeen Magazine*

Reception Given At Synagogue

RABBI AND MRS. Abraham A. Kertes were honor guests on their 25th anniversary when about 50 members of the Jewish church honored them in the recreation room of the Synagogue.

Herman Pickus, president of the Synagogue, extended greetings after which Mrs. Leonard Ribnick, president of Hadassah; Leonard Ribnick, president of B'Nai Brith, and others appeared on the program.

The honor guests were presented a treasure chest on behalf of the group. The presentation was made by Mrs. Herschel Premack, president of the ladies aid.

THE CITY'S JEWISH COMMUNITY gathered in the recreation room of the Synagogue, when about 50 guests honored Rabbi and Mrs. Abraham A. Kertes on their silver wedding anniversary. Jewish Ladies Aid and Hadassah Society arranged the entertainment. Pictured at the gathering, left to right, Mrs. Herschel Premack pins a corsage on Mrs. Kertes, while Mrs. Julius Premack puts a boutonniere on the Rev. Mr. Kertes as Mrs. Herman Pickus looks on. (Photo by Graf)

Aberdeen Daily News,
Apr 15, 1956

CHAPTER 11

YEARS OF MANY CHANGES

RABBI GLASSMAN 1957

RABBI SAMUEL GLASSMAN arrived in Aberdeen from Steubenville, Ohio, in March 1957. His wife, Faye, and their daughter, Linda, arrived a short time later. A native of New York, Rabbi Glassman studied music at the Juilliard School in New York City before becoming a rabbi. He served in the South Pacific during World War II as a chaplain's assistant.[455] During their short time in Aberdeen, he provided a thorough explanation of the Passover holiday in a local news article.[456]

While the later 1950s brought multiple, short-term rabbis to Aberdeen, those years of transitions did not hinder the growth of Aberdeen's Hadassah chapter. Various artifacts indicate that the chapter was especially strong during those years.

Courtesy of Leslie Martin

A RABBI'S HOME

In 1958, Congregation B'nai Isaac purchased a home to serve as a residence for its rabbis. It was maintained as such through 1975, when it was sold.[457]

RABBI EMANUEL EISENBERG 1958

The congregation had a new rabbi by August 1958. Rabbi Emanuel Eisenberg moved to Aberdeen with his wife, Mara, and their seven-year-old son, Harry. Rabbi Eisenberg had been in the United States for a decade. Born in Austria and educated in Israel,[458] he celebrated his 31st birthday shortly after his arrival in Aberdeen.[459]

Mara Eisenberg was welcomed to Aberdeen along with other newcomers at a Welcome Wagon picnic held at Mina Lake.[460]

Rabbi Emanuel Eisenberg lights Hanukkah candles. *Aberdeen Daily News*, December 6, 1958

Rabbi Eisenberg became involved in multifaith work in the community.[461] The community continued its tradition of raising funds for those in need.

The community had many events and holiday programs including children's plays. At the Hanukkah program in 1958, the children of the synagogue staged *Joseph and His Brothers*, directed by Bea Premack. The play featured Robert Schpok, Steven Frank, Paul Guttmann, Harry Eisenberg, and Barry Feinstein.[462] The Ladies Aid presented *The Diary of Anne Frank* at the same program.[463]

Rabbi Eisenberg's tenure at Congregation B'nai Isaac was short-lived; he tendered his resignation just months after arriving, although he stayed for a year.[464] Despite their short time in Aberdeen, it seems that they were well-liked, and the women of the congregation gave a farewell luncheon for Mara Eisenberg at the Alonzo Ward Hotel.[465]

Joseph and His Brothers was performed at Congregation B'nai Isaac. Back row from left: Steven Frank, Paul Guttman, Harry Eisenberg, and Barry Feinstein. Robert Schpok is in the foreground. *Aberdeen Daily News*, December 13, 1958

RABBI DR. ABRAHAM KERTES,
KERTES II YEARS: 1959-1964

Congregation B'nai Isaac hired Rabbi Kertes again and he and Margaret Kertes returned in 1959. With their second tenure, the synagogue regained some stability for the next few years.[466] The rabbi jumped right back into his work with non-Jewish community organizations[467] in addition to the Jewish community.[468]

Martin's, a store owned by Hanna and Martin Hochster, included in one of its advertisements a notice of an upcoming lecture to be given by Rabbi Kertes.[469]

Aberdeen Daily News,
April 10, 1960

ABERDEEN: A JEWISH HISTORY

In July 1959, Rabbi Kertes wrote to the United Synagogue of America, the umbrella group for the Conservative movement, asking whether women could be included in such rituals as congregational singing and having an *aliyah* (blessing of the Torah on the bima). There are no records of an official response, although the organization, perhaps not so subtly, sent a copy of the brochure, *Standards for Synagogue Practice*. The rabbi formed a choir of women and children to assist with High Holy Days services but there are no other indications that he expanded the role of women in the congregation's ritual life.[470]

In 1964 Rabbi Dr. Kertes took a medical leave to seek help for his failing eyesight and did not return.[471] He retired to California, where he died the following year.[472] It is not confirmed, but it is thought that perhaps Margaret Kertes died in Israel.[473]

Courtesy of Leslie Martin

Courtesy of Leslie Martin

RABBI FINKEL 1965

Rabbi Elliot Finkel was the next rabbi to spend a short time in Aberdeen, so short, in fact, that only one mention of him is found in the newspapers.[474]

Community elders remember that when he arrived, he was in the process of divorcing his wife and "needed to establish that he was a good guy." Apparently, he stayed long enough to do just that, brought his wife to town for one day to formalize the divorce, and that was the end of his tenure in Aberdeen.[475]

CHAPTER 12

RABBI BENJAMIN MAZOR: 1967 - 1969

RABBI BENJAMIN AND ESTHER MAZOR and their two young sons, Isaiah (now Avishay) and Adam Aaron, arrived in Aberdeen in the winter of 1967. Esther Mazor remembered it being bitterly cold, with the snow coming almost to their knees.[476]

Rabbi Mazor, Aberdeen, 1968 Courtesy of Mazor family

Rabbi Mazor had miraculously escaped the *Shoah* (Hebrew for catastrophe, it is used to refer to the Holocaust) by fleeing with his parents to Siberia and then making his way to Palestine, where he became a rabbi. In 2022, years after his death, Esther shared details of his life, their marriage, and how they came to Aberdeen.[477]

Born in Poland in 1935 as Benjamin Gesundheit, Rabbi Mazor descended from an esteemed rabbinical family. His great-great-grandfather was Rabbi Yaakov "Yukele" Gesundheit, who served as Chief Rabbi of Warsaw from 1870-1874.[478] As the Germans approached in World War II, Benjamin, then age seven, and his parents fled into the Soviet interior.

"In Siberia, my husband's father died, perhaps of cold or hunger, and my husband was left there with his mother. His mother somehow heard of a possibility of saving her son by taking him to Tashkent, Bukhara, (in what is now Uzbekistan) to be part of the first youth *aliyah*—return to the Jewish homeland of Palestine." His mother did get him to Tashkent, to perhaps a community center, leaving him there with only a note with

Courtesy of Mazor family

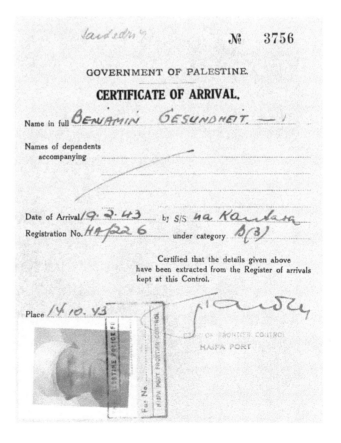

ABERDEEN: A JEWISH HISTORY

his name pinned to his jacket. From Tashkent, he was among a group of 1000 Jewish children who were sent to Tehran, Iran, where they remained for about six months. From Tehran, the children were sent to Alexandria, Egypt, and finally on to Palestine. Later, these rescued children of the first youth aliyah to Palestine (a project of Hadassah founder Henrietta Szold's) would become known as *Yeldai Tehran* (Children of Tehran).[479]

The Children of Tehran, mostly orphans, arrived in Palestine in 1943.[480]

He changed his name to Mazor, the Hebrew equivalent of Gesundheit, or "to your health,' and became an ordained rabbi and schochet in Israel.

In his adopted young country, Mazor served in the Israeli army in the mid-1950s.

Benjamin Mazor with beard looking at camera, February, 1955, Israel, Courtesy of Mazor family

Esther Mazor remembered that after his ordination in Israel and just several months after they were married, he was sent as a schochet and *bodek* (checks items to confirm that they are kosher) to Brazil. There were few cows in Israel at the time, so kosher slaughter was done in Brazil and the meat was sent frozen to Israel. On his way back to Israel from Brazil, he stopped in New York, and it was there that he received an offer to teach in Cleveland, Ohio. He planned to stay in the United States for only a year, but they remained for the rest of their lives. From Cleveland they went to Aberdeen, at which time they had been in the United States for five years.

Although ordained as an Orthdox rabbi,[481] Rabbi Mazor made clear upon his arrival in Aberdeen that he didn't advocate tradition for tradition's sake or the following of rules without understanding their meaning. He was interested in modern ways of living and understanding of the religious trends of the times.[482]

Left: Rabbi Benjamin and Esther Mazor, Aberdeen, circa late 1960s, Courtesy of Mazor family

Right: Mazor family—Rabbi Benjamin, Esther, Isaiah (now Avishay) and Adam Aaron, Aberdeen, circa late 1960s, Courtesy of Mazor family

ESTHER MAZOR

Esther Mazor lives in New York City and also spends time in Ramat Gan, Israel. Born in Israel, she trained as a nurse at Hadassah Hospital. She shared many stories about her family's years in Aberdeen in interviews in February 2022.[483]

Two such stories revealed the lengths to which they went to make sure everyone who wanted kosher meat had kosher meat. Typically, it was shipped in from Omaha, Minneapolis, and Sioux City. A Mr. Levy–perhaps

Sam, although she didn't recall–who owned a grocery store in town, made a deal with Rabbi Mazor to do some ritual slaughtering of meat at a farm near Aberdeen. Rabbi Mazor and Mr. Levy built the equipment that they needed, *kashered* (the process by which items are made kosher) the knives and packed it all up to take to the farm. They left around 6 p.m. one evening, and as the hour grew later and later, Esther became worried. The farm was only 17 miles away. What could possibly be taking so long, she wondered.[484]

The plan was for Rabbi Mazor to *schect* (slaughter) a heifer at the farm. Levy, who was also a butcher, would cut it into a variety of cuts of meat. Since there are parts of the animal that aren't kosher in any case, the farmer was happy that he would get to keep the "bottom half" of the animal.[485]

Upon their arrival, the farmer told them that he had done whatever he could to help prepare so they could get right to work. Rabbi Mazor and Levy walked into the barn to a scene they had not expected: the cow was hanging with no head and dripping blood. They explained to the farmer that they needed a living cow, not a dead one, so they had to start afresh with a different heifer.[486]

The second heifer was brought to the barn and Rabbi Mazor took out his big knife, which the farmer referred to as a machete, and did the quick cuts required for kosher slaughtering. He then opened the cow to check the lungs, another requirement for kosher meat. The farmer was amazed and said it was the most humane killing he had ever seen. Then came the salting and soaking processes required for kashering meat, and finally, the meat was ready for Levy to butcher.[487]

Rabbi Mazor finally arrived home at about four o'clock in the morning, safe and sound, much to Esther's relief, with a bit of explaining to do. More than 50 years later, she remembered the cuts of meat wrapped in wax paper, including delicacies like tongue and lungs, which they stored in the deep freeze in their basement.[488]

Esther also recalled receiving a letter years ago from a Jewish man in Schenectady, New York, whose son was a new doctor and recently married. Through the U.S. military, the couple would soon be stationed at the medical corps of an Indian reservation in Eagle Butte, South Dakota, and the father reached out to the Mazors to make a connection. The couple would need kosher meat.[489]

Of course they would help this couple who would be living more than 100 miles away. At least once, the Mazors ordered the meat, including kosher ducks from Omaha, and drove 168 miles with two kids to the reservation where the couple was stationed.[490] (The doctor, James Strosberg, remembered them bringing kosher goose, as well as their dog, "Tiran.")[491]

While at Eagle Butte delivering kosher meat to the couple, Esther Mazor purchased a piece of Indigenous art. More than a half century later it still hangs in her New York City apartment.[492]

Original art purchased at Eagle Butte in the late 1960s, Courtesy of Mazor family

In 1967, shortly after the Six Day War, Esther traveled with her two young sons to Israel. She recalled that they took a very small plane from Aberdeen to Minneapolis, where they connected to Chicago, and finally to New York, before flying to Israel.[493]

Esther shared a story from their early years in Aberdeen.

"I was at home with the two boys one day and heard the doorbell ring. The door was glass, so I could see who was on the other side. It was a lady wearing a hat with a huge ribbon on it. She was carrying a basket. At that time, I had been in the United States for only four years, so my English wasn't as good as it is now. When I opened the door, the lady wearing the hat started talking so fast that I couldn't understand what she was saying."[494]

Small plane from Aberdeen, first leg of trip to Israel, Esther, Isaiah (now Avishay) and Aaron Mazor, 1967, Courtesy of Mazor family

The woman in the hat was a representative from the Welcome Wagon. She gave Esther coupons for local businesses and invited her an upcoming get-together at the Alonzo Ward Hotel.[495]

"There must have been a thousand women there," she said. "It was packed. There was singing and talking and food and drink. They held a meeting, and I was asked what I was interested in organizing. I said I would like to learn to play bridge."[496]

A bridge club soon formed, and the women met weekly at one another's homes. Esther remembered one of the women in particular, a very pale and blonde Scandinavian woman by the name of Mecklenberg. Her husband was a dentist and worked for the U.S. health services. They were also foster parents. Esther said she remembered her because she was a newcomer too. Esther was the only Jewish person in the bridge group.[497]

About those coupons in the welcome basket: one was for a beauty school in town. Esther appreciated the introduction, and scheduled her hair appointments and manicures there the entire time the Mazors lived in Aberdeen.[498]

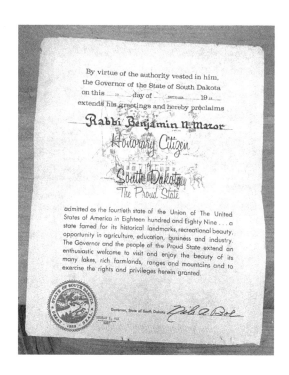

Abe Pred, then a senator in the South Dakota State Legislature, recommended that Rabbi Mazor be named an honorary citizen of South Dakota.[499]

Esther described Gail Pickus as a marvelous artist. The Mazors had a photograph of Rabbi Shaul Brook, who oversaw Rabbi Mazor's ordination in Israel. Gail created a beautiful painting based on the photo.[500]

Painting of Rabbi
Shaul Brook by Gail
Pickus, late 1960s,
Courtesy of Mazor
family

Esther had a particularly Jewish version of a fish story.

"Mr. Premack—Udell—was an avid fisherman. Many Sunday mornings, when I went out to get the newspaper, a carp would be waiting alongside it. One Sunday, there was this gigantic carp. Apparently, most people didn't like carp but it was perfect to make gefilte fish." She made the delicacy often and shared it with the Preds, Pickuses, and others.[501]

The hospital in Aberdeen, St. Luke's, had a refresher course for nurses. Rabbi Mazor was asked on several occasions to give lectures on Judaism to attendees. One night, he was asked what his wife did, and he replied that she was a nurse. Shortly thereafter, Esther Mazor was taking the nursing refresher courses with the other women.[502]

The Mazors appreciated the friendliness of Aberdonians and the warm welcome their family received, and delighted in the quiet, open spaces of their town.[503]

Esther Mazor, pictured at far left. A Star of David is barely visible on her Hadassah Hospital nurses cap. Courtesy of Mazor family.

Rabbi and Esther Mazor spent their time in Aberdeen not just nurturing the local Jewish community, which they certainly did, but also engaging enthusiastically in interfaith and community work.[504]

Rabbi Mazor presented the Boy Scouts' Ner Tamid award to Brian Friedman for extensive study and participation in religion,[505] and the Girl Scouts' Menorah Award to Ellen Premack.[506]

In addition to their family and professional responsibilities, both Rabbi[507] and Esther[508] Mazor found time to model for a local store.

Rabbi Mazor presented the Ner Tamid award to boy scout, Brian Friedman. This award is given to scouts for religious studies. *Aberdeen Daily News*, February 11, 1968

Rabbi Mazor presented the Menorah Award to girl scout, Ellen Premack. Premack was the first girl to earn this award in the Nyoda Girl Scout Council. *Aberdeen Daily News*, April 7, 1968

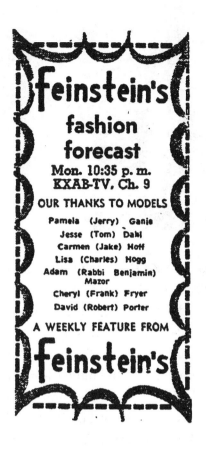

feinstein's
fashion
forecast

Mon. 10:35 p. m.
KXAB-TV, Ch. 9

OUR THANKS TO MODELS

Pamela (Jerry) Ganje

Jesse (Tom) Dahl

Carmen (Jake) Hoff

Lisa (Charles) Hogg

Adam (Rabbi Benjamin)
Mazor

Cheryl (Frank) Fryer

David (Robert) Porter

A WEEKLY FEATURE FROM

feinstein's

Models For Style Show Announced

MODELS for the Welcome Wagon style show were chosen when the group met on the mezzanine of the Downtowner Friendship Inn.

Those selected were Mrs. Kenneth Bryant, Mrs. Betty Bartholomew, Mrs. W i l l i a m Linzbach, Mrs. Douglas Rogers, Mrs. William Clapper, Mrs. R. E. Mecklenburg, Mrs. Carl Anderson, Mrs. Dennis Stern, Mrs. D. H. Bruce, Mrs. Walter Henderson and Mrs. Benjamin Mazor.

Reservations for the style show March 4-5 may be made by contacting Mrs. Bruce or Mrs. Bryant Pierce.

Mrs. David Lias, president of the evening group was a guest. Hostesses were Mrs. Clara Hubbell, Mrs. Lyda Euneau and Mrs. Lloyd Pallie.

A valentine tree hung with cupids, hearts and lovebirds was the head table centerpiece. Bridge winners were Mrs. Joe Dean and Mrs. Ethel Holst. Winners at canasta were Mrs. Harvey Schneider and Mrs. William Bartz. The special prize was won by Mrs. Arthur Kittlesland.

Left: *Aberdeen Daily News*, Mar 27, 1967

Right: *Aberdeen Daily News*, Feb 16, 1968

Courtesy of Premack family

And sometimes, clothing business and Jewish organizational business ended up on the same page!

Pictured Left to Right: Shirley Coval, Rabbi Mazor, Sally Friedman, Eleanor Frank. Courtesy of Mazor family

Esther Mazor was the speaker at the 1967 Hadassah Donor dinner, held at the Alonzo Ward Hotel. She discussed the Hadassah Medical Center in Israel and her work there as a student nurse and later as a Registered Nurse. The event included the installation of officers: President Jeanne Schpok; Vice President Leda Levy; Secretary Gail Pickus; and Treasurer Bea Premack. Carol Feinstein, who had made the dinner arrangements, was the toastmistress. Ladies Aid officers were also introduced that evening: President Sally Friedman; Vice President Sue Pred; and Secretary-Treasurer Shirley Coval. Mrs. Morris Strauss of Atlanta, Georgia, was in attendance as a guest of her daughter, Marion Guttmann.[509]

A middle-aged man in Aberdeen who was a judge came to the Mazors' home one year for a Passover seder–1967, '68 or maybe '69, Esther said. When he arrived, he presented them with a beautiful illustrated Haggadah. Esther said that they used it every year thereafter when they had a seder in their home. Their guest was Judge Moses Lindau, whose name came up several times in my research. Born in Iowa in 1910 to German Jewish immigrants, Moses Landau practiced law in Aberdeen before becoming a Brown County judge.[510] And sometimes, clothing business and Jewish organizational business ended up on the same page!

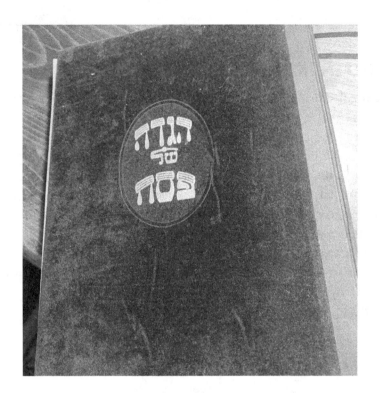

Gift from Judge Moses
Lindau, Courtesy of
Mazor family

JUDGE MOSES LINDAU

Judge Moses "Mose" Lindau recalled that Rabbi Perman was rabbi when he moved to Aberdeen. Some years later, he married Rose Berkman Schloff, a widow from St. Paul, and adopted her son, Mark. Rose became active in Hadassah and Ladies Aid, and Mark in BBYO.[511]

Mose was a founder of Aberdeen's Boys Club and the Dakota Home for Children and was an incorporator and board member of the South Dakota Northeastern Mental Health Center.[512]

Lindau recalled a warm and friendly community, however, he mentioned that during his time in Aberdeen, the son of a police officer painted a swastika on the door of the *shul* (synagogue). A judge placed the boy on probation and required that he make restitution.[513]

When the Lindaus' son, Mark, was 13, there was no resident rabbi in the community so there was no formal bar mitzvah. Mark was confirmed later with Bonnie Frankman, Sharon Premack, Nancy Schpok, and Debbie and Pamela Seltzer.[514]

The Lindaus retired to Portland, Oregon, where both died in the 1990s.[515]

Undated Photo
Courtesy of
Premack family

Rabbi Mazor teaches Hebrew classes. From left: Brian Friedman, Judy Premack, Rabbi Mazor, Wendy Feinstein, and David Pickus. *Aberdeen Daily News*, March 31, 1968

The Mazors left Aberdeen for Pennsylvania by the summer of 1969 but sent news of the birth of their daughter to their former community.[516]

By the High Holy Days in 1967, receptions following the services were being held in congregants' private homes, reflecting a community shrinking in size.[517]

LADIES AID AND HADASSAH IN RECENT YEARS

For many years, Ladies Aid held rummage sales, which were well attended in part because the stores donated new items for the events.[518] Herschel and Bea Premack recalled that, at one point, Ladies Aid lost the downtown space they had used. They relocated to the synagogue but there was some concern that people might feel uncomfortable coming to a synagogue. As it turned out, people lined up around the block, and Ladies Aid made $350–a considerable amount back then. Ladies Aid also held an annual brunch at the synagogue that was open to the public. Much later, they held bake sales.

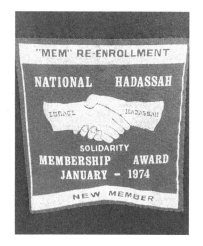

"The girls used to sell cheesecake," as Herschel put it. Bea explained that they sold them as a Hadassah fundraiser at the city's annual Arts in the Park festival. "It got to be that people thought cheesecake was a Jewish recipe," Bea said.[519] The selling of cheesecakes at the event began in 1979 as the brainchild of Joan Altman.[520]

Bea Premack

The Jewish Press, Feb 11, 2005, Courtesy of Premack family

THE PREMACKS' DEEP COMMITMENT TO THEIR COMMUNITY

The first time I interviewed the Premacks, in May 2018, at a point near the end of our nearly two-hour long conversation, Herschel said, "You have to come downstairs with me for a minute." I turned off the recorder and followed him to their basement, where he showed me a full wall of certificates chronicling Bea's decades of involvement in Jewish and other community organizations.

Among the groups represented on the wall were Ladies Aid, Hadassah, South Dakota Arts Council, the Aberdeen Area Arts Council, Northern State University, Chamber of Commerce, Aberdeen Development Corporation, Governor's Award for the Arts, Dakota Dance, Oz Festival, the local Diversity Coalition, American Association of University Women, and the League of Women Voters.[521]

"Bea and a couple of the other girls are responsible for keeping the synagogue alive," Herschel said. "On top of that, they are also responsible for making the city aware that there are Jewish people living here and active in organizations that represent the Jewish community."

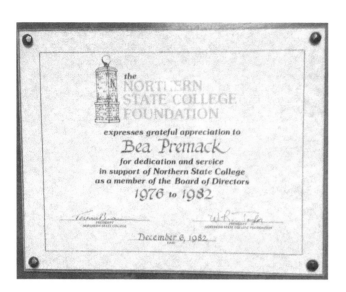

Courtesy of Premack
family

It is no surprise that Bea Premack, like Gail Pickus many years later, was also named a First Lady of Aberdeen, in 1975.[522]

Bea was recognized in 2021 for having been a charter member of South Dakota Public Broadcasting.[523]

Over the years, Herschel was a regular visitor to any Jews who were hospitalized locally, Bea told me. He had a special role in reaching out in another very specific way, as well. It seems that the Chamber of Commerce developed a habit of contacting Herschel whenever Jews were visiting Aberdeen and considering moving there. Barred from asking anything specific about religion, the Chamber of Commerce would call Herschel and use a code such as, "You know there's some people who came into my office today and I think you'd really like to meet them." And then the Premacks would meet with them. Some came and settled in Aberdeen, others did not. Once, the Premacks received a phone call from someone considering a move who asked, "Do you have grocery stores in Aberdeen?"[524]

DR. JAMES AND MARGO STROSBERG

Dr. James Strosberg and his wife, Margo, were among those who came to the region at this time. From 1968-70, he was stationed at the Public Health Service Indian Hospital at Eagle Butte, South Dakota, 173 miles southwest of Aberdeen. They had come from Schenectady, New York.[525]

Congregation B'nai Isaac became central to their lives. Dr. Strosberg recalled the same story that Esther Mazor had shared with me about the Mazors bringing kosher meat to Eagle Butte. Kosher meat came to them thereafter via a "laundry man" named Elmer making his dry-cleaning run. At first, they were the only Jews at the hospital but by their second year they were joined by two other Jewish doctors and a Jewish dentist.[526]

One year for Yom Kippur, the Strosbergs and the other Jewish doctors and their wives—the Dickmans and the Pragers—rented an airplane, which was run by the local undertaker, and flew from Eagle Butte to Aberdeen to attend services and observe the holiest day on the Jewish calendar. The Mazors had left Aberdeen by then and Rabbi Berglas was leading the congregation.[527]

Bea and Herschel Premack hosted the visitors for the evening meal before Yom Kippur began. The Strosbergs stayed at the home of a Public Health Service employee in Aberdeen, who apparently had asked the rabbi what Jews could eat. She ordered tuna fish on paper plates for the next day, but they couldn't eat it because, of course, it was Yom Kippur.[528]

Dr. Kenny Prager and Dr. Bob Dickman each led part of the service, and Dr. Strosberg had the honor of chanting *Mafter Yonah* (the Torah reading specific to Yom Kippur day). The rabbi commented in his sermon about the six of them being brave to fly in a small plane.[529]

The travelers were in a bit of a rush. Eagle Butte didn't have an actual airport. There was only a landing strip with no lights, which meant that they would have to leave Aberdeen in time to land while it was still daylight. That was a problem, as Jewish holy days begin and end in the evening. Yom Kippur wasn't over until the final blowing of the *shofar* (ram's horn).[530]

Dr. Strosberg told the rabbi of their dilemma. Rabbi Berglas replied that he forbade them from desecrating the sanctity of the holy day. Therefore, he declared, they would blow the shofar at three o'clock in the afternoon, "ending" the day early. And that is what happened.[531]

Of the trip home to Eagle Butte, Dr. Strosberg said, "I remember flying back over the Missouri river with the moon coming up over one side and the sun going down on the other, and having the box lunch of tuna fish sandwiches," that they couldn't eat earlier. "That was the best Yom Kippur I can ever remember." Congregation B'nai Isaac touched their lives and would be a part of them forever, he said. He expressed deep appreciation for their efforts that helped them keep kosher during their years in Eagle Butte.[532]

CHAPTER 13

RABBI JOSEPH BERGLAS: 1969-1971

RABBI JOSEPH BERGLAS assumed the pulpit in June 1969 following the departure of the Mazors. He and his wife, Frances, were both born in Poland, where he completed his education and obtained his rabbinical degree. Each fled in 1939, then met and married as refugees. Rabbi Berglas spent five years at a displaced persons camp in Oslo, Norway, serving Jewish war refugees. They lived in Canada for fifteen years, where he served as rabbi, cantor, and Hebrew teacher at various times in different locations, and sometimes as all three.[533]

Rabbi Joseph Berglas, *Aberdeen Daily News*, Sep 28, 1969

Rabbi Berglas commented on the kindness and friendliness of the reception that he and his family had received. Like his predecessors, he engaged in interfaith work. Just a few months into his residency in Aberdeen, he appeared as the guest speaker at the local Scandinavian Lutheran Church making a presentation to the American Lutheran Church Women (ALCW).[534]

Rabbi Berglas had 18 students under his tutelage in the fall of 1969.[535] He wrote an article for the *Aberdeen Daily News* about the bat mitzvah of Wendy Feinstein in September of that year, which was accompanied by her photo.[536] At that time, bat mitzvahs were a fairly recent practice in Jewish life.

"From Biblical times to present," he wrote, "Jewish tradition has emphasized the value and importance of women. The Matriarchs, or mothers of the nation, were accorded the same respect down through the ages as were the Patriarchs. They have been surrounded by a halo of beauty, virtue, and wisdom. The bat mitzvah is a manifestation of that attitude."

Days later, the local news reported on Rosh Hashanah, referring to it as "Yom Hadin," (Day of Judgment). Rabbi Berglas explained that the holiday marked the beginning of the Jewish year 5730, adding, "Introspection is the order of these solemn days. We are reminded that we, as adults, ought to be cognizant of our mortal shortcomings." [537]

Wendy Feinstein's Bat Mitzvah. *Aberdeen Daily News*, September 7, 1969

WENDY FEINSTEIN is pictured as she appeared during the Bat Mitzva ceremonies in the Synagogue B'Nai Isaac. She celebrated the Bat Mitzva, which signifies her completion of the first step in her religious training and her full membership in the congregation. (American-News Photo)

Bat Mitzva For Wendy Feinstein

YOUTH GROUP

The youth group of Congregation B'nai Isaac hosted a regional convention for United Synagogue Youth (USY) in May 1971. This was an extraordinary undertaking and an honor for the congregation. This was the first time that such a small USY chapter had hosted the event.[538]

Held at the Holiday Inn, the convention drew nearly 100 Jewish youth from Canada, Minnesota, Nebraska, Colorado, Missouri and North Dakota,[539] as well as other parts of South Dakota.[540]

Brian Friedman and Ellen Premack served as co-chairs, and other Aberdeen youth, including Dave Pickus, Judy Premack, Wendy Feinstein, Mike Pickus, Marjorie Frank, and Marc Feinstein, played key roles in this event. The weekend agenda included an address by Rabbi Joseph Wiesenberg, a beloved and legendary regional United Synagogue official.[541] Known to generations of USYers as Rabbi Joe, he and his late wife, Eva, were Holocaust survivors.

Another special guest at the convention was a young Danny Siegel, who became active in USY at a young age and had served as international president. He later became a leading figure in reinvigorating the discussion of tzedakah and *tikkun olam* (repairing the world) in Jewish communities.[542] A poet and self-described author of twenty-nine and one-half books, he has written on topics as diverse as *mitzvah* (literally commandment but also a good deed) heroism, personalized tzedakah, and Talmudic quotes about living the Jewish life well.[543]

Moved by the small but mighty congregation, Siegel wrote a poem entitled "*Beyt haknesset*: a *chavurah* for worship, study & community, Psalm 55, For the Jews of B'nai Isaac of Aberdeen, South Dakota." (Beyt haknesset is Hebrew for synagogue and chavurah is a study group.) A similar version of the poem with the dedication, "To Herschel," hangs in the Premack family home.

Courtesy of Congregation B'nai Isaac

5736/1975 September 15   Volume 1, No. 2

Richard Kneip Visits Aberdeen

On July 8, Governor Richard Kneip came to Aberdeen to talk to the Jewish Community about his recent trip to Russia. Attending that meeting were three USYers and many outstanding people from the Jewish Community.

Gov. Kneip praised the Aberdeen Jewish Community for bringing to his attention the great problems that Russian Jews were facing, before he left on his trip. He also added that other Jews around the country had contacted the other Governors that were going with him about the Soviet Jewry problem.

While in Russia, Gov. Kneip said, "We discoused the Soviet Jewry problem with many Soviet Officials only to get a response, if any, of 'Don't interfere with our internal offairs'". Once when Gov. Kneip brought up the Soviet Jewry question, the Soviet official stood up and walked out of the room.

Gov. Kneip, while in Russia, visited Dr. Lerner, a prominent soviet Jewish activist, and both discussed the Jackson Admendment. After a great length of argument, both pro and con, they came to the conclution that the Jackson Admendment was good because it brought world attention to the Soviet Jewry problem.

Afterwords, Gov. Kneip answered many questions from the Aberdeen Jewish Community.

USY SWIM PARTY

The USYers got together June 29 and did a little swimming. They swam for about an hour then babysat at Adam Altman's birthday party. The purpose was simply to have a good time, and we sure did. Our thanks go to the Altmans for the use of their pool.

ELECTIONS

Our meeting started the same as usual, but when it was over a new Presidentand new officers had been elected. Jon Pickus was elected pres, taking the job from Paul Premack. Paul was a very good president and we thank him very much for all he's done for our chapter. Other officers were: Paul Premack, Vice President; Rick Walter, Secretary; Paul Premack, Treasurer; and Corresponding Secretary, Mike Fred. It looks like a good year!

HERZL CAMP

Herzl campthis year was just as good as it was last year. There was one new thing. It was an Israeli day where they give you Israeli food, andsome special programs and study groups. Otherwise camp was very much the same. The spirit was high, the food rotten, and everyoneseemed to have a great time.

Courtesy of Congregation B'nai Isaac

Aberdeen's USY chapter was called K'ton Ton, a reference to its small size (*k'ton* is the Hebrew word for small). Like its parent congregation, this USY chapter was active and involved. A two-page issue of the *Kton Ton Gazette* from September 1975, written by chapter members, is rich with insights into youth activities at B'nai Isaac. Featured is a report on a visit from the governor of South Dakota, Richard Kneip, who came to Aberdeen to speak with the Jewish community about his trip to Russia. He praised the community for calling his attention to the issue of Soviet Jewry. The newsletter also mentions a swim party for USYers at the Altmans' home, after which the teens babysat at the young Adam Altman's birthday party. Reports were provided on the summer at Herzl Camp and USY camp, and yard work performed at the synagogue by the chapter members.

Courtesy of author

Also promoted were regional USY opportunities, including a conclave. Several of those who had been active in the 1971 regional convention had graduated from high school by this time, leaving only four members in the local chapter. The article on chapter elections contained no surprises. All four members were elected as officers.

BEST SMALL CHAPTER

EMTZA REGION USY

1973

In addition to USY, the synagogue's young people were involved with B'nai Brith Youth Organization (BBYO), an organization that is open to all branches of Judaism; and Young Judaea, a Zionist youth organization.[544]

While no news could be located about the departure of Rabbi Berglas from Aberdeen, there is no further reference to him in the local news after May of 1971. A gravestone found in a North Miami Beach cemetery indicates that he died in 1993. Interestingly, his first name is spelled "Josef" on the stone.[545]

CHAPTER 14

1971 TO THE PRESENT: THE YEARS WITHOUT A FULL-TIME RABBI

RABBI BERGLAS WAS ABERDEEN'S last full-time rabbi. After he left in the early 1970s, leadership was assumed by congregants. The congregation also hired various clergy members over the years to lead High Holy Days services.[546]

For decades, Herschel Premack has led Friday evening services. Services on the High Holy Days these days are shorter than they were with rabbinical leadership, but Herschel said they do their best to include "the important parts." The community had been quite fortunate, he said, because of the many helpful people who have assisted in conducting services. Sometimes people would simply show up and offer up their skills, he said. For example, when Dr. James and Margo Strosberg returned for services during this time, she knew all of the tunes for the prayers and songs and led the congregation that year. A few years ago, a man by the name of Bruce Klein showed up and said, "I know this part of the service. I'll help you with it."[547]

For several years the community hired David Gordon, who came from Wisconsin with his wife, Susan, to preside over either Rosh Hashanah or Yom Kippur services. David was hired again in 2018 to conduct Yom Kippur services, marking the last time an individual from outside of the congregation was brought in to officiate at High Holy Days services.[548]

David and Susan Gordon, Courtesy of Congregation B'nai Isaac

Adam Altman, Susan and David Gordon, Courtesy of Congregation B'nai Isaac

SUNDAY SCHOOL AND
HEBREW SCHOOL

Unsigned and undated drawing, believed to have been created by a Sunday school student Courtesy of Congregation B'nai Isaac

For many years Bea Premack and Gail Pickus taught Hebrew school and Sunday school respectively. For a time, Sunday school met in Gail's home, and the kids learned Jewish cooking and enjoyed other fun Jewish learning experiences. In these years and even before, Sunday school students regularly performed plays at the Purim and Hanukkah holidays. Bea taught the kids how to read Hebrew in preparation for their b'nai mitzvah.[549]

Sunday school students created models of the B'nai Isaac sanctuary and the State of Israel. Courtesy of Leslie Martin

ADAM ALTMAN

Around the time of Rabbi Berglas's departure from Aberdeen in the early 1970s, Adam Altman was born in Iowa City, where his father was completing medical school. His family moved to Aberdeen in 1973, where Adam grew up. He spent some time in other places during college and thereafter, and returned to Aberdeen full time in 2006, where he practices law.[550]

Altman remembered Congregation B'nai Isaac as a fun place to be when he was growing up. He recalls playing games, including *dreidel* (Hanukkah spinning top game) in the synagogue's basement.[551]

As a Sunday school student, he was involved in refurbishing the large 3-dimensional map of Israel created by students who preceded him. Gail Pickus, one of the synagogue's longest serving Sunday school teachers, was Adam's teacher. He remembers a couple of classmates who were Soviet Jews. Altman continues to attend synagogue on occasion, and has enjoyed helping with groundskeeping in recent years. Altman holds the synagogue and the community close to his heart.[552]

Aberdeen's chapter celebrated Hadassah's 60th anniversary in 1972.[553] Noted as Hadassah committee chairs that year were Gail Pickus, Carol Feinstein, Bess Premack, Sue Pred, Sally Friedman, and Eleanor Frank.[554]

Aberdeen Daily News, February 13, 1972

ITEMS THAT were made in Israel and were given as awards to the Aberdeen chapter of Hadassah are compared by Mmes. Manley Feinstein, David Deutsch and Al Coval. The awards were given for participation in the Jewish National fund, Israel education services, and Youth Aliyah programs. Mrs. Deutsch is a regional vice president from Minnesota; Mrs. Feinstein is also a regional vice president; and Mrs. Coval is a past regional officer. (American-News Photo)

Left: *Aberdeen Daily News*, March 05, 1972

Right: *Aberdeen Daily News*, August 30, 1972

A local Hadassah fashion show featured Israeli fashions in 1974.[555] Hadassah fashion shows were much anticipated events in the community, with the 1977 event receiving extensive coverage in the local news. As with so many Jewish community events, the fashion shows were also fundraisers.[556]

Unidentified women modeling Israeli fashions, *Aberdeen Daily News*, September 22, 1974

THE FEINSTEIN FAMILY

In 1974, Carol Feinstein was elected as a delegate to the South Dakota State Democratic Convention. She served as secretary of the Brown County Democratic Party for 10 years.[557] Carol was honored in 1975 for her work in international endeavors with the American Field Service (AFS).[558]

Carol Feinstein, left, modeling flapper dress as part of a Bicentennial Style Show. *Aberdeen Daily News*, September 12, 1976

Flapper dress worn by Carol Feinstein   *Connie Siegel in 1930s creation*   *Jean Lantsberger models 1895 gown*

Courtesy of Aberdeen Magazine

Carol and Manley Feinstein live in the Denver area near their daughter, Wendy.[559] Their son Barry lives in Jerusalem,[560] and son, Marc, was a member of the South Dakota House of Representatives from 2005-2015.[561]

The synagogue's newsletter, *Practically the Whole Megillah*, from May 1, 1980, contains probably one of the most unusual things ever written in a synagogue newsletter. At that time, the Premacks lived out in the country. In a section referring to Brochin's, the Judaica store that existed for many years in Minneapolis, a note advised that Bea would be stopping there in

May, so if anyone wanted anything, they should let her know. That in itself isn't unusual, but the parenthetical statement that followed is: "Stop and see the new colt at Premack's".[562]

A 1984 article co-written by Bea Premack and former Aberdonian Marcia Lawson states, among other things, that the congregation had dwindled to 15 families, about the same number of Jews who lived in Aberdeen in 1910. [563]

THE MIRACLE OF THE TORAH COVER

as written by Herschel Premack and shared with the author

Traditional Jewish mysticism holds that four things can annul the decree that seals a person's fate: alms, prayer, change of name, and change of deeds. Sometimes Jewish people who are ill will change their names in hopes of preventing death from finding them. This story is an example of that belief put into practice.

As this happened back in the late 1920s or early '30s, you are getting this second hand.

I believe that it was a young Joe Sudow who was gravely ill, and to ward off the evil spirits, his mother hand-made a new Torah cover and sewed a different/new name on the front so evil spirits would not recognize her ill child. Joe recovered from his illness and, apparently, all was soon forgotten.

During B'nai Isaac's 90th anniversary celebration, Joy Sudow Sager and her family visited, and while at the synagogue, she recalled the incident and inquired about the Torah cover.

To her surprise, Bea Premack went to the cabinet used to store Torah covers and pulled out that very Torah cover and returned it to the Sudow family.

Joy was filled with a mixture of joy and gratitude as the Torah cover made by her mother's hand, to save her sick brother, was returned for the family to have as a keepsake and heirloom.

BEN VICTOR

Benjamin Victor arrived in Aberdeen in 2001 to study art, specifically sculpture, at Northern State University. Although Jewish, the Bakersfield, California, native had not had much exposure to Jewish life and was interested in learning more about his heritage. During his years in Aberdeen, Congregation B'nai Isaac became a second home to him, and the Jews of Aberdeen a second family.[564]

During the time he served on the synagogue's grounds and aesthetics committee, there was discussion of the condition of the wooden Ten Commandments above the synagogue's front door: they were rotting and decaying, and the paint chipping. The committee considered refinishing it but Victor volunteered to replace the wooden original with a bronze version so it would last forever.

Courtesy of Dale Bluestein

ABERDEEN: A JEWISH HISTORY

Aberdeen War Memorial. Courtesy of benjaminvictor.com

Victor received his first big commission while only a sophomore: the Aberdeen War Memorial sculpture at the Aberdeen Regional Airport.[565]

His second commission made him a national figure at age 26. This commission was for a sculpture depicting Sarah Winnemucca, a Native American author, activist, educator, and spokesperson for the Northern Paiute.[566] It was a considerable honor for such a young artist, as the sculpture's destination was the National Statuary Hall Collection in the U.S. Capitol in Washington, D.C., representing the state of Nevada. The bronze sculpture was dedicated in 2005.[567]

Sarah Winnemucca. Courtesy of benjaminvictor.com

Victor is the youngest sculptor ever to be represented in the Hall,[568] and in 2019 he became the only living artist to have three works in that space.[569] He is known for his exceptional ability to capture the human figure in great detail.

These two early commissions launched a career that has produced sculptures for sites around the world.[570]

Victor remained in Aberdeen until 2014 and now lives in Boise, Idaho. He remembers being enthusiastically welcomed by the congregation and the city. Of B'nai Isaac he said, "I felt so loved by that small community. They treated me with so much patience. I didn't know much about my Jewish ancestry, and they took so much time with me to teach me about the history of Judaism, the faith and practice, and the Hebrew language. It added a richness to my life that was missing before. It was a wonderful time to be a part of the community and I really miss it. They treated every single one of us as if we were their family."[571] In June of 2022, during a walking tour of downtown Aberdeen, local historian Troy McQuillan, pointed out a building on the west side of Main Street that formerly housed a Jewish-owned business. According to McQuillan, Ben Victor had recently purchased that building to house his art studio, and has plans to move back to Aberdeen, with his family, in the near future.

In my recent interview with him, Victor mentioned Nathan Green, a congregant he befriended during his time in Aberdeen. Green, who had developmental disabilities, loved being at the synagogue. Congregants took turns picking him up from the nearby town where he lived to take him to services, where he greeted everyone.[572] Nathan Green was the brother of Arthur Green, whose memories of life in Aberdeen are noted in Chapter 8. Nathan passed away in February 2021,[573] and his wife, Theresa, passed away just six weeks later.[574]

Congregation B'nai Isaac in 2022 counts a handful of dedicated people. The current board includes President Jerry Taylor; Vice President Gail Pickus; Treasurer Joyce Kimmel, a transplant of several decades from the East Coast; and Secretary Matt Perreault, a newcomer to town along with his wife, Liz Sills, and their toddler, Remy.

Sills, Perreault, and Remy, are among the newest Jews in Aberdeen, having arrived during the summer of 2016. They both work at Northern State University, where Liz teaches communications studies and Matt works in admissions.[575]

Perreault, originally from Connecticut, and Sills, from Indiana, met while doing graduate work in Louisiana. While there, Sills had found information online about Congregation B'nai Isaac, surprised to find a synagogue in a town the size of Aberdeen. After relocating, they walked into the synagogue lobby on a Friday just before services. They remembered a look of shock coming over the faces of the five or six people sitting there at seeing new faces. They were instantly welcomed and have been a part of the community since. They admitted, though, to experiencing a bit of culture shock upon arriving in a city smaller than some of the educational institutions they had attended.[576]

Perreault mentioned that although the Jewish community is small, the synagogue serves the general community in other ways. For example, Board President Jerry Taylor and others regularly welcome non-Jews into the synagogue and give mini lessons on Judaism.[577]

Herschel Premack at left. Yelduz Shrine Horse Patrol. Courtesy of Premack family

Perreault is also involved with the Freemasons, thanks to Herschel and Bea Premack. He said that the Freemasons will not serve pork at monthly Masonic luncheons out of respect for the Premacks.[578]

The Premacks are fixtures in Aberdeen and very well respected, Perreault remarked. Referring to their place in the Jewish community, he added, "They are not only the Jewish ambassadors and matriarch and patriarch of the Jewish community of Aberdeen, but also all of South Dakota."

Jerry Taylor has been president of the congregation for a number of years. Speaking of the Premacks' dedication to the synagogue, he said, "He (Herschel) and Bea have kept the synagogue open and going through the sheer force of their will."[579]

Courtesy of Congregation B'nai Isaac

Today, South Dakota has the smallest Jewish population of any state, only 400 in 2021. In the tenth least diverse state, those identifying as Jewish represent less than one-tenth of one percent of the population.[580]

In March 2021, the beloved home of Congregation B'nai Isaac was listed on the South Dakota State Register of Historic Places.[581]

These stories are evidence of the vibrant Jewish community that once thrived in Aberdeen. The close-knit community prospered and contributed to the vitality of this midwestern prairie city.

For almost a century and a half, Jewish people have been part of the story of Aberdeen, from pioneer Jews to those living there today. They celebrated life and created connections that remain strong, even among those who have moved away. For those who have passed, may their memories be always for a blessing.

EPILOGUE

IN THE MIDDLE OF JUNE 2022, along with a dozen fellow travelers, I journeyed from Minneapolis, Minnesota by coach to Aberdeen, South Dakota. There we met several others who had either driven separately from the Twin Cities or had come to join us from other locations. In total, we were about 20 individuals, and by our presence, we increased the local Jewish population greatly for a period of just under forty-eight hours.

Our purpose was to spend a weekend with Aberdeen's Jewish community, to celebrate Shabbat together and to mark 105 years of Congregation B'nai Isaac.

That the current congregation, which numbers fewer than a dozen, continues to meet weekly to mark the Sabbath, and comes together for the Jewish High Holy Days and other dates on the Jewish calendar, is nothing short of remarkable.

Debby McNeil reads from old yahrzeit board, while Margie Calmenson Howell and Sisters Kathleen and Mary Lou of Presentation Sisters look on, Courtesy of Dale Bluestein

As you have read, Congregation B'nai Isaac dates to 1917, but an organized Jewish community in Aberdeen goes back to at least 1909. Since incorporating in 1917, the synagogue has been in continuous operation, despite not having had a full-time rabbi since the early 1970s.

It was an honor to spend time with the local community, where we were moved greatly as Herschel Premack led Kabbalat Shabbat services on the same bima his parents had wed a full century earlier, and his children had celebrated their b'nai mitzvot.

Courtesy of Leslie Martin

Courtesy of Synagogue360.com

ABERDEEN: A JEWISH HISTORY

Courtesy of Leslie
Martin

Courtesy of Leslie
Martin

Courtesy of Dale
Bluestein

Courtesy of Dale
Bluestein

ABERDEEN: A JEWISH HISTORY

A sign above the stairway from the synagogue's lobby heading down-stairs encourages visitors to come downstairs for refreshments, led us down, not for refreshments, but to see where generations had celebrated, learned, and played.

Courtesy of Leslie Martin

Courtesy of author

Dinner followed at the Alonzo Ward hotel building. While the building no longer functions as a hotel, we were able to use a private room there and enjoy a delicious dinner catered by resident restaurant, Roma.

Saturday morning brought an excellent tour of downtown Aberdeen, where local historian, Troy McQuillan, did a wonderful job of taking us back in time.

Troy McQuillan (back to camera) leading tour of downtown Aberdeen, June 18, 2022, Courtesy of Leslie Martin

The K.O. Lee Library graciously hosted the Jewish Historical Society of the Upper Midwest and our guests as we officially launched this publication, along with A stop along the way, a gorgeous video created by the unparalleled Dale Bluestein. Aberdonians were out in force to learn more about Aberdeen's Jews of both yesteryear and today.

Book launch at K.O. Lee library, June 18, 2022, Herschel Premack, Robin Doroshow, Leslie Martin, Courtesy of Dale Bluestein

Courtesy of Dale Bluestein

ABERDEEN: A JEWISH HISTORY

Back on our hotel patio later that evening, many of us gathered to close out the Sabbath with Havdalah, the service that separates the holy Sabbath from the rest of the week. Prairie winds made it impossible to keep the Havdalah candle lit, but it was still a lovely time to be together.

Courtesy of Dale Bluestein

Sunday morning, before heading back home, Patricia Kendall, executive director of the Dacotah Prairie Museum, gave our group a private tour, which was a wonderful way to end a very special weekend.

Dale Bluestein, Robin Doroshow, Bea and Herschel Premack, Juliana Sellers at Dacotah Prairie Museum, Courtesy of Leslie Martin

Courtesy of Dale
Bluestein

ADDITIONAL PHOTOS

Fan Premack, Mattie Feinstein, Helen
Ribnick, Corrine Pickus playing mah
jongg, undated photo, Courtesy of
Premack family

Facing camera, Minnie Salinsky,
Gussie Amdur back to camera, Fan
Premack, Corrine Pickus, undated
photo, Courtesy of Premack family

Sam Levy and Sam
Smilo (formerly
Smolowitz) between
unidentified woman
and unidentified
man, undated photo,
Courtesy of Premack
family

Bill & Sarah Ribnick, Corinne & Herman Pickus, Sam Calmenson, circa 1947, Courtesy of Premack family

Herschel Premack, Sophie & Jake Parkans, Ben Rubin, undated photo, Courtesy of Premack family

Sophie Radin, Evalyn Liszt Schwartz, Jean Schpok, Sonia Pred, Liszt farewell, Sherman Hotel, Sept 1955, Courtesy of Premack family

Top Left: Courtesy of Synagogues360.com

Top Right: Original ark, Courtesy of Leslie Martin

Bottom Left: Ladies Aid Cup, Courtesy of author

Right: Herschel Premack blowing Shofar, undated photo, Courtesy of Congregation B'nai Isaac

Below: Courtesy of author

Courtesy of Dale Bluestein

USYers visit B'nai
Isaac, 2015, Courtesy
of Congregation B'nai
Isaac

Hazon visits B'nai
Isaac, 2012, Courtesy
of Congregation B'nai
Isaac

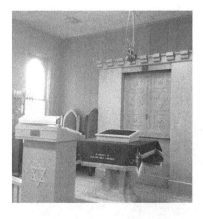

Left: Gail Pickus,
Herschel and Bea
Premack, 90th
anniversary of
Congregation B'nai
Isaac, 2007, Courtesy
of Congregation B'nai
Isaac

Right: Courtesy of
author

Kabbalat Shabbat, June
2022, Courtesy of Leslie
Martin

ABERDEEN: A JEWISH HISTORY

Presentation
Sisters attend
Kabbalat
Shabbat,
June 2022,
Courtesy of
Leslie Martin

ACKNOWLEDGMENTS

WITH GRATITUDE TO the dozens of past and current residents of Aberdeen, South Dakota, who generously shared their memories and stories with me. You welcomed me warmly whether we met in person, or communicated via phone call, video call, or email. For the few who remain in Aberdeen, you have my abundant gratitude for opening your homes and synagogue to me on multiple occasions and embracing me without reservation. Also, thank you to the descendants of former Aberdonians who shared what had been passed down, adding richness to this history.

Special thanks go to Jackie Ormand, Curator of Collections, and Levi Margolis, Curatorial Assistant, at the Dacotah Prairie Museum; Troy McQuillen, Creative Director at McQuillen Creative Group; Kate Dietrick, Archivist at the Nathan and Theresa Berman Upper Midwest Jewish Archives at the University of Minnesota; Stephanie Forsland, for German translation; and Ralph Levitt, Zachary Baker, and Meyer Weinshel for Yiddish translation.

I am indebted to the historians and writers who came before me. Their works provided strong foundational information for this book.

With appreciation to my family—Rich, Theo and Raina—who allowed mewho allowed me to take over the dining room table for longer than I had anticipated and for picking up slack around the house.

Abundant thanks to my colleagues: Dale Bluestein, Juliana Sellers, and Julie Tarshish for all of your work in helping make this book a success (and for holding things together when I was deep in the weeds).

To Julie and Ryan and their team at Mayfly Design, you have my great appreciation.

Finally, and especially, endless gratitude to my editor, Leslie Martin, without whom this book simply wouldn't have been possible.

SELECTED BIBLIOGRAPHY

Bender, Rebecca E., and Kenneth M. Bender, *Still*, Fargo, ND: North Dakota State University Press, 2019

McQuillen, Troy, *Images of America: Aberdeen*, Charleston, SC: Arcadia Press, 2013

Radin, Beryl A., *Leaving South Dakota*, Herndon, VA: Mascot Books, 2017

Schloff, Linda M., *And Prairie Dogs Weren't Kosher*, St. Paul, MN: Minnesota Historical Society Press, 1996

Sherman, William C., *Plains Folk: North Dakota's Ethnic History*, Fargo, ND: North Dakota Institute for Regional Studies, 1983

Sherman, William C., *Prairie Mosaic: An Ethnic Atlas of Rural North Dakota*, Fargo, ND: North Dakota Institute for Regional Studies, 1983

Sorin, Gerald, *A Time for Building: The Third Migration 1880-1920*, Baltimore, MD: The Johns Hopkins University Press, 1992

ENDNOTES

1. Isadore Singer, *The Jewish Encyclopedia*, 1906 edition (Jerusalem: Encyclopaedia Judaica, 1972.

2. Lance Nixon, "Promised Land," (2014).

3. Ibid.

4. Nixon, "Promised Land."

5. Ibid.

6. Ibid.

7. Native Knowledge 360, https://americanindian.si.edu/nk360/plains-belonging-nation/oceti-sakowin (accessed November 21, 2021).

8. Elizabeth Prine Pauls, "Native American Self-Names." *Encyclopedia Britannica*, March 6, 2008, https://www.britannica.com/topic/Native-American-Self-Names-1369572 (accessed February 1, 2022).

9. Department of the Interior, National Park Service, *National Register of Historic Places Registration Form*, 1988, https://npgallery.nps.gov/GetAsset/e4d214df-f599-46c8-a8a8-8e775b2f4236 p. 3, section 8 (accessed January 1, 2022).

10. History.com editors, "South Dakota," https://www.history.com/topics/us-states/south-dakota (accessed September 25, 2021).

11. Helen Bergh, et. al., *Early History of Brown County, South Dakota*, (USGenWeb Archives) (http://files.usgwarchives.net/sd/brown/ehbc/ehbc-fulltext.txt, p. 12 (accessed October 3, 2021).

12. Aberdeen Area Chamber of Commerce, *History of Aberdeen*, https://aberdeensd.com/living-here/history-of-aberdeen/ (accessed October 5, 2021).

13. Dacotah Prairie Museum, Brown County, South Dakota, *Unit 1: How Aberdeen Was Founded*, https://brown.sd.us/dacotah-prairie-museum/for-educators/aberdeen-history-lessons/how-aberdeen-was-founded (accessed July 9, 2021).

14. Ibid.

15. Dacotah Prairie Museum, Brown County, South Dakota, *Unit 5. Aberdeen Railroad Depots: Centers for Activity*, https://brown.sd.us/dacotah-prairie-museum/for-educators/aberdeen-history-lessons/aberdeen-railroad-depots (accessed August 1, 2021).

16. South Dakota Public Broadcasting, *J.L.W.Zietlow and his Dakota Central Telephone Company*, https://www.sdpb.org/blogs/images-of-the-past/jlwzietlow-and-his-dakota-central-telephone-company/ (accessed October 15, 2021).

17. Ibid.

18. South Dakota State Historical Society, *The Dakota Fairy Tales of L. Frank Baum*, https://www.sdhspress.com/journal/south-dakota-history-30-1/the-dakota-fairy-tales-of-l-frank-baum/vol-30-no-1-the-dakota-fairy-tales-of-l-frank-baum.pdf (accessed October 28, 2021).

19. Encyclopedia of the Great Plains, *BAUM, L. FRANK (1856-1919)*, http://plainshumanities.unl.edu/encyclopedia/doc/egp.lt.003 (accessed October 28, 2021)

20. South Dakota Hall of Fame, *Legacy L. Frank Baum*, https://sdexcellence.org/L._Frank_Baum_2002 (accessed November 22, 2021)

21. Sons of Jacob Cemetery, https://sojnorthdakota.org/history/(accessed November 09, 2021).

22. "Dan Eisenberg Dry Goods Store Ad, *Bismarck Weekly Tribune*, June 12, 1885. https://www.newspapers.com/clip/88636503/dan-eisenberg-dry-goods-store-ad/(Accessed November 01, 2021).

23. Helen Graf Strauss Oral History interview by Dr. Robert G. Webb. Brown County Museum and Historical Society Oral History Program, December 26, 1978.

24. Don Artz, "The Town in the Frog Pond, Stories of Builders. Buildings. and Business in Aberdeen's Commercial Historic District," (Aberdeen, Memories, Inc, 1991) http://aberdeenareahistory.org/files/original/8e9a8d5c9c79dc07cbe33a75d101db91.pdf p. 41 (accessed October 15, 2021).

25. "Open to the Public, The Golden Eagle Clothing House Opens Wide Its Doors to the Public," *Aberdeen Weekly News*, October 7, 1887, https://www.genealogybank.com/doc/newspapers/image/v2%3A12A7F5A3C13E62AA%40GB3NEWS-1145F8009F2E1610%402410552-1145F8022F305E38%406-1145F807B4FBA4F8 (accessed November 10, 2021).

26. "City in Brief," *Aberdeen Daily News*, April 1, 1893, https://aberdeennews.newsbank.com/doc/image/v2:114175180414EFE8@NGPA-SDAN-115A50273959BB70@2412555-115A5027C36625D0@2-115A50293116C1D8@City%20in%20Brief?search_terms (accessed November 10, 2021).

27. "The Week in Society," *Aberdeen American*, August 26, 1906, https://www.genealogybank.com/doc/newspapers/image/v2%3A117034F05215C2C0%40GB3NEWS-116A0DF994A500F0%402417449-116A0DFA8B206B50%406-116A0DFBFA23E170.

28. Helen Graf Strauss Oral History interview by Dr. Robert G. Webb. Brown County Museum and Historical Society Oral History Program, December 26, 1978.

29. "To be Big Year for Building Total Cost of Building under Way is near Two Hundred Thousand," *Aberdeen American*, March 23, 1916, https://www.genealogybank.com/doc/newspapers/image/v2%3A117034F05215C2C0%40GB3NEWS-117BFBD1975B4B38%402420946-117BFBD1CD704EC0%405-117BFBD314F45970 (accessed September 2, 2021)

30. "Notice: Strauss Clothing House Will Be Closed All Day Monday, November 28th, in memory of David Strauss," *Aberdeen American-News*, November 27, 1932, https://www.genealogybank.com/doc/newspapers/image/v2%3A114175180414EFE8%40GB3NEWS-1211093B0FE3FA58%402427039-120B7639EA0318B0%401-120B7639EA0318B0 (accessed September 2, 2021)

31. Elinor F. Strauss and Helen Graf Strauss, "Biography of Anna Graf Strauss (Mrs. David Strauss)," Undated, signed by authors.

32. "Will of Strauss Names 19 Heirs," *Aberdeen Evening News*, December 14, 1932, https://www.genealogybank.com/doc/newspapers/image/v2%3A114175180414EFE8%40GB3NEWS-12110A02EB7198E8%402427056-120CBF9A82C11FB8%400-120CBF9A82C11FB8 (accessed September 2, 2021)

33. Helen Graf Strauss Oral History interview by Dr. Robert G. Webb. Brown County Museum and Historical Society Oral History Program, December 26, 1978.

34. Ibid.

35. Ibid.

36. "Jewish in Aberdeen: 'We became the teachers,'" *Aberdeen Daily News*, June 7, 1992, https://www.genealogybank.com/doc/newspapers/image/v2%3A114175180414EFE8%40GB3NEWS-121CEE4D61E300C8%402448781-121A958950B22798%4029-121A958950B22798%40?fname=&mname=&lname=Strauss&rgfromDate=&rgtoDate=&formDate=&formDateFlex=exact&dateType=range&kwinc=B%27nai%20Isaac&kwexc=&sort=old&h=14 (accessed September 2, 2021)

37. "Ancestry.com," relational database, *https://www.ancestry.com/* (https://search.ancestry.com/cgi-bin/sse.ll?indiv=1&dbid=8561&h=625934&tid=&pid=&queryId=c8db1129c784d7df4afa8b5ca8ddd023&usePUB=true&_phsrc=PWt1019&_phstart=success Source: May 20, 2021), Hiram A. Jacobs and Carola Strauss marriage date; South Dakota Marriage Records, 1905-2016.

38. "Tribute to Helen Graf Strauss," *Aberdeen Daily News*, June 14, 1998 https://www. genealogybank.com/doc/newspapers/image/v2%3A114175180414EFE8%40GB3NEW S-12218037625B93F8%402450979-121FE482A7852060%4011-121FE482A7852060%4 0?h=15&fname=&mname=&lname=Strauss&rgfromDate=&rgtoDate=&formDate=&form DateFlex=exact&dateType=range&kwinc=B%27nai%20Isaac&kwexc=&sort=old&sid=h xsqxjfogjovhilaerqvrmlcpyqadsmo_wma-gateway009_1645150060425 (accessed September 2, 2021)

39. Aberdeen City Directory, 1887-88 (E.A. Frazier & Co, 1888) p.34 http://digitalcollections.northern.edu/digital/collection/local/id/13635 (accessed September 8, 2021)

40. "Grand Opening," *Aberdeen Weekly News*, September 4, 1885 https://www.gene alogybank.com/doc/newspapers/image/v2%3A12A7F5A3C13E62AA%40GB3NEWS-11 45F517824E58E8%402409789-1145F5178D85E618%400-1145F5190C842D88%40Adver tisement?h=2&fname=&mname=&lname=&rgfromDate=1885&rgtoDate=1885&form Date=&formDateFlex=exact&dateType=range&kwinc=%22Goodman%22%20%22Kas triner%22&kwexc=&sort=old&sid=rinvwcgayunflblypnaqsopanxnyznrc_wma-gate way009_1649106907662 (accessed April 1, 2022).

41. "A Grand Spring Opening," *Aberdeen Daily News*, March 11, 1888 https://aberdeen news.newsbank.com/doc/image/v2:114175180414EFE8@NGPA-SDAN-1145FA3AD9FF 6D10@2410708-1145FA3B52531210@3?search_terms (accessed September 8, 2021)

42. "The City in Brief," *Aberdeen Daily News*, July 20, 1890 https://aberdeennews.news bank.com/doc/image/v2:114175180414EFE8@NGPA-SDAN-115C80EE3827F618@2411569-115C80EE6CC44808@3-115C80EF62FB5E38@The+City+in+Brief?search_terms (accessed September 8, 2021)

43. "Advertisements," *Aberdeen Daily News*, 1885-1890https://aberdeennews. newsbank.com/search?date_from=1885&date_to=1890&text=Kastriner%20 &pub%5B0%5D=114175180414EFE8&content_added=&sort=old&page=25 (accessed September 8, 2021)

44. "Personal" *Aberdeen Daily News*, August 25, 1889 https://aberdeennews.newsbank.com/ doc/image/v2:114175180414EFE8@NGPA-SDAN-1145FCB559CA10E8@2411240-1145FC B66E264908@8-1145FCB8E642E818@Personal?search_terms (accessed September 9, 2021)

45. "Born," *Aberdeen Daily News*, January 19, 1888 https://aberdeennews.newsbank.com/ doc/image/v2:114175180414EFE8@NGPA-SDAN-1145FB451E608CE0@2410656-1145FB 45B0270E90@3-1145FB47204926E8@Birth+Notice?search_terms (accessed September 10, 2021)

46. "Died" *Aberdeen Daily News*, April 3, 1888 https://aberdeennews.newsbank.com/doc/ image/v2:114175180414EFE8@NGPA-SDAN-1145FA642EC995B8@2410731-1145FA64B6C 00D60@3-1145FA65EDE0F6F0@Mortuary+Notice?search_terms (accessed September 10, 2021)

47. "The City in Brief," *Aberdeen Daily News*, July 7, 1891 https://aberdeennews.newsbank.com/doc/image/v2:114175180414EFE8@NGPA-SDAN-1146002EFB6A4038@2411921-1146002F8D8BE158@3-11460031297B1848@The+Ci ty+in+Brief?search_terms (accessed September 10, 2021)

48. "The City in Brief," *Aberdeen Daily News*, November 4, 1890 https://aberdeennews.newsbank.com/doc/image/v2:114175180414EFE8@NGPA-SDAN-115C8166B9E31B68@2411676-115C816709803488@5-115C816862FC2570@The+Ci ty+of+Brief?search_terms (accessed September 10, 2021).

49. "Personal," *Aberdeen Daily News*, October 30, 1890 https://aberdeennews.newsbank. com/doc/image/v2:114175180414EFE8@NGPA-SDAN-115C817209DA1458@2411671-115C81723431C160@2-115C817309004E58@Personal?search_terms (accessed September 10, 2021)

50. Aberdeen City Directory, 1899-1900 (Scollard Directory Company, 1899) p. 39 http://digitalcollections.northern.edu/digital/collection/local/id/11880

51. "Charles Goodman Dead," *Aberdeen Daily News*, August 27, 1907 :https://aberdeennews.newsbank.com/doc/image/v2:114175180414EFE8@ NGPA-SDAN-117EED9EA08E9070@2417815-117EED9EFA62F9C8@3-117EED A0B8F59E88@Mortuary+Notice?search_terms

52. Aberdeen City Directory, 1889-90 (Chas. Pettibone & Company, 1889) p. 76; 86 http://digitalcollections.northern.edu/digital/collection/local/id/12080

53. "Aberdeen, South Dakota," *Encyclopedia Britannica*, 2005, https://www.britannica.com/ place/Aberdeen-South-Dakota (accessed April 1, 2022)

54. Goldie Smilowitz Krystal interview recorded by Bea Premack on November 23, 1987, as cited in "A History of the Jewish Community of Aberdeen, South Dakota, 1887-1964," by Bernice Premack.

55. Ibid.

56. "Advertisement" *Aberdeen Daily News*, February 18, 1909 https://www.genealogybank.com/doc/newspapers/image/v2%3A114175180414EFE8%40GB 3NEWS-117C07FAE6DF0108%402418356-117C07FB21B59F98%403-117C07FC620CB49 0%40%255BMetropolitan%253B%2BTailors%253B%2BManager%255D?h=2&fname=isa dore&mname=&lname=kraywetz&rgfromDate=&rgtoDate=&formDate=&formDateFlex =exact&dateType=range&kwinc=&kwexc=&sid=ybeeoqagoyenbuszdbtptpeensbiwcbp_ wma-gateway009_1645285948082

57. "Between the Cossacks to See Who Can Tell the Biggest Yarn" *St. Paul Daily Globe*, January 29, 1895 https://www.genealogybank.com/doc/newspapers/image/v2%3A16A0C- 1CA030E9955%40GB3NEWS-165A01AD32004A5C%402413223-165A01B8E044F180%402 -165A01B8E044F180%40?h=1&fname=Isaac&mname=&lname=kraywetz&kwinc=&kwex c=&rgfromDate=&rgtoDate=&formDate=&formDateFlex=exact&dateType=range&pro cessingtime=&addedFrom=&addedTo=&sort=old&sid=jjxlttjxjcyctfdbwxbvxbpxtykheilr_ wma-gateway003_1645286210732

58. "Ancestry.com," relational database, *https://www.ancestry.com/* (https://www.ancestry .com/discoveryui-content/view/16342078:6482?tid=&pid=&queryId=c15f05cb3f06aab 09220dc9acebc2246&_phsrc=PWt1020&_phstart=successSource: January 10, 2022) World War I Draft Registration Card, National Archives and Records Administration.

59. "Sons of Issac" (sic), *Aberdeen Weekly News*, January 25, 1917 https://www.genealogybank.com/doc/newspapers/image/v2%3A12A 7F5A3C13E62AA%40GB3NEWS-12144E86DD194B88%402421254-1214 12AC97C5C8F0%404-121412AC97C5C8F0%40?h=4&fname=&mname=&lname=Kray wetz&rgfromDate=&rgtoDate=&formDate=&formDateFlex=exact&dateType =range&kwinc=Jewish&kwexc=&sid=iksckydrkuctbxwyvloxwnsijzycwljd_wma-gate way008_1645288064868

60. "Ancestry.com," relational database, *https://www.ancestry.com/* (https://www.ancestry. com/discoveryui-content/view/413434:70800?tid=&pid=&queryId=7c38f5f8a58cb0b9f9b b8a14a5734d8c&_phsrc=PWt613&_phstart=successSource: January 15, 2022) U.S. Natural ization Index, 1849-1985.

61. "Between the Cossacks to See Who Can Tell the Biggest Yarn," January 29, 1895.

62. "City Local News" *Oakes Republican*, July 20, 1905 https://chroniclingamerica.loc.gov/ lccn/sn88076145/1905-07-20/ed-1/seq-5/#date1=1777&index=2&rows=20&words=Kray wetz&searchType=basic&sequence=0&state=&date2=1963&proxtext=kraywetz+&y=0&x =0&dateFilterType=yearRange&page=1 (accessed April 4, 2022).

63. "Society," *Minneapolis Star Tribune*, April 22, 1900 https://www.newspapers.com/image/180285471/?article=46b3f30e-879b-498b-876 4-5e500d136528&focus=0.447842,0.73478395,0.58233726,0.7604555&xid=3398&_ ga=2.93307165.1848440393.1645147228-2113274208.1636493498

64. "Ancestry.com," relational database, *https://www.ancestry.com/* (https://www.ancestry.com/discoveryui-content/view/292278:2561?tid=&pid=&queryId=c27ed6734af2fb6ea713ae846fd648cb&_phsrc=PWt615&_phstart=successSource: January 15, 2022) United States Marriage Index 1849-1950.

65. "Ancestry.com," relational database, *https://www.ancestry.com/* (https://www.ancestry.com/family-tree/person/tree/177984868/person/122316818495/facts?_phsrc=PWt620&_phstart=successSource: January 15, 2022) Minnesota, U.S., Territorial and State Censuses, 1849-1905.

66. "Ancestry.com," relational database, *https://www.ancestry.com/* (https://www.ancestry.com/discoveryui-content/view/102253053:60525?tid=&pid=&queryId=26284fbec6c6d8872f3bf35c765e2f03&_phsrc=PWt625&_phstart=successSource: January 15, 2022) U.S. Obituary Index, 1891-2003.

67. "Ancestry.com," relational database, *https://www.ancestry.com/* (https://www.ancestry.com/mediaui-viewer/tree/177984868/person/122316798407/media/4ae85984-1836-4e78-ad4c-a4765e69243d?_phsrc=PWt600&_phstart=successSource: January 15, 2022). St. Paul Globe, January 28, 1902.

68. "Ancestry.com," relational database, *https://www.ancestry.com/* (https://www.ancestry.com/discoveryui-content/view/589961:60160?tid=&pid=&queryId=a87570501eb9fd4112d135c02af19ba0&_phsrc=PWt629&_phstart=successSource: January 15, 2022). South Dakota State Census, 1915.

69. Ancestry.com," relational database, *https://www.ancestry.com/* (https://www.ancestry.com/family-tree/person/tree/177984868/person/122316821415/facts?_phsrc=PWt632&_phstart=successSource: January 15, 2022). 1910 United States Federal Census.

70. "Starts Relief Campaign," Aberdeen Weekly News, February 1, 1917 https://www.genealogybank.com/doc/newspapers/image/v2%3A12A-7F5A3C13E62AA%40GB3NEWS-12144EB904C4F668%402421261-121412ACB3BF6FC0%404-121412ACB3BF6FC0%40?h=3&fname=&mname=&lname=Kraywetz&rgfromDate=&rgtoDate=&formDate=&formDateFlex=exact&dateType=range&kwinc=Jewish&kwexc=&sid=iksckydrkuctbxwyvloxwnsijzycwljd_wma-gateway008_1645288064868

71. "Sons of Issac" (sic), January 25, 1917

72. "Prairie Flower Camp Party," *Aberdeen Daily News*, March 31, 1917 https://www.genealogybank.com/doc/newspapers/image/v2%3A114175180414EFE8%40GB3NEWS-11932C98D9EAD788%402421319-11932C9902BEE180%404?fname=&mname=&lname=&kwinc=%22mrs.%20i%20kraywetz%22&kwexc=&sort=old&rgfromDate=&rgtoDate=&formDate=&formDateFlex=exact&dateType=range&processingtime=&addedFrom=&addedTo=&sid=dytepbvunegameqfyqdmwzckkbikuskh_wma-gateway008_1645294913242

73. "Society," *Aberdeen American*, February 10, 1917 https://aberdeennews.news-bank.com/doc/image/v2%3A117034F05215C2C0%40NGPA-SDAN-11B2BBCE01348090%402421270-11B2BBCE190FA258%405-11B2BBCE839EBA30%40Society?search_terms=%22I%2BKraywetz%22%2BMrs.&text=%22I%20Kraywetz%22%20Mrs.&pub%255B0%255D=117034F05215C2C0&content_added=&date_from=&date_to=&sort=old&pdate=1917-02-10

74. "Talks on Tailoring," *Aberdeen American*, January 4, 1910 https://www.genealogybank.com/doc/newspapers/image/v2%3A117034F05215C2C0%40GB3NEWS-1183C117F8F135A0%402418676-1183C119E7A77188-1183C123CDBD1318?h=32&fname=&mname=&lname=Kraywetz&kwinc=&kwexc=&sort=old&rgfromDate=1891&rgtoDate=1930&formDate=&formDateFlex=exact&dateType=range&processingtime=&addedFrom=&addedTo=&page=2&sid=mgtoisiqtitohurlqhpwicgmjafvytlb_wma-gateway008_1645220405583

75. "Notice of First Meeting of Creditors," *Aberdeen Weekly News*, November 15, 1917
https://www.genealogybank.com/doc/newspapers/image/v2%3A12A
7F5A3C13E62AA%40GB3NEWS-12144FFDF4DB7A98%402421548-121412AF0AB18C8
0%403-121412AF0AB18C80%40?h=11&fname=&mname=&lname=Kraywetz&kwinc=
consumer&kwexc=&rgfromDate=&rgtoDate=&formDate=&formDateFlex=exact&
dateType=range&processingtime=&addedFrom=&addedTo=&sort=old&sid=lrrklydgtrqa
vyybdmoabgoraaloqkss_wma-gateway008_1647986710842

76. "Rudoph Kraywetz Killed," *Aberdeen Daily News*, December 27, 1918
https://www.genealogybank.com/doc/newspapers/image/v2%3A114175180414EFE8%40GB
3NEWS-11A8884AF5A00AE8%402421955-11A8884B40F306D8%407-11A8884C76625918%4
0Rudolph%2BKraywetz%2BKilled?h=2&fname=rudolph&mname=&lname=kraywetz&rgfr
omDate=&rgtoDate=&formDate=&formDateFlex=exact&dateType=range&kwinc=&kwex
c=&sid=vfyzkjdvptyqvsqwauczoaeyjmejmxhb_wma-gateway003_1645292154407

77. "Rudolph Harold Kraywetz, mascot of camp 2094," *Modern Woodman*, August, 1916,
Vol. 33, No. 8 https://babel.hathitrust.org/cgi/pt?id=mdp.39015016796982&view=1up&se
q=21&skin=2021

78. " Starts Relief Campaign," February 1, 1917

79. "Advertisement," *Aberdeen American*, May 9, 1909
https://www.genealogybank.com/doc/newspapers/image/v2%3A117034F
05215C2C0%40GB3NEWS-1188B9D231020158%402418431-1188B9D
3520FDB08%402-1188B9D5A62628B8%40Advertisement?h=136&f
name=&mname=&lname=&kwinc=%22Metropolitan%20Tailors%22&kw
exc=&sort=old&rgfromDate=1891&rgtoDate=1930&formDate=&formDateFlex=exact&da
teType=range&processingtime=&addedFrom=&addedTo=&page=9&sid=tdpyukfhteomao
vrwssrncfsgvktptvs_wma-gateway014_1645219887416

80. "Ancestry.com," relational database, *https://www.ancestry.com/*
(https://www.ancestry.com/discoveryui-content/view/65866842:6061: January 15, 2022)
1920 Federal Census.

81. "Ancestry.com," relational database, *https://www.ancestry.com/*
(https://www.ancestry.com/discoveryui-content/view/191770668:60525?tid=&pid=&que
ryId=47b1cdc81165cec4eed8c238ca4bce1d&_phsrc=PWt646&_phstart=successSource:
January 15, 2022) Find a Grave 1600-current.

82. "Ancestry.com," relational database, *https://www.ancestry.com/* (https://www.ancestry.
com/discoveryui-content/view/502534170:1171?tid=&pid=&queryId=add92c45c873a6d4b
8daa91719c48b97&_phsrc=PWt648&_phstart=successSource: January 20, 2022) Missouri
Marriage Records, 1805-2002.

83. "Auto-Pedestrian Accidents Kill Two," *Daily Nonpareil*, April 6, 1959 https://www.gene
alogybank.com/doc/newspapers/image/v2%3A14A9EA648C1E88E0%40GB3NEWS-1599C
2F9F5E21978%402436665-15987C9DF2B0D5DA%4015-15987C9DF2B0D5DA%40?h=1&f
name=hannah&mname=&lname=diehl&rgfromDate=1959&rgtoDate=1959&formDate=&
formDateFlex=exact&dateType=range&kwinc=&kwexc=&sid=cjsbuovnbhubrclhpfhpes
clpdxcbuma_wma-gateway001_1649116178668.

84. Aberdeen City Directory, 1903-04 (John H. Ley, 1904)p. 128. http://digitalcollections.
northern.edu/digital/collection/local/id/13830 (accessed January 15, 2022)

85. Helen Graf Strauss Oral History interview by Dr. Robert G. Webb. Brown County
Museum and Historical Society Oral History Program, December 26, 1978.

86. "Aberdeen's Jewish Community Began Nearly a Century Ago," *Aberdeen Daily News*,
January 29, 1984
https://www.genealogybank.com/doc/newspapers/image/v2%3A114175180414EFE8%40GB
3NEWS-1215FC8D5CC6BAD0%402445729-121413A7B8375B80%4077-121413A7B8375B80%
40?h=36&fname=&mname=&lname=Mazor&rgfromDate=&rgtoDate=&formDate=&form
DateFlex=exact&dateType=range&kwinc=&kwexc=&sort=old&page=2&sid=btlfjkggffxj
pylixuirnljmzahyfetv_s074_164444507531

87. "Wedding Announcement," *Black Hills Daily Register*, January 29, 1910 https://www. newspapers.com/image/91658280/?image=91658280&words=&article=06feb66f-5592-4b5 1-9321-8c201a8b9f02&focus=0.019067949,0.88994086,0.17945817,0.92754558&xid=3398&_ ga=2.232879517.2075853818.1647526087-2113274208.1636493498&ancestry=true.

88. "New York Store Opens," *Aberdeen Daily News*, February 14, 1910 https://aberdeennews.newsbank.com/doc/image/v2:114175180414EFE8@NGPA-SDAN-117C091C0FC206F0@2418717-117C091D9BBE7290@7-117C09211A13D3B8@ New+York+Store+Opens+I.+Salinsky+Begins+Business+in+Fine+Room+of+New+Build ing?search_terms

89. "Ancestry.com," relational database, *https://www.ancestry.com/* (https://www.ancestry. com/discoveryui-content/view/1032144889:2469?_phsrc=PWt212&_phstart=successSou rce&gsln=salinsky&ml_rpos=30&queryId=8f79b3d61e0d337ccb75bfb70fac2b05: January 31, 2022) U.S. City Directories, 1822-1995.

90. Goldie Smilowitz Krystal interview recorded by Bea Premack on November 23, 1987 as cited in "A History of the Jewish Community of Aberdeen, South Dakota, 1887-1964, by Bernice Premack.

91. "Aberdeen's Jewish Community Began Nearly a Century Ago," January 29, 1984.

92. Ibid.

93. "Popular Young Man Will Be Married," *Aberdeen Daily News*, July 3, 1913 https://aberdeennews.newsbank.com/doc/image/v2:114175180414EFE8@NGPA-SDAN-11826E2B2413A820@2419952-11826E2B89FB9E48@3-11826E3056C6CB98@Popu lar+Young+Man+Will+be+Married?search_terms

94. "Advertisement," *Aberdeen Daily News*, January 18, 1916 https://aberdeennews.newsbank.com/doc/image/v2:114175180414EFE8@ NGPA-SDAN-118B43CFA4E82A78@2420881-118B43CFDCF9FFD0@4-118B43D 06296FEE8@Advertisement?search_terms

95. "Lasts Rites Held Over Little Lucile Knapp," *Aberdeen American*, May 4, 1907 https://aberdeennews.newsbank.com/doc/image/v2:117034F05215C2C0@NGPA-SDAN-11728BB8CD7B1490@2417700-11728BB94B978398@7-11728BBB047678A8@ Last+Rites+Held+over+Little+Lucile+Knapp?search_terms

96. "Perry-Foltz nuptials," *Aberdeen American*, May 11, 1907 https://aberdeennews.newsbank.com/doc/image/v2:117034F05215C2C0@ NGPA-SDAN-11728B5D4CCB0258@2417707-11728B5DB1CB3910@6?search_terms

97. "Popular Young Man Will Be Married," July 3, 1913.

98. "Poison Ivy," *Aberdeen American*, August 5, 1913 https://aberdeennews.newsbank.com/doc/image/v2:117034F05215C2C0@NGPA-SDAN-117C01BA351591B0@2419985-117C01BA6462B668@5-117C01BB6EF7AE80@ Mines+with+Poison+Ivy?search_terms

99. "'Reds at Length Win Tournament," *Aberdeen American*, September 3, 1913 'https://aberdeennews.newsbank.com/doc/image/v2:117034F05215C2C0@NGPA-SDAN-11 7C021388626490@2420041-117C021459BB5760@6-117C0215AAC2D2B8@%22Reds%22+at +Length+Win+Tournament?search_terms

100. "Women's Golf Tournament," *Aberdeen American*, September 25, 1914 https://aberdeennews.newsbank.com/doc/image/v2:117034F05215C2C0@ NGPA-SDAN-117F2AEA3AA13378@2420401-117F2AEB4DA5B6A0@2-117F2AE C5B2F6D48@Women%27s+Golf+Tournament+Play+is+to+Start+at+Country+ Club+at+Oce+and+Run+to+October+15?search_terms

101. "Calmenson Co. Doubles Store by Adding Another Frontage," *Aberdeen American*, May 28, 1916 https://aberdeennews.newsbank.com/doc/image/v2:117034F05215C2C0@ NGPA-SDAN-1183BB2E45421D78@2421012-1183BB2FBADE2508@2-1183BB345DDA5198@ Calmenson%20Co.%20Doubles%20Store%20by%20Adding%20Another%20Front age%20Clothing%20Business%20Developed%20by%20Advertising?search_terms

102. "Name Collar for the Country Club," *Aberdeen American*, June 8, 1917 https://aberdeennews.newsbank.com/doc/image/v2:117034F05215C2C0@ NGPA-SDAN-11B2BBB8A36A48C0@2421388-11B2BBB8E729C5A8@5-11B2BBB942E2A9A8@ Name%20Collar%20for%20the%20Country%20Club?search_terms

103. Gail Pickus, Bea and Herschel Premack interview recorded by author, May 18, 2018.

104. "Max Rosen is Taken in Death," *Aberdeen Daily News*, January 23, 1951. https://aberdeennews.newsbank.com/doc/image/v2:114175180414EFE8@NGPA-SDAN-120F1F0629BAC8F8@2433670-120CBFFEF43860B0@11-120CBFFEF43860B0@?search_terms

105. "Calmenson Clothiers Organize Ball Team," *Aberdeen American*, March 15, 1916 https://aberdeennews.newsbank.com/doc/image/v2:117034F05215C2C0@ NGPA-SDAN-117BFB1DD2CCF918@2420938-117BFB1F074BF738@4-117BFB21D0C75190@ Calmenson%20Clothiers%20Organize%20Ball%20Team?search_terms (accessed March 20, 2021)

106. "Advertisement," *Aberdeen Daily News*, August 3, 1917 https://aberdeennews.newsbank.com/doc/image/v2:114175180414EFE8@ NGPA-SDAN-119F2FC752A99E50@2421444-119F2FC78CA81CC0@4?search_terms

107. "Farmers Unite In Webster," *Aberdeen American*, May 18, 1909 https://aberdeennews.newsbank.com/doc/image/v2:117034F05215C2C0@NGPA-SDAN-1188B8EF67F61658@2418445-1188B8EF71AAD800@0-1188B8F044323800@Farm ers+Unite+in+Webster+Get+Together+in+Project+to+Erect+New+Cooperative+Elevator? search_terms

108. "Advertisement," *Aberdeen American*, September 3, 1921 https://aberdeennews.newsbank.com/doc/image/v2:117034F05215C2C0@NGPA-SDAN-11B3C20825EDD6C0@2422936-11B3C20842E4EFB0@5-11B3C20900B61930@Advertise ment?search_terms

109. "Calmenson's The Style Center of Good Clothes," *Aberdeen American*, November 21, 1921 https://aberdeennews.newsbank.com/doc/image/v2:117034F05215C2C0@NGPA-SDAN-11A891E068939A90@2423015-11A891E0C9ACE9D8@6

110. Ibid.

111. Ibid.

112. Ibid

113. "Come See Hat Worn by Tom Mix," *Aberdeen American*, June 26, 1924 https://aberdeennews.newsbank.com/doc/image/v2:117034F05215C2C0@NGPA-SDAN-120A6A6BDE7C65C8@2423963-120880256B020280@5-120880256B020280@?search_terms

114. Kinky Friedman, "The Transcendence of True Cowboys," Tampa Bay Times, March 19, 1991 https://www.tampabay.com/archive/1991/03/19/the-transcendence-of-true-cowboys/

115. Ben Calmenson written recollections sent to Bea Premack,1987.

116. "Officers Install New O.E.S. Executives," *Aberdeen Daily News*, December 14, 1927 https://www.genealogybank.com/doc/newspapers/image/v2%3A114175180414EFE8%40GB 3NEWS-121264A6C9256A58%402425229-120A76B9C3E06A98%401-120A76B9C3E06A9 8%40?h=2&fname=rose&mname=&lname=calmenson&rgfromDate=&rgtoDate=&form Date=&formDateFlex=exact&dateType=range&kwinc=&kwexc=&sid=tkksbqrmstgyizsd bobcvsrnfsdzworz_wma-gateway002_1645471946719

117. "Pioneer Aberdeen Pharmacist Busy Predmetsky Bldg," Aberdeen Daily News, March 30, 1924 https://aberdeennews.newsbank.com/doc/image/v2:114175180414EFE8@NGPA-SDAN-120DBAD28CF46418@2423875-120B14DF90D98D88@0

118. "Advertisement," *Aberdeen Daily News*, November 24, 1916
https://aberdeennews.newsbank.com/doc/image/v2:114175180414EFE8@NGPA-SDAN-119F2B268F25E248@2421192-119F2B26B549BD28@2-119F2B2782F59D38@Advertise
ment?search_terms

119. "Predmestky's," *Aberdeen American*, February 7, 1917
https://aberdeennews.newsbank.com/doc/image/v2:117034F05215C2C0@
NGPA-SDAN-11B2BBC967FA8328@2421267-11B2BBC9A41C4EF8@14-11B2BB
CB16671B80@Predmestky%27s?search_terms

120. Ibid.

121. Sam Salinsky oral history recorded by Gail Pickus and Joanne Brock, March 18, 1974, and cited in A History of the Jewish Community of Aberdeen, South Dakota, 1887-1964 by Bernice Premack.

122. William C. Sherman, *Plains Folk* (Fargo:North Dakota Institute for Regional Studies, 1988) p.393.

123. William C. Sherman, Jewish Settlement in North Dakota Collection, MS334, Institute for Regional Studies, NDSU, Fargo. https://library.ndsu.edu/AS2.pub/repositories/3/ (accessed November 22, 2021).

124. National Archives, https://www.archives.gov/education/lessons/homestead-act (accessed September 7, 2021)

125. Ibid.

126. "Ashley Jewish Homesteaders Cemetery," *Jewish American Society for Historic Preservation*, http://www.jewish-american-society-for-historic-preservation.org/mdpa/ash leynorthdakota.html (accessed November 14, 2021)

127. William C. Sherman and Thomas D. Isern, *Prairie Mosaic: An Ethnic Atlas of Rural North Dakota*, p. 53.

128. Max Wishek and Dr. Leo Cohen interview by William C. Sherman, circa 1980. MDSU Institute for Regional Studies and University Archives (Fargo, ND) as cited in *Still*, by Rebecca E. Bender and Kenneth M. Bender, (Fargo: North Dakota State University Press, 2019).

129. *The Volga Germans*, https://www.volgagermans.org/(accessed January 20, 2022).

130. Janet E.Schulte, "Proving up and Moving up": Jewish Homesteading Activity in North Dakota, 1900-1920" (1990). *Great Plains Quarterly* Volume 10, no. 4 (2010) p. 228-44. https://digitalcommons.unl.edu/greatplainsquarterly/398

131. Ibid

132. Ibid

133. Schulte, "Proving Up and Moving Up,"236-37.

134. Sherman, *Plains Folk*, 395.

135. *The Wishek News*, 1916, as cited in Plains Folk, 395.

136. Schulte, "Proving Up and Moving Up,", 238-39.

137. Sherman, *Plains Folk*.

138. Quanrud, Ted, "Old Jewish Cemeteries in N.D. Show Once-Large Community," *Grand Forks Herald*, December 6, 1987, https://www.ashleyjewishcemetery.org/wp-con tent/uploads/2021/05/oldcemetery.pdf

139. Sherman, *Plains Folk*, 395

140. Ibid.

141. "Wishek, N.D., Congregation presents Sefer (sic) Torah to Gemilus Chesed; Dissolves, *American Jewish World*, August 23, 1935, https://www.nli.org.il/en/newspa pers/amjwld/1935/08/23/01/article/49/?e=-------en-20--1--img-txIN%7ctxTI-------------1 (accessed November 10, 2021)

142. https://www.ashleyjewishcemetery.org/history/, (accessed November 20, 2021)

143. Goldie Smilowitz Krystal interview recorded by Bea Premack on November 23, 1987 as cited in https://www.genealogybank.com/doc/newspapers/image/v2%3A114175180414EFE8%40GB3NEWS-11932D14108B88E0%402421300-119 32D143B28C298%404?fname=&mname=&lname=&kwinc=Rabbi&kwexc=&rgfrom Date=1/1/1914&rgtoDate=1/1/19112/31/19244&formDate=&formDateFlex=exact&date Type=range&processingtime=&addedFrom=&addedTo=&sid=tzagjgjwtavtqesndmsx jvfxahgqloba_wma-gateway001_1642540877740.

144. Quanrud,"Old Jewish Cemeteries in N.D. Show Once-Large Community," Grand Forks Herald, December 6, 1987.

145. "Ancestry.com," relational database, *https://www.ancestry.com/* (https://www.ancestry.com/discoveryui-content/view/75149827:61747: November 30, 2021) N.D. State Death Certificates, 1908-2007.

146. "Ancestry.com," relational database, *https://www.ancestry.com/* (https://www.ancestry.com/discoveryui-content/view/8663145:1246?tid=&pid=&queryId=31a029dcafe 464ced7047ff3705f3344&_phsrc=PWt98&_phstart=successSource: November 30, 2021) U.S. General Land Office Records, 1796-2015.

147. Bea and Herschel Premack interview, by author, May 19, 2018.

148. Ibid.

149. Ibid.

150. Telephone call with Herschel Premack and author, March 2, 2022.

151. https://www.legacy.com/us/obituaries/houstonchronicle/name/sybil-balasco-obitu ary?id=8965257 (accessed January 14, 2022)

152. Bea and Herschel Premack interview with author, May 19, 2018.

153. History Committee of Brown County Museum and Historical Society, Brown County History. Aberdeen, South Dakota: North Plains Press, 1980, as cited in A History of the Jewish Community of Aberdeen, South Dakota, 1887-1964 by Bernice Premack.

154. Oral History interview with Sam Salinsky conducted by Gail Pickus and Joanne Brock on March 18, 1974. Dacotah Prairie Museum, Aberdeen, South Dakota as cited in A History of the Jewish Community of Aberdeen, South Dakota, 1887-1964 by Bernice Premack.

155. Lance Nixon, "Promised Land," *Capital Journal*, July 25, 2014 https://www.capjournal.com/news/promised-land/article_4d363024-13c0-11e4-8907-0019bb2963f4.html

156. Pierre M. Meste, "History of the Knights of the Macabee" (sic) *TNGenWeb Project*, https://www.tngenweb.org/crocketttn/organizations/knights_macabee_history.php (accessed June 12, 2021).

157. Oral History Interview with Sam Salinsky conducted by Gail Pickus and Joanne Brock on March 18, 1974. Dacotah Prairie Museum, Aberdeen, South Dakota as cited in A History of the Jewish Community of Aberdeen, South Dakota, 1887-1964 by Bernice Premack.

158. "The Jewish New Year," *Aberdeen Daily News*, September 13, 1901, https://aberdeen news.newsbank.com/doc/image/v2:114175180414EFE8@NGPA-SDAN-1195D6FF2966FB D8@2415641-1195D6FF4DC3CDC0@2-1195D700089AC240@The+Jewish+New+-Year.+It+Begins+Tonight+and+is+Observed+with+Feasting+and+Joy?search_terms

159. Articles of Incorporation (copy) provided by Congregation B'nai Isaac..

160. "Rabbi Hess in Charge," *Aberdeen Daily News*, May 5, 1917, https://www.genealogybank.com/doc/newspapers/image/v2%3A114175180414EFE8%40GB 3NEWS-11932BC620535848%402421354-11932BC64775D5F8%403-11932BC6FB 4B2748%40Rabbi%2BHess%2Bin%2BCharge?h=3&fname=&mname=&lname=&k winc=Hess&kwexc=&rgfromDate=1/1/1914&rgtoDate=1/1/1918&formDate=&formDateFlex =exact&dateType=range&processingtime=&addedFrom=&addedTo=&sid=gdbxwjyellfad vcvdxrnhbvcvaarxrhe_wma-gateway010_1642443239294

161. "geni.com," commercial genealogy and social networking, (https://www.geni.com/people/Rabbi-Julius-Hess/4465645056110039939: August 12, 2021) Find A Grave.

162. "geni.com," commercial genealogy and social networking, (https://www.geni.com/people/Moyshe-Yoelson/2489156: August 12, 2021) 1940 U.S. Federal Census.

163. "Al Jolson American Singer," *Encyclopedia Britannica*, 2021 https://www.britannica.com/biography/Al-Jolson (accessed November 22, 2021).

164. Jerry Klinger, "The Jewish Homesteads of North Dakota," *San Diego Jewish World*, May 28, 2017 https://www.sdjewishworld.com/2017/05/28/the-jewish-homesteaders-of-north-dakota/(accessed May 12, 2021).

165. "Rabbi, Honor Guest at Meeting," *Aberdeen Daily News*, March 12, 1917 https://www.genealogybank.com/doc/newspapers/image/v2%3A114175180414EFE8%40GB3NEWS-1 1932D14108B88E0%402421300-11932D143B28C298%404?fname=&mname=&lname=&k winc=Rabbi&kwexc=&rgfromDate=1/1/1914&rgtoDate=1/1/19112/31/19244&formDate=& formDateFlex=exact&dateType=range&processingtime=&addedFrom=&added To=&sid=tzagjgjwtavtqesndmsxjvfxahgqloba_wma-gateway001_1642540877740 (accessed February 1, 2021).

166. Ibid.

167. Ibid.

168. "Deed Record #97," p. 531, July 11, 1917. Register of Deeds, Brown County Court House, Aberdeen, South Dakota as cited in "A History of the Jewish Community of Aberdeen, South Dakota, 1887-1964, by Bernice Premack.

169 *Aberdeen News*, March 10, 2017

170 "Deed Record #97," p. 531, July 11, 1917. Register of Deeds, Brown County Court House, Aberdeen, South Dakota as cited in "A History of the Jewish Community of Aberdeen, South Dakota, 1887-1964, by Bernice Premack.

171. "Notable Week for Local Jews First Time New Year Will be Observed in Our Synagogue," *Aberdeen American*, September 16, 1917 https://www.genealogybank.com/doc/newspapers/image/v2%3A117034F05215C 2C0%40GB3NEWS-119D2FB9F4CBBF40%402421488-119D2FBA75506448%4018-1 19D2FBC83F10880%40Notable%2BWeek%2Bfor%2BLocal%2BJews%2BFirst%2B Time%2BNew%2BYear%2BWill%2Bbe%2BObserved%2Bin%2BOur%2BSyna gogue?h=4&fname=&mname=&lname=hess&kwinc=north%20dakota%20jewish&k wexc=&rgfromDate=1890&rgtoDate=1919&formDate=&formDateFlex=exact&date Type=range&processingtime=&addedFrom=&addedTo=&sid=daaqqnazspiznmwcsvj foicnsybrqekr_wma-gateway010_1642538036464 (accessed May 12, 2021).

172. Menachem Posner, "What to Expect at a Hachnasat Sefer Torah Parade," https://www.chabad.org/library/article_cdo/aid/3212196/jewish/What-to-Expect-at-a-Hachnasat-Sefer-Torah-Parade.htm (accessed January 18, 2022).

173. "Aberdeen Jews Dedicate New Synagogue on Sunday," *Aberdeen Daily News*, September 6, 1917 https://aberdeennews.newsbank.com/doc/image/v2:114175180414EFE8@NGPA-SDAN-119F2FEEB8C318F0@2421478-119F2FEEF33CE 5C8@3-119F2FF02C2671C8@Aberdeen+Jews+to+Dedicate+New+Synagogue+next+Sun day?search_terms (accessed April 10, 2021).

174. "Notable Week for Local Jews First Time New Year Will be Observed in Our Synagogue," September 16, 1917

175. "Ner Tamid," *Encyclopedia Britannica*, https://www.britannica.com/topic/ner-tamid (accessed March 30, 2022).

176. "Notable Week for Local Jews First Time New Year Will be Observed in Our Synagogue," September 16, 1917

177. *Aberdeen News*, July 14, 2014

178. Camilla Ghisleni, "What is Vernacular Architecture?" *ArchDaily*, November 25, 2020 https://www.archdaily.com/951667/what-is-vernacular-architecture

179. Synagogues360, https://synagogues-360.anumuseum.org.il/tour/congregation-bnai-isaac/

180. "Hub Jews Celebrate Thanksgiving," *Aberdeen Daily News*, October 2, 1917 https://
aberdeennews.newsbank.com/doc/image/v2:114175180414EFE8@NGPA-SDAN-119F2EAA
A40DD3F0@2421504-119F2EAACCF780F8@1-119F2EABB4C0BED8@Hub+Jews+Celebrat
ed+Thanksgiving+Special+Services+at+Synagogue+Last+Night+-+Week+of+Rejoicing?
search_terms

181. "Purim Services Start Saturday Night," *Aberdeen Daily News*, March 12, 1919
https://aberdeennews.newsbank.com/doc/image/v2:114175180414EFE8@NGPA-
SDAN-11A88851DA09FC30@2422030-11A888522AC69F60@7-11A8885379F9D3D0@
Purim+Services+Start+Saturday+Night+Jewish+Festival+and+Purim+Party
+to+Help+Poor+Sunday+Night?search_terms

182. "Tzedakah 101," *My Jewish Learning* https://www.myjewishlearning.com/article/tzeda-
kah-101/(accessed March 31, 2022).

183. "Jews to Give $1200 to War Relief," *Aberdeen Daily News*, May 21, 1918. https://www.
usdinflation.com/amount/1200/1918 (accessed March 31, 2022).

184. "Inflation of $1,200 since 1918," *USD Inflation* https://www.usdinflation.com/
amount/1200/1918 (September 24, 2021).

185. "Jews to Give $1200 to War Relief," May 21, 1918.

186. Ibid.

187. "Churches of Aberdeen Make Influence felt in Community's Life," *Aberdeen American*, December 19, 1921 https://www.genealogybank.com/doc/newspapers/image/
v2%3A117034F05215C2C0%40GB3NEWS-11A8920EE0242E10%402423043-11A8920F
052955B8%400-11A8920F3A110550%40Churches%2Bof%2BAberdeen%2BMake%2BInflu
ences%2BFelt%2Bin%2BCommunity%2527s%2BLife%2BFirst%2BHouse%2Bof%2BWor
ship%2BWas%2BEstablished?h=1&fname=&mname=&lname=&kwinc=%22Churches%20
of%20Aberdeen%22&kwexc=&rgfromDate=1919&rgtoDate=1922&formDate=&formDate
Flex=exact&dateType=range&processingtime=&addedFrom=&addedTo=&sid=azfqsbefc
drsmyttqhlsdeutvxzpzsx0_wma-gateway010_1649188907973 (accessed May 1, 2021).

188. "What Society is Doing," *Aberdeen American*, https://www.genealogybank.com/
doc/newspapers/image/v2%3A117034F05215C2C0%40GB3NEWS-119D2F1A1979FCE8
%402421413-119D2F1A610FF188%404-119D2F1B1CE965D0%40What%2BSociety%2B
is%2BDoing?h=25&fname=&mname=&lname=hess&kwinc=north%20dakota%20jew
ish&kwexc=&rgfromDate=1890&rgtoDate=1919&formDate=&formDateFlex=exact&da
teType=range&processingtime=&addedFrom=&addedTo=&page=1&sid=daaqqnazspizn
mwcsvjfoicnsybrqekr_wma-gateway010_1642538036464https://www.genealogybank.
com/doc/newspapers/image/v2%3A117034F05215C2C0%40GB3NEWS-119D2F1A1979F
CE8%402421413-119D2F1A610FF188%404-119D2F1B1CE965D0%40What%2BSo
ciety%2Bis%2BDoing?h=25&fname=&mname=&lname=hess&kwinc=north%20
dakota%20jewish&kwexc=&rgfromDate=1890&rgtoDate=1919&formDate=&
formDateFlex=exact&dateType=range&processingtime=&addedFrom=&added
To=&page=1&sid=daaqqnazspiznmwcsvjfoicnsybrqekr_wma-gateway010_1642538036464
(accessed February 12, 2021).

189. "Plan Young Peoples' Hebrew Association," *Aberdeen American*, August 7, 1917 https://
www.genealogybank.com/doc/newspapers/image/v2%3A117034F05215C2C0%40GB
3NEWS-119D2F31B63BAAC0%402421448-119D2F31D4DC64A0%401-119D2F3283D5B8
50%40Plan%2BYoung%2BPeoples%2527%2BHebrew%2BAssociation%2BDiscuss%2B
Plans%2Bat%2BMeeting%2Bat%2BResidence%2Bof%2BRabbi%2BHess%2BLast?h=1&f
name=&mname=&lname=&rgfromDate=&rgtoDate=&formDate=08/07/1917&formDate
Flex=exact&dateType=date&kwinc=Hebrew&kwexc=&sid=wvrqaggxfqibrbdsknrwb
bqlzdtjsxbq_s074_1642627586821 (accessed February 21, 2021).

190 "Ancestry.com." relational database, https://www.ancestry.com/discoveryui-content/
view/66599187:7602

191. Ibid.

192. "Aberdeen Jottings," *American Jewish World*, March 8, 1918, Vol. 6, No. 26 https://

umedia.lib.umn.edu/item/p16022coll529:11549/p16022coll529:11543?child_index
=10&facets%5Bcollection_name_s%5D%5B%5D=The%20American%20Jewish%20
World&facets%5Bcontributing_organization_name_s%5D%5B%5D=University%20
of%20Minnesota%20Libraries%2C%20Nathan%20and%20Theresa%20Berman%20
Upper%20Midwest%20Jewish%20Archives.&q=Abraham%20Hess&query=Hess&side
bar_page=1&sort=date_created_sort%20asc%2C%20title_sort%20asc&utf8=%E2%9C%93
(accessed November 3, 2021).

193. "Daughter of Rabbi Hess Buys Bond for her Soldier Husband," *Aberdeen Daily News*,
April 22, 1918 https://aberdeennews.newsbank.com/doc/image/v2:114175180414EFE8@
NGPA-SDAN-119F2C29D1749120@2421706-119F2C2A358B5A08-119F2C2CE8150068?
search_terms (accessed June 12, 2021).

194. "Social Events," *Aberdeen Daily News*, February 20, 1922 https://www.genealogybank.
com/doc/newspapers/image/v2%3A114175180414EFE8%40GB3NEWS-11B3C04BB208A
B88%402423106-11B3C04BCEDE9848%407-11B3C04C6E200B60%40So
cial%2BEvents?h=2&fname=&mname=&lname=Hess&kwinc=%22double%20
wedding%22&kwexc=&rgfromDate=2/20/1922&rgtoDate=2/20/1922&formDate=&
formDateFlex=exact&dateType=range&processingtime=&addedFrom=&added
To=&sid=cbsjljlzqnlyfysihryimbyzubskiude_wma-gateway011_1649189771076 (accessed
May 22, 2021).

195. "Society," *Aberdeen American*, June 18, 1918
https://www.genealogybank.com/doc/newspapers/image/v2%3A117034F
05215C2C0%40GB3NEWS-119D3208F6F2D948%402421763-119D320926462C08
%404-119D3209DF6FC290%40Society?h=1&fname=&mname=&lname=&rgfrom
Date=6/18/1918&rgtoDate=6/18/1918&formDate=6/18/1918&formDateFlex=exact&date
Type=date&kwinc=Self%20Denial&kwexc=&sid=zugzpuwysrwjbkfgmuttbwmxqglozmdb_
wma-gateway011_1642632794612 (accessed March 21, 2021).

196. Ibid.

197. "Honor Draftee in Social Events," *Aberdeen Daily News*, June 18, 1918 https://aber-
deennews.newsbank.com/doc/image/v2:114175180414EFE8@NGPA-SDAN-119F2D
C9B0567F18@2421763-119F2DC9EC7A9CA8@3-119F2DCB2D0C5558@Honor%20Draft
ees%20in%20Social%20Event?search_terms (accessed March 31, 2021).

198. "Ribnicks Hosts in Honor of Son," Aberdeen American, April 28, 1920
https://aberdeennews.newsbank.com/doc/image/v2:117034F05215C2C0@
NGPA-SDAN-11ADDEA068C2B140@2422443-11ADDEA079F883E0@4-11AD
DEA0C0EA8710@Society+the+Whole+of+Life?search_terms (accessed April 5, 2021).

199. Aberdeen City and Brown County Directory, 1919 (R.L. Polk and Company, 1919) p.
31 http://digitalcollections.northern.edu/digital/collection/local/id/12180/rec/1(accessed
July 3, 2021).

200. "For God's Sake Help!" *Aberdeen Daily News*, March 22, 1919
https://aberdeennews.newsbank.com/doc/image/v2:114175180414EFE8@NGPA-SDAN-
11A88842D4C02240@2422040-11A88842EDCE97D0@2-11A8884384EE2D30@Advertise
ment?search_terms (accessed August 10, 2021).

201. "Ruin, Starvation, Death," *Aberdeen American*, March 23, 1919 https://aber
deennews.newsbank.com/doc/image/v2:117034F05215C2C0@NGPA-SDAN-
11A5A62ED94C3628@2422041-11A5A62F17806B20@5-11A5A630083FE488@
Advertisement?search_termshttps://aberdeennews.newsbank.com/doc/image/
v2:117034F05215C2C0@NGPA-SDAN-11A5A62ED94C3628@2422041-11A5A62F
17806B20@5-11A5A630083FE488@Advertisement?search_terms (accessed August 10,
2021).

202. Gail Pickus, Bea and Herschel Premack interview recorded by author, May 18, 2018.

203. Aberdeen City Directory, 1917 as cited in A History of the Jewish Community of
Aberdeen, South Dakota, 1887-1964 by Bernice Premack.

204. Gail Pickus, Bea and Herschel Premack interview recorded by author, May 18, 2018.

205. Leona Premack Arnold and Julius Premack oral history conducted by Paul Premack, 1976, and cited in A History of the Jewish Community of Aberdeen, South Dakota, 1887-1964 by Bernice Premack.

206. "Jewish Wine Delivered to Rabbi Last Evening," *Aberdeen Daily News*, https://aberdeennews.newsbank.com/doc/image/v2:114175180414EFE8@NGPA-SDAN-11A5A FA4B3D370D8@2422423-11A5AFA4E4FB1E08@0-11A5AFA554F50168@Jewish+Wine+De livered+to+Rabbi+Last+Evening?search_terms (accessed January 5, 2022).

207. "Jewish Wine Goes to Jail," *Aberdeen Daily News*, https://aberdeennews.newsbank.com/doc/image/v2:114175180414EFE8@NGPA-SDAN-11A5AEF18F02A6C0@2422421-11A5AEF1A01DA630@0-11A5AEF230DA1A80@Jew ish+Wine+Goes+to+Jail+over+100+Gallons+of+Wine+for+Celebration+of+Passover+Con fiscated+by+Sheriff?search_terms (accessed January 5, 2022).

208. "Rabbi Hess Case was Continued," *Aberdeen American*, https://www.genealogy bank.com/doc/newspapers/image/v2%3A117034F05215C2C0%40GB3NEWS-11ADD E97935975F0%402422431-11ADDE979E86E160%401-11ADDE97CA34ABC0%40Rabbi%2B Hess%2BCase%2BWas%2BContinued?h=2&fname=&mname=&lname=Hess&rgfrom Date=1/1/1914&rgtoDate=1/1/19112/31/19244&formDate=&formDateFlex=exact&dateType=range&k winc=Hess&kwexc=&sid=yhchvxmgtpsbtcqfcbdihdpiexozjxtx_s072_1642539755369 (accessed January 5, 2022).

209. Conversations between Brown County court personnel and author, January 10, 2022.

210. "Advertisement," *The Jewish Daily News* (Yiddishe Tagblatt) November 20, 1921 https://www.nli.org.il/en/newspapers/?a=is&oid=ytb19211120-01.2.109&type=nlilogicalsec tionpdf&e=-------en-20-ytb-1--img-txIN%7ctxTI-%d7%90%d7%91%d7%a2%d7%a8%d7%9 3%d7%99%d7%9f-------North+America-----1 (accessed January 14, 2022).

211. Levitt, Dr. Ralph, email message to author, February 28, 2022.

212. "Aberdeen's Jewish Community Began Nearly a Century Ago," January 29, 1984.

213. Ibid.

214. Baker, Zachary M., email message to author, February 28, 2022. Zachary M. Baker, Reinhard Family Curator *Emeritus* of Judaica and Hebraica Collections, Stanford University Libraries.

215. Jerry, Klinger, "Congregation Sons of Israel, First Jewish House of Worship in South Dakota," The Historical Marker Database, 2019, https://www.hmdb.org/m.asp?m=134205 (accessed February 10, 2022).

216. "Rabbi Hess Leaves for Sioux Falls Synagogue," *Aberdeen Daily News*, February 25, 1922https://aberdeennews.newsbank.com/doc/image/v2:114175180414EFE8@NGPA-SDAN-11B3C050E0CF17F8@2423111-11B3C050E8B5A180@1-11B3C0511C1F66E0@Rab bi+Hess+Leaves+for+Sioux+Falls+Synagogue?search_terms (accessed February 17, 2022).

217. "New Rabbi in Services for Purim Festival," *Aberdeen Daily News*, March 9, 1922 https://www.genealogybank.com/doc/newspapers/image/v2%3A114175180414E FE8%40GB3NEWS-11B3C060F76B9388%402423123-11B3C061107BDD28%402-11B3C 0616AF9A9C8%40New%2BRabbi%2Bin%2BServices%2Bfor%2BPurim%2BFesti val%2BRecent%2BLeader%2Bin%2BCharge%2Bof%2BLocal%2BCongregation%2Bto%2B Mark%2BHoly%2BDay?h=4&fname=&mname=&lname=&kwinc=Rabbi&kwexc=&rgfrom Date=1/1/1914&rgtoDate=1/1/19112/31/19244&formDate=&formDateFlex=exact&date Type=range&processingtime=&addedFrom=&addedTo=&sid=tzagjgjwtavtqesndmsx jvfxahgqloba_wma-gateway001_1642540877740 (accessed February 22, 2022).

218. "Rabbi Segal Corrects Errors Appearing in Journal," *Aberdeen Journal*, March 15, 1922 https://www.genealogybank.com/doc/newspapers/image/v2%3A120864088679F 70D%40GB3NEWS-120D13945EFA1978%402423129-1208DA94557D6760%405-1208DA

94557D6760%40?h=2&fname=&mname=&lname=segal&kwinc=&kwexc=&sort=old&rg
fromDate=1922&rgtoDate=1923&formDate=&formDateFlex=exact&dateType=range&pro
cessingtime=&addedFrom=&addedTo=&sid=hpinwctfgxcoqglnooxjpqdecgxweqwn_
wma-gateway005_1643665870367 (accessed February 22, 2022).

219. "Passover Services Held at Synagogue," *Aberdeen Daily News*, April 13, 1922 https://
www.genealogybank.com/doc/newspapers/image/v2%3A114175180414EFE8%40GB3NEWS
-11B3C0936AFF3F78%402423158-11B3C0936ECBB898%400-11B3C093B29E82E8%40Pass
over%2BServices%2BHeld%2Bat%2BSynagogue?h=6&fname=&mname=&lname=segal&k
winc=&kwexc=&sort=old&rgfromDate=1922&rgtoDate=1923&formDate=&formDateFlex
=exact&dateType=range&processingtime=&addedFrom=&addedTo=&sid=hpinwctfgxco
qglnooxjpqdecgxweqwn_wma-gateway005_1643665870367 (accessed February 22, 2022).

220. "Items of Interest in the Jewish World," *The Hebrew Standard*, May 12, 1922, p. 4
https://www.nli.org.il/he/newspapers/hebstd/1922/05/12/01/article/8/?e=-------he-20--1--
img-txIN%7ctxTI-------------1(accessed May 5, 2021).

221. "A History of the Jewish Community of Aberdeen, South Dakota, 1887-1964," by
Bernice Premack.

222. "Society," The Aberdeen American, November 18, 1922
https://aberdeennews.newsbank.com/doc/image/v2:117034F05215C2C0@NGPA-
SDAN-11ADDFB3E1482FF8@2423377-11ADDFB3F44E1F18@3-11ADDFB4615AF0C0@
City+Society+State+Edited+by+Mrs.+Dean+Potter+Delightful+Parties+on+Social+Pro
gram?search_terms (accessed September 12, 2021)

223. "Premack Marriage License," https://spaces.hightail.com/space/iD4HcGCVsz/files/
fi-ee14bca0-2073-4d7a-94a6-903ac3b01039/fv-ca2d1106-11a3-4276-ae7d-893ac89fd632/
IMG_0314.jpeg

224. "Society Events," *Aberdeen American*, October 29, 1922 https://aberdeennews.
newsbank.com/doc/image/v2:117034F05215C2C0@NGPA-SDAN-11ADDFA070849F
B0@2423357-11ADDFA090B79638@7-11ADDFA10B433590@Society+Events?search_terms

225.

226. https://aberdeennews.newsbank.com/doc/image/v2:117034F05215C2C0@NGPA-
SDAN-11ADDFA070849FB0@2423357-11ADDFA090B79638@7-11ADDFA10B433590@
Society+Events?search_terms

227. Gail Pickus, Bea and Herschel Premack interview recorded by author, May 18, 2018.

228. Bea and Herschel Premack interview recorded by author, May 19, 2018.

229. "'Dear Abby' advice columnist Pauline Friedman Phillips dies at age 94," *Aberdeen
News*, January 17, 2013
https://www.aberdeennews.com/story/news/2013/01/17/dear-abby-advice-columnist-
pauline-friedman-phillips-dies-at-age-94/46262357/ (accessed December 4, 2021).

230. "PaknTreger," *Yiddish Book Center*, 2014 https://www.yiddishbookcenter.org/lan
guage-literature-culture/pakn-treger/bintel-brief (accessed December 5, 2021).

231. "'Dear Abby' advice columnist Pauline Friedman Phillips dies at age 94," January 17,
2013.

232. Leona Premack Arnold and Julius Premack interview recorded by Paul Premack,
1976, as cited in "A History of the Jewish Community of Aberdeen, South Dakota, 1887-
1964," by Bernice Premack.

233. "Synagogue Purchased in 1917," *Aberdeen Daily News*, January 25, 1976 https://
aberdeennews.newsbank.com/doc/image/v2:114175180414EFE8@NGPA-SDAN-
121850612DDAA1D8@2442803-12145406D88392E0@42-12145406D88392E0@?search_
terms (accessed May 12, 2021).

234. Gail Pickus, Bea and Herschel Premack interview recorded by author, May 18, 2018.

235. Karol, Barbara, "Phone conversation with author," March 1, 2022.

236. "Wedding Anniversary," *Aberdeen Weekly News*, February 16, 1922.
https://www.genealogybank.com/doc/newspapers/image/v2%3A12A

7F5A3C13E62AA%40GB3NEWS-11A890BE11D6C9A8%402423102-11A890BE750CD750
%405-11A890BFCFAFA7D0%40Corn%2Bis%2BCalled%2BBarometer%2Bof%2BProsper
ity%2Bfor%2BFarmers%2Bin%2BAll%2BSections%2Bof%2BState?h=7&fname=max&m
name=&lname=amdur&kwinc=&kwexc=&sort=old&rgfromDate=1915&rgtoDate=1955&
formDate=&formDateFlex=exact&dateType=range&processingtime=&addedFrom=&ad
dedTo=&sid=apgdrzxdzamsyyfjgntkqgytvjlcosmp_wma-gateway008_1646275867174

237. "Plans for Zionist Campaign are being Rapidly Completed," *Aberdeen American*, February 9, 1919, https://www.genealogybank.com/doc/newspapers/ image/v2%3A117034F05215C2C0%40GB3NEWS-11A5A67D16B35EF0%402421999-11A5A67D66B6A8E8%409-11A5A67EDAA551D0%40Plans%2Bfor%2BZi onist%2BCampaign%2BAre%2BBeing%2BRapidly%2BCompleted%2BCam paign%2Bto%2BAid%2Bin%2BRaising%2B%25249%252C000%252C000%2Bfor%2B the%2BRestoration?h=3&fname=&mname=&lname=&kwinc=aberdeen%20%22max%20 amdur%22&kwexc=&sort=old&rgfromDate=&rgtoDate=&formDate=&formDateFlex =exact&dateType=range&processingtime=&addedFrom=&addedTo=&sid=nznqhivhfx axgsqrkhljsxavojvyqiop_wma-gateway005_1646279457602

238. "Hadassah Circle Meeting," *Aberdeen Journal*, January 7, 1922 https://www.genealogybank.com/doc/newspapers/image/v2%3A120864088679F 70D%40GB3NEWS-120D12CF5C677430%402423062-120CBF14D1717440%404-120CBF 14D1717440%40?h=14&fname=&mname=&lname=Amdur&rgfromDate=&rgtoDate=& formDate=&formDateFlex=exact&dateType=range&kwinc=men%27s%20store&kwex c=&sort=old&sid=jcrzeuihbnclsntuujmupxvsehsboygk_wma-gateway005_1646280173334

239. Karol, Barbara, "Phone conversation with author," March 1, 2022.

240. Ibid.

241. "Ancestry.com," relational database, *https://www.ancestry.com/* (https://search.ancestry.com/cgi-bin/sse.dll?indiv=1&d-bid=8561&h=297442&tid=&pid=&queryId=e980899a0e829236e008f380941ddf1e&use PUB=true&_phsrc=PWt718&_phstart=successSource: February 9, 2022) South Dakota Marriages, 1905 -2017.

242. "Debaters Win District Meet," Aberdeen Daily News, February 23, 1934 https:// aberdeennews.newsbank.com/doc/image/v2:114175180414EFE8@NGPA-SDAN-1211FF 14CF5114E0@2427492-120B765387D31128@1-120B765387D31128@?search_terms (accessed February 21, 2021).

243. "Minnesota delegation to the first National Economic Conference for Israel, Minneapolis, Minnesota," *Minnesota Digital Library*, https://collection.mndigital.org/cata log/jhs:500#?c=&m=&s=&cv=&xywh=-1259%2C0%2C6702%2C3395

244. https://louwineshop.com/

245. Amdur, Louis, emails with author, March 2022.

246. "Advertisement," *Aberdeen Daily News*, October 17, 1919 https:// www.genealogybank.com/doc/newspapers/image/v2%3A114175180414E FE8%40GB3NEWS-11B11E7CE4D0F8F8%402422249-11B11E7C EEB8A5C8%402-11B11E7D3B44BEA8%40Advertisement?h=15&fname=&mname=&l name=&rgfromDate=&rgtoDate=&formDate=&formDateFlex=exact&dateType=range&k winc=Sudow%27s&kwexc=&sort=old&sid=lgawwvweszxyrzhnftquoaniqwqfqmid_ wma-gateway014_1646274905918

247. "Advertisement," *Aberdeen Daily News*, July 16, 1920. https://aberdeennews.newsbank.com/doc/image/v2:114175180414EFE8@ NGPA-SDAN-11CACA3746E79FB8@2422522-11CACA375D11D178@5-11CACA37D 5EDE440@Advertisement?search_terms

248. "Advertisement," *Aberdeen Daily News*, September 22, 1922.https://aberdeen news.newsbank.com/doc/image/v2:114175180414EFE8@NGPA-SDAN-120C54C6E21F D700@2423320-120A6B4BC275E200@4-120A6B4BC275E200@?search_terms

249. "Advertisement," *Aberdeen Daily News*, October 6, 1922. https://aberdeennews.newsbank.com/doc/image/v2:114175180414EFE8@NGPA-SDAN-120 C556D9E44C780@2423334-120A6E0FAB6E8F90@4-120A6E0FAB6E8F90@?search_terms

250. Leona Premack Arnold and Julius Premack oral history conducted by Paul Premack, 1976, and cited in A History of the Jewish Community of Aberdeen, South Dakota, 1887-1964 by Bernice Premack.

251. "Hyman Truck Started with Just One Vehicle," *Aberdeen Daily News*, June 17, 1956. https://aberdeennews.newsbank.com/doc/image/v2:114175180414EFE8@NGPA-SDAN-121267153782B568@2435642-120F08395070B1C8@91-120F08395070B1C8@?search_terms

252. Schneier, Betsy Rosenbaum emails with author, February - March 2022.

253. "World War I - Jewish Soldiers in the Russian Army," *IDF and Defense Establishment Archives*, https://archives.mod.gov.il/sites/English/Exhibitions/The_Jewish_Combatant_Collection/Pages/Jewish-soldiers-in-the-Russian-Army.aspx (accessed March 30, 2022).

254. Schneier, Betsy Rosenbaum emails with author, February - March 2022.

255. Ibid.

256. "Ancestry.com," relational database, *https://www.ancestry.com/* https://www.ancestry.com/discoveryui-content/view/900077786:61305?tid=&pid=&queryId=b f33eb6063957e881516d404c0c63ab5&_phsrc=PWt239&_phstart=successSource. 1920 U.S. Federal Census.

257. "Ancestry.com," relational database, *https://www.ancestry.com/* https://www.ancestry.com/discoveryui-content/view/201320:62035?tid=&pid=&queryId=357b21aa02825f632a 4262f93ea3167c8&_phsrc=PWt233&_phstart=successSource. 1920 U.S. Federal Census.

258. Lieberman, Victor, "The Early History," https://bnaiisraelnd.org/history/.

259. Silberg, Beryl Hardin, "Phone conversation with author," March 1, 2022.

260. "Virtual Jewish World: North Dakota, United States," *Jewish Virtual Library*, jewishvirtuallibrary.org. J

261. Lieberman, Victor, "The Early History," https://bnaiisraelnd.org/history/.

262. Schneier, Betsy Rosenbaum emails with author, February - March 2022.

263. Ben Calmenson written recollections sent to Bea Premack,1987.

264. "Main Street at Noon," *Aberdeen Evening News*, October 15, 1929 https://aberdeennews.newsbank.com/doc/image/v2:114175180414EFE8@NGPA-SDAN-1221828AE7D D17E8@2425900-120CB7B8A01A8D38@0-120CB7B8A01A8D38@?search_terms

265. "Social Activities," *Aberdeen American*, November 28, 1924 https://aberdeennews.newsbank.com/doc/image/v2:117034F05215C2C0@NGPA-SDAN-120A6CC9440C9730@2424118-1208805CF1CA42F8@1-1208805CF1CA42F8@?search_terms

266. Ibid.

267. Gail Pickus, Bea and Herschel Premack interview recorded by author, May 18, 2018.

268. Ibid.

269. "Franklin Premack Obituary," *New York Times*, April 8, 1975 https://timesmachine.nytimes.com/timesmachine/1975/04/08/76551326.html?pageNumber=40

270. "Premack Award Suspended," Minnesota Journalism Center, *University of Minnesota, School of Journalism and Mass Communication*, http://mjc.umn.edu/events/premack.html.

271. "Premack Principle," *Science Direct*, https://www.sciencedirect.com/topics/psychology/premack-principle#:~:text=Premack's%20Principle-,Premack's%20principle%20(or%20the%20differential%20probability%20hypothesis)%20refers%20to%20reinforcing,a%20more%20desired%20behavior%20afterward.&text=The%20more%20highly%20desirable%20behavior,%2C%20albeit%20less%20enjoyable%2C%20activity.

272. "Ann James Premack obituary," *VC Star*, https://www.vcstar.com/obituaries/vcs024442.

273. Ibid.

274. Ibid.

275. Ibid.

276. Ibid.

277. "David Premack obituary," *University of Pennsylvania Almanac*, https://almanac.upenn.edu/archive/volumes/v62/no2/obit.html

278. Ann James Premack and David Premack, "Teaching Language to an Ape," Scientific American, October 1972. https://www.scientificamerican.com/article/teaching-language-to-an-ape/

279. "David Premack obituary," *Psychonomic Society*, https://www.psychonomic.org/page/obituaries

280. Gail Pickus, Bea and Herschel Premack interview recorded by author, May 18, 2018.

281. "Bat Dor Dance Company," 1975 https://www.israeldance-diaries.co.il/wp-content/uploads/2018/10/ANNUAL1975_companies_premeieres.pdf

282. Gail Pickus, Bea and Herschel Premack interview recorded by author, May 18, 2018.

283. "City under Canvass for Jewish Funds People throughout Town Will be Asked to Help Save Starving People," *Aberdeen Daily News*, April 5, 1922, https://www.genealogybank.com/doc/newspapers/image/v2%3A114175180414EFE8%40GB3NEWS-11B3C0896A117860%402423150-11B3C08999A477E8%407-11B3C08A724EE030%40City%2Bunder%2BCanvass%2Bfor%2BJewish%2BFunds%2BPeople%2Bthroughout%2BTown%2BWill%2Bbe%2BAsked%2Bto%2BHelp%2BSave%2BStarving%2BPeople?h=4&fname=ben&mname=&lname=brussel&rgfromDate=1920&rgtoDate=1930&formDate=&formDateFlex=exact&dateType=range&kwinc=&kwexc=&sort=old&sid=qcsqlcthgmdarrseaovcyebtueswbcrf_wma-gateway008_1648612049559

284. "The Devastating Spanish Flu in Aberdeen," *Aberdeen Magazine*, September/October, 2020 https://aberdeenmag.com/2020/09/the-devastating-spanish-flu-in-aberdeen/

285. Ibid.

286. "Hadassah Minutes Book," November, 1921 to July, 1928. Nathan and Theresa Berman Upper Midwest Jewish Archives, University of Minnesota.

287. "Will Celebrate the Dedication of the New Hebrew University," *Aberdeen American*, March 31, 1925 https://aberdeennews.newsbank.com/doc/image/v2:117034F05215C2C0@NGPA-SDAN-120A6F539E7CA060@2424241-12088060F139A388@7-12088060F139A388@?search_terms

288. "Local Jews to Journey to Dakota Conference," *Aberdeen Daily News*, February 14, 1926 https://www.genealogybank.com/doc/newspapers/image/v2%3A114175180414EFE8%40GB3NEWS-120F2114814685D8%402424561-120929642D87CAD0%405-120929642D87CAD0%40?h=3&fname=&mname=&lname=hardin&rgfromDate=&rgtoDate=&formDate=&formDateFlex=exact&dateType=range&kwinc=%22united%20jewish%22&kwexc=&sid=euxqcrpcvxyeiizxlqmxihzbvqlolpqy_wma-gateway003_1649205406640

289. "Inflation Calculator," *CPI Inflation Calculator*, https://www.in2013dollars.com/us/inflation/1926?amount=15000

290. "Local Jews to Journey to Dakota Conference," February 14, 1926

291. "Drive to Raise Fund of $5,000 in Aberdeen for Jewish Welfare, *Aberdeen Daily News*, May 14, 1926 https://www.genealogybank.com/doc/newspapers/image/v2%3A114175180414EFE8%40GB3NEWS-120F5832C323B9E8%402424650-120D097B0CF71780%404-120D097B0CF71780%40?h=5&fname=&mname=&lname=hardin&rgfromDate=&rgtoDate=&formDate=&formDateFlex=exact&dateType=range&kwinc=%22united%20jewish%22&kwexc=&sid=euxqcrpcvxyeiizxlqmxihzbvqlolpqy_wma-gateway003_1649205406640

292. "$5,000 in 1926 value today," *CPI Inflation Calculator*, https://www.in2013dollars.com/us/inflation/1926?amount=5000#:~:text=%245%2C000%20in%201926%20is%20equivalent,cumulative%20price%20increase%20of%201%2C475.15%25.

293. "Aberdeen Jews Do Their Part Toward Helping Palestine," *Aberdeen Daily News*, September 18, 1926

294. "$1400 in 1926 value today," *Dollar Times*, https://www.dollartimes.com/inflation/

inflation.php?amount=1400&year=1926

295. "Hadassah Minutes Book," November, 1921 to July, 1928. Nathan and Theresa Berman Upper Midwest Jewish Archives, University of Minnesota.

296. "Hadassah Sewing for Orphans," *Aberdeen Journal*, May 25, 1921 https://www.genealo gybank.com/doc/newspapers/image/v2%3A120864088679F70D%40GB3NEWS-120D0E1E 6CAA5F38%402422835-120C7C0274D77F10%402-120C7C0274D77F10%40?h=4&fname=& mname=&lname=&rgfromDate=1921&rgtoDate=1921&formDate=&formDateFlex=exact& dateType=range&kwinc=Hadassah&kwexc=&sid=kgowdrrwldwrmbbbjtreypytmfhzuqka_ wma-gateway020_1649206321353

297. "Hadassah Sewing Club," *Aberdeen Journal*, November 9, 1921 https://www. genealogybank.com/doc/newspapers/image/v2%3A120864088679F70D%40GB 3NEWS-120D121BEEC5FBD8%402423003-120CBB2996E01C10%404-120CB B2996E01C10%40?h=3&fname=&mname=&lname=&rgfromDate=1921&rgtoDate=1921& formDate=&formDateFlex=exact&dateType=range&kwinc=Hadassah&kwexc=&sid=k gowdrrwldwrmbbbjtreypytmfhzuqka_wma-gateway020_1649206321353

298. "Announcements, *Aberdeen Daily News*, December 11, 1921 https://www. genealogybank.com/doc/newspapers/image/v2%3A120864088679F70D%40GB 3NEWS-120D121BEEC5FBD8%402423003-120CBB2996E01C10%404-120CB B2996E01C10%40?h=3&fname=&mname=&lname=&rgfromDate=1921&rgtoDate=1921& formDate=&formDateFlex=exact&dateType=range&kwinc=Hadassah&kwexc=&sid=k gowdrrwldwrmbbbjtreypytmfhzuqka_wma-gateway020_1649206321353

299. "Society," *Aberdeen American*, January 8, 1922 https://www.genealogybank.com/doc/ newspapers/image/v2%3A117034F05215C2C0%40GB3NEWS-11ADDF1853F33D20%4024 23063-11ADDF185ED81670%401-11ADDF1887BAE1C0%40Society%2BMiss%2BZola%2B Friel%2BEditor?h=1&fname=&mname=&lname=&kwinc=Hadassah&kwexc=&rgfrom Date=1922&rgtoDate=1922&formDate=&formDateFlex=exact&dateType=range&process ingtime=&addedFrom=&addedTo=&sort=old&sid=cgqgqiyklyrtoxccknqxvzqngnmpfzbz_ wma-gateway017_1649206602462

300. "Announcements," *Aberdeen Journal*, March 18, 1922 https://www.genealogybank. com/doc/newspapers/image/v2%3A120864088679F70D%40GB3NEWS-120D139C0FB 5BE68%402423132-120CC2CE33E9FE48%404-120CC2CE33E9FE48%40?h=10&fname =&mname=&lname=&kwinc=Hadassah&kwexc=&rgfromDate=1922&rgtoDate=1922& formDate=&formDateFlex=exact&dateType=range&processingtime=&added From=&addedTo=&sort=old&sid=cgqgqiyklyrtoxccknqxvzqngnmpfzbz_wma-gate way017_1649206602462

301. "Society," *Aberdeen Daily News*, February 8, 1922 https://www.genealogybank.com/doc/newspapers/image/v2%3A114175180414EFE8%40GB 3NEWS-11B3C032B5ADD240%402423094-11B3C032DA4E9A98%407-11B3C0339B8D 2D48%40Social%2BEvents%2BMiss%2BZola%2BFriel%2BEditor?h=8&fname=&m name=&lname=&rgfromDate=1915&rgtoDate=1950&formDate=&formDateFlex=exact& dateType=range&kwinc=Hadassah&kwexc=&sort=old&sid=tlejcxyytcxmujrhqgqenpdck gyddjnk_wma-gateway014_1642886943742

302. "City Federation Meeting," *Aberdeen Journal*, March 7, 1922 https://www.genealogy bank.com/doc/newspapers/image/v2%3A120864088679F70D%40GB3NEWS-120D137E AECE48D8%402423121-120CC24BEB4BC938%404-120CC24BEB4BC938%40?h=2& fname=&mname=&lname=&rgfromDate=&rgtoDate=&formDate=&formDateFlex =exact&dateType=range&kwinc=%22City%20Federation%22%20Hadassah&kwex c=&sort=old&sid=agxgkzcqizriknybsyzxxehxqvzvgkru_wma-gateway017_1649207145811

303. "Hadassah Club Members Hold Meeting," *Aberdeen Daily News*, May 10, 1922 https://www.genealogybank.com/doc/newspapers/image/v2%3A114175180414E FE8%40GB3NEWS-11B3C02AC2646D40%402423185-11B3C02AD14641A8%402-11B3C

02B473C3FC8%40Activities%2Bon%2Bthe%2BSocial%2BCalendar?h=18&fname=&m
name=&lname=&rgfromDate=1915&rgtoDate=1950&formDate=&formDateFlex=exact&
dateType=range&kwinc=Hadassah&kwexc=&sort=old&page=1&sid=tlejcxyytcxmujrhqgq
enpdckgyddjnk_wma-gateway014_1642886943742

304. Ibid.

305. "Hadassah Sewing Circle," *Aberdeen Journal*, March 1, 1922
https://www.genealogybank.com/explore/newspapers/all/usa/south-dakota/aberdeen/
aberdeen-journal?fname=&mname=&lname=&rgfromDate=&rgtoDate=&formDate=&
formDateFlex=exact&dateType=range&kwinc=toothbrush%2C%20Hadassah&kwexc=%20

306. "Bridge Tea Given at Country Club," *Aberdeen Daily News*, May 21, 1925
https://www.genealogybank.com/doc/newspapers/image/v2%3A114175180414E
FE8%40GB3NEWS-120F0F0AB510CEF0%402424292-120C61DC19772A40%4010
-120C61DC19772A40%40?h=55&fname=&mname=&lname=&rgfromDate=1915&rg
toDate=1950&formDate=&formDateFlex=exact&dateType=range&kwinc=Hadas
sah&kwexc=&sort=old&page=3&sid=tlejcxyytcxmujrhqgqenpdckgyddjnk_wma-gate
way014_1642886943742

307. "Hadassah Members Anticipate Lecture," *Aberdeen Daily News*, December 7, 1926
https://aberdeennews.newsbank.com/doc/image/v2%3A114175180414EFE8%40NG
PA-SDAN-120F5B551C212FE8%402424857-120929BA1C6B8EF8%403-120929BA1C6B8E
F8%40?search_terms=Hadassah%2Bsocial%2Bworker&text=Hadassah%20social%20
worker&pub%255B0%255D=114175180414EFE8&sort=old&pdate=1926-12-07

308. "Dinner Party at Sudow Home for Speaker," *Aberdeen Daily News*, December 9, 1926
https://aberdeennews.newsbank.com/doc/image/v2:114175180414EFE8@NGPA-SDAN-
120F5B57011008A0@2424859-120929BAB2A67610@1-120929BAB2A67610@?search_terms

309. Ibid.

310. "Jewish Holiday Observed By Women," *Aberdeen Daily News*, October 20, 1927 https://
aberdeennews.newsbank.com/doc/image/v2:114175180414EFE8@NGPA-SDAN-1212590CE-
2D2A088@2425174-120A76B5189B8F80@1-120A76B5189B8F80@?search_terms

311. "Noted Pianist Guest of Honor," *Aberdeen Daily News*, February 28, 1922 https://aber
deennews.newsbank.com/doc/image/v2:114175180414EFE8@NGPA-SDAN-1212590CE
2D2A088@2425174-120A76B5189B8F80@1-120A76B5189B8F80@?search_terms

312. "Advertisement," *Aberdeen Daily News*, January 24, 1934 https://aberdeennews.news
bank.com/doc/image/v2:114175180414EFE8@NGPA-SDAN-1211FE33ED249C30@2427462-
120D29B8F824AE40@2-120D29B8F824AE40@?search_terms

313. "Advertisement," *Aberdeen Daily News*, January 26, 1934
https://aberdeennews.newsbank.com/doc/image/v2:114175180414EFE8@NGPA-SDAN-
1211FE3A53712088@2427464-120D29FE0B59E628@4-120D29FE0B59E628@?search_term

314. Gail Pickus, Bea and Herschel Premack interview recorded by author, May 18, 2018.

315. "The Following Stores Closed," *Aberdeen Daily News*, September 21, 1928 https://
aberdeennews.newsbank.com/doc/image/v2:114175180414EFE8@NGPA-SDAN-
12135D4024EC2DD0@2425511-120A76D65380C858@7-120A76D65380C858@?search_
terms

316. "Advertisement," *Aberdeen Daily News*, November 15, 1928 https://www.
genealogybank.com/doc/newspapers/image/v2%3A114175180414EFE8%40GB
3NEWS-12135F3701E031B0%402425566-12115D411E1B7D30%404-12115D411E1B
7D30%40?h=3&fname=&mname=&lname=&kwinc=%22Ben%20Brussel%22&kwex
c=&sort=bst&rgfromDate=1920&rgtoDate=1930&formDate=&formDateFlex=exact&date
Type=range&processingtime=&addedFrom=&addedTo=&sid=bdpeiqqlazwsqaoxihxpdsy
frwinfbft_wma-gateway014_1645154214138

317. "Announcement," *Aberdeen Daily News*, April 11, 1923 https://www.genealogybank.
com/doc/newspapers/image/v2%3A114175180414EFE8%40GB3NEWS-120C5C08D3A3B
5C0%402423521-120AC7B00A34AFA8%402-120AC7B00A34AFA8%40?h=19&fname=be

n&mname=&lname=brussel&rgfromDate=1920&rgtoDate=1930&formDate=&formDate
Flex=exact&dateType=range&kwinc=&kwexc=&sort=old&page=1&sid=qcsqlcthgmdarr
seaovcyebtueswbcrf_wma-gateway008_1648612049559

318. "Myer Kadesky Moves Store to Frederick," *Aberdeen American*, April 23, 1925
https://www.genealogybank.com/doc/newspapers/image/v2%3A117034F05215C
2C0%40GB3NEWS-120A6FCD1B59ADB0%402424264-120880904207E1D8%403
-120880904207E1D8%40?h=26&fname=ben&mname=&lname=brussel&rgfrom
Date=1920&rgtoDate=1930&formDate=&formDateFlex=exact&dateType=range&k
winc=&kwexc=&sort=old&page=1&sid=qcsqlcthgmdarrseaovcyebtueswbcrf_wma-gate
way008_1648612049559

319. "Ancestry.com," relational database, *https://www.ancestry.com/* (https://www.ancestry.
com/discoveryui-content/view/110451452:2442?tid=&pid=&queryId=c020881b5a95f1322
874d7b929d4434b&_phsrc=PWt968&_phstart=successSource: June 22, 2021) 1920 U.S.
Federal Census.

320. "Ancestry.com, relational database, *https://www.ancestry.com/*
(https://www.ancestry.com/discoveryui-content/view/110927259:6224?tid=&pid=&query
Id=35830ae0784c9b601a239b2339c973c3&_phsrc=PWt1038&_phstart=successSource: June
22, 2021) 1930 U.S. Federal Census.

321. https://glorecords.blm.gov/details/patent/default.aspx?accession=185916&doc
Class=SER&sid=u0045sks.yw4

322 Ancestry.com - https://www.ancestry.com/discoveryui-content/view/668067:8561

323. "James Cash Penney and The Golden Rule," https://fs.blog/james-cash-penney-and-
the-golden-rule/

324. Telephone call with Herschel Premack and author, March 2, 2022.

325. Ibid.

326. Ibid.

327. "Hadassah Chapter to Sponsor Party," *Aberdeen Daily News*, March 5, 1928 https://
aberdeennews.newsbank.com/doc/image/v2%3A114175180414EFE8%40NGPA-SDAN-
12134CCD43DC6358%402425311-12100EB474985330%402-12100EB474985330%40?search_
terms=K%2BC%2Bpurim%2BGlee&text=K%20C%20purim%20Glee&pub%255B0%255D=
114175180414EFE8&sort=old&pdate=1928-03-05

328. "Hadassah Mothers Annually Invite," *Aberdeen Daily News*, December 29, 1930 https://
aberdeennews.newsbank.com/doc/image/v2:114175180414EFE8@NGPA-SDAN-1221D8625
0637EE0@2426340-121F7E28D7AD7E30@2-121F7E28D7AD7E30@?search_terms

329. "Mrs. Schwartz Heads Northwest Regional Hadassah," *Jewish Telegraphic Agency*,
November 24, 1930
https://www.jta.org/archive/mrs-schwartz-heads-northwest-regional-hadassah

330. "Mrs. Sam Sudow," *Aberdeen Daily News*, May 28, 1931 https://aberdeen
news.newsbank.com/doc/image/v2:114175180414EFE8@NGPA-SDAN-1221DE
66A16020E0@2426490-120A766DB0CEFEC0@7-120A766DB0CEFEC0@?search_terms

331. "Hadassah Society Women," *Aberdeen Daily News*, September 24, 1931
https://www.genealogybank.com/doc/newspapers/image/v2%3A114175180414E
FE8%40GB3NEWS-1221E05BD397E650%402426609-120A767D88AFDC98%403-1
20A767D88AFDC98%40?h=180&fname=&mname=&lname=&rgfromDate=1915&rg
toDate=1950&formDate=&formDateFlex=exact&dateType=range&kwinc=Hadas
sah&kwexc=&sort=old&page=11&sid=tlejcxyytcxmujrhqgqenpdckgyddjnk_wma-gate
way014_1642886943742

332. "Bnai (sic) Brith Lodge Will Hold Dance," *Aberdeen Daily News*, November 21,
1926 https://www.genealogybank.com/doc/newspapers/image/v2%3A114175180414E
FE8%40GB3NEWS-120F5AE9E6129118%402424841-120929B693AE6808%409-12

0929B693AE6808%40?h=25&fname=&mname=&lname=&rgfromDate=&rgtoDat
e=&formDate=&formDateFlex=exact&dateType=range&kwinc=Amdur%20
men%27s&kwexc=&sort=old&page=1&sid=sypiubbztgzgbviedclmydhfmhryjmfa_
wma-gateway011_1646281263117

333. "Fargo Lawyer Will Address Bnai (sic) Brith," *Aberdeen Daily News*, May 15,
1927 https://www.genealogybank.com/doc/newspapers/image/v2%3A114175180414E
FE8%40GB3NEWS-1221E05BD397E650%402426609-120A767D88AFDC98%403-1
20A767D88AFDC98%40?h=180&fname=&mname=&lname=&rgfromDate=1915&rg
toDate=1950&formDate=&formDateFlex=exact&dateType=range&kwinc=Hadas
sah&kwexc=&sort=old&page=11&sid=tlejcxyytcxmujrhqgqenpdckgyddjnk_wma-gate
way014_1642886943742

334. "Lashkowitz, Harry, 1889-1963," *Social Networks and Archival Context*, https://snacco
operative.org/ark:/99166/w6gf2nxc (accessed January 15, 2022).

335. "Personals," *Aberdeen Daily News*, January 10, 1929, https://aberdeennews.newsbank.
com/doc/image/v2:114175180414EFE8@NGPA-SDAN-1213626A2E092418@2425622-
120A76DE46B890D8@1-120A76DE46B890D8@?search_terms

336. "Society Notes," *Aberdeen Daily News*, December 14, 1926 https://aberdeen
news.newsbank.com/doc/image/v2:114175180414EFE8@NGPA-SDAN-120F5B5FE
90BEB58@2424864-120929BC50B753D0@1?pdate=1926-12-14

337. "Name Leaders for Boys' Annual Camp, *Aberdeen Daily News*, May 14, 1929 https://
aberdeennews.newsbank.com/doc/image/v2:114175180414EFE8@NGPA-SDAN-12136A57E
F6E0F30@2425746-120A76E902B709B0@1-120A76E902B709B0@?search_terms

338. "Couple Surprises Friends with Marriage," *Aberdeen Daily News*, February 29, 1928
https://aberdeennews.newsbank.com/doc/image/v2:114175180414EFE8@NGPA-SDAN-
12134C9CB9507088@2425306-120A76BFAB1A4188@11-120A76BFAB1A4188@?search_
terms

339. "Hebrew Ceremony at Alonzo Ward is Brilliant," *Aberdeen Daily News*, August 6, 1928
https://aberdeennews.newsbank.com/doc/image/v2:114175180414EFE8@NGPA-SDAN-
1213584BEB352840@2425465-1211150039F61AB0@2-1211150039F61AB0@?search_terms

340. "Ehrlich Buys Jewelry Store," *Aberdeen Daily News*, February 28, 1932 https://aber
deennews.newsbank.com/doc/image/v2:114175180414EFE8@NGPA-SDAN-1221E28C
0B8A1DE8@2426766-120A768EB5C2F850@1-120A768EB5C2F850@?search_terms

341. "Spiritual Leader Named," *American Jewish World*, Vol. 25, No. 39, May 28, 1937
https://umedia.lib.umn.edu/item/p16022coll529:37680/p16022coll529:37667?child_
index=11&facets%5Bcontributing_organization_name_s%5D%5B%5D=University%20
of%20Minnesota%20Libraries%2C%20Nathan%20and%20Theresa%20Berman%20
Upper%20Midwest%20Jewish%20Archives.&q=%20Hardin&query=Hardin&sidebar_
page=1&sort=&utf8=%E2%9C%93

342. "geni.com," commercial genealogy and social networking, (https://www.geni.com/
people/Rabbi-Aaron-Hardin/6000000000313074753: March 10, 2022) Find a Grave Index,
1600 - current.

343. Levy, Bea, Phone conversation with author, February 15, 2022.

344. Weinshel, Meyer, email message to author, February 15, 2022.

345. "Advertisement," *Aberdeen Daily News*, May 14, 1915 https://www.genealogy
bank.com/doc/newspapers/image/v2%3A114175180414EFE8%40GB3NEWS-120F1F
75657B5A28%402433692-120CC00767B0FED8%405-120CC00767B0FED8%40?h=13&fna
me=&mname=&lname=&rgfromDate=&rgtoDate=&formDate=&formDateFlex=exact&da
teType=range&kwinc=%22Pioneer%20Wrecking%22&kwexc=&sort=old&sid=kakamzgg
blsehporhstcvlsvrefrgtyh_wma-gateway011_1645153064400

346. Levy, Bea, Phone conversation with author, February 15, 2022.

347. Ibid.

348. Zivotofsky, Dr. Ari Z., "What's the Truth about . . . "Planting" Knives to Kasher

Them?" *Jewish Action: The Magazine of the Orthodox Union*, Spring, 2019 https://jewishaction.com/religion/jewish-law/whats-the-truth-about-planting-knives-to-kasher-them/

349. Levy, Bea, Phone conversation with author, February 15, 2022.

350. Levy, Bea, Phone conversation with author, February 15, 2022.

351. Ibid.

352. Ibid.

353. Jonathan Kamel, "Kamel: Walk to Remember shows Northwestern's progress in Jewish integration" *The Daily Northwestern*, April 9, 2013. https://dailynorthwestern.com/2013/04/09/opinion/kamel-walk-to-remember-shows-northwesterns-progress-in-jewish-integration/#

354. "Mrs. Louise Fedje to Present Pupils in Piano Recital, *Aberdeen Daily News*, June 3, 1935 https://aberdeennews.newsbank.com/doc/image/v2:114175180414EFE8@NGPA-SDAN-121216341C049798@2427957-121105DEEB8868C0@2-121105DEEB8868C0@?search_terms

355. "Pfitzner Classes in Recital Tonight," *Aberdeen Daily News*, November 28, 1932 https://aberdeennews.newsbank.com/doc/image/v2:114175180414EFE8@NGPA-SDAN-121109434785DF70@2427040-120B7639F6CBF440@1-120B7639F6CBF440@?search_terms

356. "Reminiscences: Aberdeen's Yesteryears," *Aberdeen Daily News*, November 13, 1959 https://aberdeennews.newsbank.com/doc/image/v2:114175180414EFE8@NGPA-SDAN-1215B7E11B092868@2436886-121028AF2F6DF3D8@3-121028AF2F6DF3D8@?search_terms

357. Levy, Bea, Phone conversation with author, February 15, 2022.

358. Ibid.

359. "Social and Personal: Minneapolis," *American Jewish World*, Vol. 26, No. 26 https://umedia.lib.umn.edu/item/p16022coll529:49395/p16022coll529:49384?child_index=5&facets%5Bcontributing_organization_name_s%5D%5B%5D=University%20of%20Minnesota%20Libraries%2C%20Nathan%20and%20Theresa%20Berman%20Upper%20Midwest%20Jewish%20Archives.&q=%22norman%20perman%22&query=Perman&sidebar_page=1&sort=date_created_sort%20asc%2C%20title_sort%20asc&utf8=%E2%9C%93

360. "Ancestry.com," relational database, *https://www.ancestry.com/* (https://www.ancestry.com/1940-census/usa/South-Dakota/Chana-Rebecca-Perman_3vlorj: June 29, 2021). 1940 U.S. Federal Census.

361. "Sioux Falls Man Marries Aberdeen Girl," *Argus Leader*, September 29, 1939 https://www.newspapers.com/image/228972618/?terms=pitts&match=1

362. "Rabbi to Conduct Ceremony Tuesday," *Rapid City Journal*, January 23, 1943 https://www.newspapers.com/image/350616675/?terms=Perman%20Rabbi&match=1

363. Jay Kirschenmann, "It's About Time: Ward turned his five cents into Aberdeen's finest hotel," *Aberdeen News*, January 24, 2020 https://www.aberdeennews.com/story/opinion/columns/2020/01/24/its-about-time-ward-turned-his-five-cents-into-aberdeens-finest-hotel/115793582/

364. "Ward Condos," https://www.wardcondos.com/

365. Arthur Green written recollections sent to Bea Premack,1987.

366. Ibid.

367. Ibid.

368. Ibid.

369. Ibid.

370. "Ancestry.com," relational database, *https://www.ancestry.com/* (https://www.ancestry.com/discoveryui-content/view/1031954316:2469?_phsrc=PWt1010&_phstart=successSource&gsln=gottesman&ml_rpos=1&queryId=7a36a2f1bdefa4d7e0826ac66114f520: June 29,

2021) U.S. City Directories, 1822-1995.

371. Wolf-Simon Greling and Gerda E.H. Koch, *Selig Sigmund Auerbach : ein deutsches Rabbinerschicksal im 20. Jahrhundert*, (Berlin, Hentrich and Hentrich, Centrum Judaicum, 2015).

372. Forsland, Stephanie, emails March, 2022.

373. Ibid.

374. Ibid.

375. "With the Rabbis," Jewish Post, *Hoosier State Chronicles*, June 3, 1949 https://newspapers.library.in.gov/?a=d&d=JPOST19490603-01.1.8&e=-------en-20--1--txt-txIN-------

376. "Church Services," *Aberdeen Daily News*, November 29, 1951 https://aberdeennews.newsbank.com/doc/image/v2:114175180414EFE8@NGPA-SDAN-120F58CA8037EC68@2433980-120CC0AAA8143548@19-120CC0AAA8143548@?search_terms

377. "Jubilee Sabbath to be Observed, *Aberdeen Daily News*, January 6, 1951 https://aberdeennews.newsbank.com/doc/image/v2:114175180414EFE8@NGPA-SDAN-120F1E92A605FE58@2433653-120CBFFA14E3ABE8@11-120CBFFA14E3ABE8@?search_terms

378. "Church Services," *Aberdeen Daily News*, February 10, 1951 https://aberdeennews.newsbank.com/doc/image/v2%3A114175180414EFE8%40NGPA-SDAN-120F1F5DB1EF5B10%402433688-120CC005DF035C90%409-120CC005DF035C90%40?search_terms=auerbach%2Bscouts&text=auerbach%20scouts&date_from=1951&date_to=1951&pub%255B0%255D=114175180414EFE8&sort=old&pdate=1951-02-10

379. "Church Services," *Aberdeen Daily News*, November 1, 1951 https://aberdeennews.newsbank.com/doc/image/v2%3A114175180414EFE8%40NGPA-SDAN-120F584EF0F5D428%402433952-120CC09491237768%4019-120CC09491237768%40?search_terms=auerbach&date_from=1951&date_to=1951&text=auerbach&pub%255B0%255D=114175180414EFE8&sort=old&page=6&pdate=1951-11-01f

380. "Church Services," *Aberdeen Daily News*, February 28, 1951 https://aberdeennews.newsbank.com/doc/image/v2:114175180414EFE8@NGPA-SDAN-120F1FB4F0C37D70@2433706-120CC00F67DD1400@11-120CC00F67DD1400@?search_terms

381. "Youth Week Observed Here," *Aberdeen Daily News*, April 22, 1952 https://aberdeennews.newsbank.com/doc/image/v2:114175180414EFE8@NGPA-SDAN-12103C6C804F5498@2434125-120CC0FC632D0CF8@11-120CC0FC632D0CF8@?search_terms

382. "Church Services," *Aberdeen Daily News*, July 7, 1951 https://aberdeennews.newsbank.com/doc/image/v2:114175180414EFE8@NGPA-SDAN-120F21CBF33B99C0@2433835-120CC0478F2647D8@9-120CC0478F2647D8@?search_terms

383. "A Founder's Day Tea Marked a Meeting of Howard-Hedger PTA," *Aberdeen Daily News*, February 18, 1951 https://aberdeennews.newsbank.com/doc/image/v2:114175180414EFE8@NGPA-SDAN-120F1F88E1ECE020@2433696-120CC00ACB86B6D0@12-120CC00ACB86B6D0@?search_terms

384. "Membership to YW to be Stressed," *Aberdeen Daily News*, March 25, 1951 https://aberdeennews.newsbank.com/doc/image/v2:114175180414EFE8@NGPA-SDAN-120F20296DD5F2A0@2433731-120CC01CA2F11568@15-120CC01CA2F11568@?search_termsbea

385. "Church Services," *Aberdeen Daily News*, September 21, 1951 https://aberdeennews.newsbank.com/doc/image/v2:114175180414EFE8@NGPA-SDAN-120F57C11E4F8198@2433911-120CC074118C08F0@9-120CC074118C08F0@?search_terms

386. "Church Services, *Aberdeen Daily News*, October 19, 1951 https://aberdeennews.newsbank.com/doc/image/v2:114175180414EFE8@NGPA-SDAN-120F5828764C96C8@2433939-120CC08A584188A0@12-120CC08A584188A0@?search_terms

387. Sadly, Skar entered a life of crime and was gunned down in Chicago only fourteen years later. Chicago Tribune, September 11, 1065.

388. "Church Services," *Aberdeen Daily News*, February 24, 1951

https://aberdeennews.newsbank.com/doc/image/v2:114175180414EFE8@NGPA-SDAN-120F1FA23A4396A0@2433702-120CC00CE06B8F80@9-120CC00CE06B8F80@?search_terms

389. "Hebrew School in City Hall,: Jewish Post, *Hoosier State Chronicles*, March 9, 1951 https://newspapers.library.in.gov/?a=d&d=JPOST19510309-01&e=-------en-20--1--txt-txIN-------

390. https://aberdeennews.newsbank.com/doc/image/v2:114175180414EFE8@NGPA-SDAN-120F20D7CDE023A8@2433773-120CC032C895DC58@23-120CC032C895DC58@?search_terms

391. "Dakota Council of B'nai Brith Opens," *Aberdeen Daily News*, May 6, 1951 https://aberdeennews.newsbank.com/doc/image/v2:114175180414EFE8@NGPA-SDAN-120F206576D1DFE0@2433745-120CC0259668B5A8@15-120CC0259668B5A8@?search_terms

392. "Annual Donor Dinner Given, *Aberdeen Daily News*, April 30, 1952 https://aberdeennews.newsbank.com/doc/image/v2:114175180414EFE8@NGPA-SDAN-12103C84DC52B798@2434133-120CC0FE50C71EC8@8-120CC0FE50C71EC8@?search_terms

393. Ibid.

394. Paul Guttmann Solomon interview recorded by author, April 27, 2021.

395. Ibid.

396. Ibid.

397. Ibid.

398. Oral History , Bea, Herschel and Gail, May 18, 2018.

399. Bea Levy interview, Feb 15, 2022

400. "New Men's Store to Open in Hub," *Aberdeen Daily News*, January 11, 1951 https://aberdeennews.newsbank.com/doc/image/v2:114175180414EFE8@NGPA-SDAN-120F1EB14EB2E4C8@2433658-120CBFFB77C10688@7-120CBFFB77C10688@?search_terms

401. https://aberdeennews.newsbank.com/doc/news/105C2F8D0E014574?[nb_api_views_search_terms]&[nb_api_views_query_string]&pdate=2004-09-19

402. Leland Frankman oral history taken by author, April 29, 2021.

403. Ibid.

404. Ibid.

405. Ibid.

406. "Rabbi Auerbach to leave and Rabbi Kertes to come to Aberdeen," *American Jewish World*, Vol. 42, No. 1, September 4, 1953 https://umedia.lib.umn.edu/item/p16022coll529:16110/p16022coll529:16023?child_index=17&page=12&q=mary%20pewe&query=kert&rows=50&sidebar_page=1&sort=title_sort%20asc%2C%20date_created_sort%20desc

407. "Rabbi Kertes Finds Friendliness Here," *Aberdeen Daily News*, January 24, 1954 https://www.genealogybank.com/doc/newspapers/image/v2%3A114175180414EFE8%40GB3NEWS-121EEC6569695D38%402434767-121DE2FBF22C21A8%4014-121DE2FBF22C21A8%40?h=11&fname=&mname=&lname=kertes&kwinc=&kwexc=&rgfromDate=1950&rgtoDate=1970&formDate=&formDateFlex=exact&dateType=range&processingtime=&addedFrom=&addedTo=&sort=old&sid=bymcupkzorxgeurgbdverhgiutlateve_wma-gateway016_1644350325749

408. Gail Pickus, Bea and Herschel Premack interview recorded by author, May 18, 2018.

409. "Rabbi Auerbach to leave and Rabbi Kertes to come to Aberdeen,"September 4, 1953 https://umedia.lib.umn.edu/item/p16022coll529:16110/p16022coll529:16023?child_index=17&page=12&q=mary%20opewe&query=kert&rows=50&sidebar_page=1&sort=title_

sort%20asc%2C%20date_created_sort%20desc

410. Premack, Herschel "Phone conversation with author," February 13, 2022.

411. "Conservative Judaism," New World Encyclopedia https://www.newworldencyclopedia.org/entry/Conservative_Judaism (accessed March 31, 2022).

412. "Aberdeen Rabbi on Committee," *Aberdeen Daily News*, February 27, 1953 https://www.genealogybank.com/doc/newspapers/image/v2%3A114175180414EFE8%40GB 3NEWS-12103E2782A2ED40%402434436-120CD8DBD7663FE8%409-120CD8DBD7663F E8%40?h=1&fname=&mname=&lname=kertes&kwinc=&kwexc=&rgfromDate=1950&rg toDate=1970&formDate=&formDateFlex=exact&dateType=range&processingtime=&ad dedFrom=&addedTo=&sort=old&sid=bymcupkzorxgeurgbdverhgiutlateve_wma-gate way016_1644350325749

413. "Kertes Family is Honored," *Aberdeen Daily News*, March 25, 1953 https:// www.genealogybank.com/doc/newspapers/image/v2%3A114175180414EFE8%40GB 3NEWS-12103EBFACBE3558%402434462-120CD8E62219D3F0%405-120CD8E62219D3F 0%40?h=3&fname=&mname=&lname=kertes&kwinc=&kwexc=&rgfromDate=1950&rg toDate=1970&formDate=&formDateFlex=exact&dateType=range&processingtime=&ad dedFrom=&addedTo=&sort=old&sid=bymcupkzorxgeurgbdverhgiutlateve_wma-gate way016_1644350325749

414. "Rabbi Kertes Finds Friendliness Here," *Aberdeen Daily News*, January 24, 1954.

415. "Memorial Day Program, *Aberdeen Daily News*, May 28, 1953 https://www. genealogybank.com/doc/newspapers/image/v2%3A114175180414EFE8%40GB 3NEWS-121009FB380B0BC0%402434526-120CD9A0CE67BE80%402-120CD9A0CE67B E80%40?h=6&fname=&mname=&lname=kertes&kwinc=&kwexc=&rgfromDate=1950&rg toDate=1970&formDate=&formDateFlex=exact&dateType=range&processingtime=&ad dedFrom=&addedTo=&sort=old&sid=bymcupkzorxgeurgbdverhgiutlateve_wma-gate way016_1644350325749

416. "Memorial Service ot Highlight Veterans Day," *Aberdeen Daily News*, November 7, 1954 https://www.genealogybank.com/doc/newspapers/image/v2%3A114175180414E FE8%40GB3NEWS-120FFF234AD404B8%402435054-120D72F003FFF0E8%405-120D 72F003FFF0E8%40?h=27&fname=&mname=&lname=kertes&rgfromDate=1950&rgto Date=1958&formDate=&formDateFlex=exact&dateType=range&kwinc=&kw exc=&sort=old&page=1&sid=utwsczjatlaomgfffrqiqpmzexshvdzg_wma-gate way010_1644362551523

417. "Several Hundred Attend Program," *Aberdeen Daily News*, November 11, 1955 https://aberdeennews.newsbank.com/doc/image/v2:114175180414EFE8@NGPA-SDAN-121250D15117F230@2435423-120F0809A4938A68@11-120F0809A4938A68@?search_terms

418. "Rabbi Kertes Finds Friendliness Here," *Aberdeen Daily News*, January 24, 1954

419. "Eleven Persons were in the Class of Naturalization," *Aberdeen Daily News*, June 16, 1954 https://www.genealogybank.com/doc/newspapers/image/v2%3A114175180414E-FE8%40GB3NEWS-121EEF3DA3209590%402434910-121D5800F4264BC8%4017-121D5800F4264BC8%40?h=22&fname=&mname=&lname=kertes&rgfromDate=1 950&rgtoDate=1958&formDate=&formDateFlex=exact&dateType=range&kwinc=&k wexc=&sort=old&page=1&sid=utwsczjatlaomgfffrqiqpmzexshvdzg_wma-gate way010_1644362551523

420. "Young Church People Invited to Synagogue," *Aberdeen Daily News*, January 20, 1954 https://www.genealogybank.com/doc/newspapers/image/v2%3A114175180414E-FE8%40GB3NEWS-121EEC5BA2109C90%402434763-121D57F5F9A34F60%405-1

21D57F5F9A34F60%40?h=10&fname=&mname=&lname=kertes&rgfromDate=1950&rgto
Date=1958&formDate=&formDateFlex=exact&dateType=range&kwinc=&kwex
c=&sort=old&sid=utwsczjatlaomgfffrqiqpmzexshvdzg_wma-gateway010_1644362551523

421. "Weekly Meditation," *Aberdeen Daily News*, February 27, 1954
https://www.genealogybank.com/doc/newspapers/image/v2%3A114175180414EFE8%40GB
3NEWS-121EECD252654A20%402434801-121DE9979414DA98%402-121DE9979414DA98%4
0?h=15&fname=&mname=&lname=kertes&rgfromDate=1950&rgtoDate=1958&formDate=
&formDateFlex=exact&dateType=range&kwinc=&kwexc=&sort=old&sid=utwsczjatlaomgff
frqiqpmzexshvdzg_wma-gateway010_1644362551523

422. Weekly Meditation," *Aberdeen Daily News*, December 4, 1954 News,https://
www.genealogybank.com/doc/newspapers/image/v2%3A114175180414EFE8%40GB
3NEWS-1210015F4E845EA0%402435081-120F0DAE4316C580%402-120F0DAE4316C580%
40?h=31&fname=&mname=&lname=kertes&rgfromDate=1950&rgtoDate=1958&formDate=
&formDateFlex=exact&dateType=range&kwinc=&kwexc=&sort=old&page=2&sid=ut
wsczjatlaomgfffrqiqpmzexshvdzg_wma-gateway010_1644362551523

423. "Church Census Sunday to Launch 3-week Religious Program Here," *Aberdeen Daily
News*, September 12, 1956
https://www.genealogybank.com/doc/newspapers/image/v2%3A114175180414E
FE8%40GB3NEWS-12135886AEA0C098%402435729-12111927E7E-
CEE98%4016-12111927E7ECEE98%40?h=79&fname=&mname=&lname=kertes&rg
fromDate=1950&rgtoDate=1958&formDate=&formDateFlex=exact&dateType=range&k
winc=&kwexc=&sort=old&page=5&sid=utwsczjatlaomgfffrqiqpmzexshvdzg_wma-gate
way010_1644362551523

424. "Rabbi Kertes to Speak at Camp," *Aberdeen Daily News*, June 26, 1955
https://www.genealogybank.com/doc/newspapers/image/v2%3A114175180414E
FE8%40GB3NEWS-12100EEB156A19F8%402435285-120D741DEE2B5600%407-120D
741DEE2B5600%40?h=46&fname=&mname=&lname=kertes&rgfromDate=1950&rg
toDate=1958&formDate=&formDateFlex=exact&dateType=range&kwinc=&k
wexc=&sort=old&page=3&sid=utwsczjatlaomgfffrqiqpmzexshvdzg_wma-gate
way010_1644362551523

425. "Ministerial Assn Hears Dr. Kertes," *Aberdeen Daily News*, December
9, 1954 https://www.genealogybank.com/doc/newspapers/image/
v2%3A114175180414EFE8%40GB3NEWS-1210018CBA380D80%402435086-12
0F103ED36879B0%4014-120F103ED36879B0%40?h=32&fname=&mname=&l
name=kertes&rgfromDate=1950&rgtoDate=1958&formDate=&formDateFlex=exact&da
teType=range&kwinc=&kwexc=&sort=old&page=2&sid=utwsczjatlaomgfffrqiqpmzexsh
vdzg_wma-gateway010_1644362551523

426. Gail Pickus, Bea and Herschel Premack interview recorded by author, May 18, 2018.

427. Ibid

.428. "Message of Hope Seen in 'Purim,'" *Aberdeen Daily News*, March 20, 1954
https://www.genealogybank.com/doc/newspapers/image/v2%3A114175180414E
FE8%40GB3NEWS-121EED1DE9F81C30%402434822-121D57FAAAC7DF
B0%409-121D57FAAAC7DFB0%40?h=16&fname=&mname=&lname=kertes&rgfrom
Date=1950&rgtoDate=1958&formDate=&formDateFlex=exact&dateType=range&k
winc=&kwexc=&sort=old&page=1&sid=utwsczjatlaomgfffrqiqpmzexshvdzg_wma-gate
way010_1644362551523

429. "New Year Message," *Aberdeen Daily News*, December 30, 1955
https://www.genealogybank.com/doc/newspapers/image/v2%3A114175180414E
FE8%40GB3NEWS-121257EE837C1AE8%402435472-120F0815E35E5628%405-120F

0815E35E5628%40?h=55&fname=&mname=&lname=kertes&rgfromDate=1950&rg
toDate=1958&formDate=&formDateFlex=exact&dateType=range&kwinc=&k
wexc=&sort=old&page=3&sid=utwsczjatlaomgfffrqiqpmzexshvdzg_wma-gate
way010_1644362551523

430. "Easter, Passover Fall on Same Day this Year," *Aberdeen Daily News*, April 17, 1954
https://www.genealogybank.com/doc/newspapers/image/v2%3A114175180414E
FE8%40GB3NEWS-121EED84CD7D2BB8%402434850-121D57FCAE1FBD40%4
01-121D57FCAE1FBD40%40?h=18&fname=&mname=&lname=kertes&rgfrom
Date=1950&rgtoDate=1958&formDate=&formDateFlex=exact&dateType=range&k-
winc=&kwexc=&sort=old&page=1&sid=utwsczjatlaomgfffrqiqpmzexshvdzg_wma-gate
way010_1644362551523

431. "Jewish Synagogue to Usher In New Year," *Aberdeen Daily News*, September 25, 1954
https://www.genealogybank.com/doc/newspapers/image/v2%3A114175180414E
FE8%40GB3NEWS-121465A130E30F78%402435011-1211651E324E5778%401-12116
51E324E5778%40?h=25&fname=&mname=&lname=kertes&rgfromDate=1950&rg
toDate=1958&formDate=&formDateFlex=exact&dateType=range&kwinc=&k
wexc=&sort=old&page=1&sid=utwsczjatlaomgfffrqiqpmzexshvdzg_wma-gate
way010_1644362551523

432. "Jewish Pentecost to be Observed," *Aberdeen Daily News*, June 4, 1954
https://www.genealogybank.com/doc/newspapers/image/v2%3A114175180414E
FE8%40GB3NEWS-121EEF022B4BD108%402434898-121D580028E2BC60%4015-121
D580028E2BC60%40?h=20&fname=&mname=&lname=kertes&rgfromDate=1950&rg
toDate=1958&formDate=&formDateFlex=exact&dateType=range&kwinc=&k
wexc=&sort=old&page=1&sid=utwsczjatlaomgfffrqiqpmzexshvdzg_wma-gate
way010_1644362551523

433. "Artist for Life," *Aberdeen Magazine*, September/October, 2015 https://aberdeenmag.
com/2015/10/artist-for-life/

434. Bea and Herschel Premack interview recorded by author, May 19, 2018.

435. "Walter W. Ross: The Founder of Beta Sigma Phi," *Beta Sigma Phi International for the
Best Friends of you Life*, https://bspinternational.org/History.php

436. "Texas 'Snowbird' Named First Lady of Aberdeen," *Aberdeen American*, March 3, 1996
https://aberdeennews.newsbank.com/doc/image/v2:114175180414EFE8@NGPA-SDAN-
121F2DBBE0802508@2450146-121D3D0F93E640E8@32-121D3D0F93E640E8@?search_
terms

437. Ibid.

438. Ibid.

439. Ibid.

440. Ibid.

441. "B'nai B'rith Elects Officers," *Aberdeen Daily News*, April 14, 1953
https://www.genealogybank.com/doc/newspapers/image/v2%3A114175180414EFE8%40GB
3NEWS-121008AE7541F8E0%402434482-120CD994C9B1A4C8%4011-120CD994C9B1A4
C8%40?h=4&fname=&mname=&lname=kertes&kwinc=&kwexc=&rgfromDate=1950&rg
toDate=1970&formDate=&formDateFlex=exact&dateType=range&processingtime=&ad
dedFrom=&addedTo=&sort=old&sid=bymcupkzorxgeurgbdverhgiutlateve_wma-gate
way016_1644350325749

442. "Audiences Informed, Entertained at Teas, *Aberdeen Daily News*, March 27, 1955
https://www.genealogybank.com/doc/newspapers/image/v2%3A114175180414E
FE8%40GB3NEWS-12103A6D7B94DA78%402435194-120F628538BD1DB0%4014-120F

628538BD1DB0%40?h=40&fname=&mname=&lname=kertes&rgfromDate=1950&rgto
Date=1958&formDate=&formDateFlex=exact&dateType=range&kwinc=&kw
exc=&sort=old&page=2&sid=utwsczjatlaomgfffrqiqpmzexshvdzg_wma-gate
way010_1644362551523

443. "11th Donor Dinner Held by Hadassah," *Aberdeen Daily News*, May 25, 1955
https://www.genealogybank.com/doc/newspapers/image/v2%3A114175180414E
FE8%40GB3NEWS-12103F0A6915D280%402435253-120F7027B447C230%4010-120
F7027B447C230%40?h=44&fname=&mname=&lname=kertes&rgfromDate=1950&rg
toDate=1958&formDate=&formDateFlex=exact&dateType=range&kwinc=&k
wexc=&sort=old&page=2&sid=utwsczjatlaomgfffrqiqpmzexshvdzg_wma-gate
way010_1644362551523

444. "Final Rites Held for W. Ribnick," *Aberdeen Daily News*, January 28, 1954
https://www.genealogybank.com/doc/newspapers/image/v2%3A114175180414EFE8%40GB
3NEWS-121EEC75F3B83C00%402434771-121D57F6A25DE1D0%4017-121D57F6A25DE
1D0%40?h=14&fname=&mname=&lname=kertes&rgfromDate=1950&rgtoDate=1958&
formDate=&formDateFlex=exact&dateType=range&kwinc=&kwexc=&sort=old&sid=ut
wsczjatlaomgfffrqiqpmzexshvdzg_wma-gateway010_1644362551523

445. A History of the Jewish Community of Aberdeen, South Dakota, 1887-1964 by Bernice
Premack.

446. "Final Rites Held for W. Ribnick," January 28, 1954.

447. "Goodman Rites Held on Friday," *Aberdeen Daily News*, June 10, 1956 https://www.
genealogybank.com/doc/newspapers/image/v2%3A114175180414EFE8%40GB3NEWS-
121266C65941B2C0%402435635-1210FF9158BD11A0%408-1210FF9158BD11A0%40?h=72&f
name=&mname=&lname=kertes&r=

448. "Local Deaths: Sam Levy," *Aberdeen Daily News*, May 15, 1971
https://www.genealogybank.com/doc/newspapers/image/v2%3A114175180414EFE8%40GB
3NEWS-1216A3EA462CBBF8%402441087-1216503504A01CD0%402-1216503504A01CD0
%40?h=10&fname=rABBI&mname=&lname=BERGLAS&kwinc=&kwexc=&sort=old&rg
fromDate=&rgtoDate=&formDate=&formDateFlex=exact&dateType=range&process
ingtime=&addedFrom=&addedTo=&sid=bikbhutnzjrayatzepuucyjrkhihigyy_wma-gate
way005_1644790311773

449. "Practically the Whole Megillah,"April 26, 1979.

450. Jay Kirschenmann, "It's About Time: Olwin Angell building downtown has housed
stores, apartments and a gym," *Aberdeen News*, September 20, 2019
https://www.aberdeennews.com/story/opinion/columns/2019/09/20/its-about-time-olwin-
angell-building-downtown-has-housed-stores-apartments-and-a-gym/44366005/

451. "Reception Given at Synagogue," *Aberdeen Daily News*, April 15, 1956 https://
www.genealogybank.com/doc/newspapers/image/v2%3A114175180414EFE8%40GB
3NEWS-121264FC4EA2B828%402435579-12103B3A30CB1E90%4011-12103B3A30CB1E90%
40?h=67&fname=&mname=&lname=kertes&rgfromDate=1950&rgtoDate=1958&formDate
=&formDateFlex=exact&dateType=range&kwinc=&kwexc=&sort=old&page=4&sid=ut
wsczjatlaomgfffrqiqpmzexshvdzg_wma-gateway010_1644362551523

452. "The Public Voice: Festival of Hanukkoh," *Aberdeen Daily News*, December 8, 1955
https://www.genealogybank.com/doc/newspapers/image/v2%3A114175180414E
FE8%40GB3NEWS-121252AF67604AB0%402435450-120F081173CB1C08%403-120F
081173CB1C08%40?h=54&fname=&mname=&lname=kertes&rgfromDate=1950&rg
toDate=1958&formDate=&formDateFlex=exact&dateType=range&kwinc=&k
wexc=&sort=old&page=3&sid=utwsczjatlaomgfffrqiqpmzexshvdzg_wma-gate
way010_1644362551523

453. "Synagogue's Mortgage is Burned," *Aberdeen Daily News*, January 17, 1956
https://www.genealogybank.com/doc/newspapers/image/v2%3A114175180414E
FE8%40GB3NEWS-121258876C90D428%402435490-120F0818256EFA30%405-120F

0818256EFA30%40?h=56&fname=&mname=&lname=kertes&rgfromDate=1950&rg
toDate=1958&formDate=&formDateFlex=exact&dateType=range&kwinc=&k
wexc=&sort=old&page=3&sid=utwsczjatlaomgfffrqiqpmzexshvdzg_wma-gate
way010_1644362551523

454. "Dr. Kertes Leaves Hub," *Aberdeen Daily News*, September 30, 1956
https://www.genealogybank.com/doc/newspapers/image/v2%3A114175180414EFE8%40GB
3NEWS-1213592BD9443B30%402435747-1211549A71E59328%408-1211549A71E59328%4
0?h=80&fname=&mname=&lname=kertes&kwinc=&kwexc=&rgfromDate=1950&rgto
Date=1970&formDate=&formDateFlex=exact&dateType=range&processingtime=&ad
dedFrom=&addedTo=&sort=old&page=5&sid=bymcupkzorxgeurgbdverhgiutlateve_
wma-gateway016_1644350325749

455. "New Rabbi Comes Here," *Aberdeen Daily News*, March 5, 1957
https://www.genealogybank.com/doc/newspapers/image/v2%3A114175180414E
FE8%40GB3NEWS-1213608C0F1A5158%402435903-1211AEA839882640%402-1211A
EA839882640%40?h=82&fname=&mname=&lname=kertes&rgfromDate=1950&rg
toDate=1958&formDate=&formDateFlex=exact&dateType=range&kwinc=&k
wexc=&sort=old&page=5&sid=utwsczjatlaomgfffrqiqpmzexshvdzg_wma-gate
way010_1644362551523

456. "Passover to be Observed," *Aberdeen Daily News*, April 9, 1957
https://www.genealogybank.com/doc/newspapers/image/v2%3A114175180414EFE8%40GB
3NEWS-121361286080C148%402435938-1211B6A24408F968%402-1211B6A24408F968%40?
h=39&fname=&mname=&lname=glassman&rgfromDate=&rgtoDate=&formDate=&formD
ateFlex=exact&dateType=range&kwinc=&kwexc=&sort=old&page=2&sid=oiyjxwlwtdcv
vcayqzhjqtzqlkuvylgp_wma-gateway016_1643169407920

457. Bea and Herschel Premack interview recorded by author, May 19, 2018.

458. "One of the Newest Families in Aberdeen," *Aberdeen Daily News*, August 10, 1958
https://aberdeennews.newsbank.com/doc/image/v2:114175180414EFE8@NGPA-SDAN-
12121173B3DCE6B8@2436426-12115AE90F65A680@16-12115AE90F65A680@?search_terms

459. "Two Parties Fete Birthday," *Aberdeen Daily News*, October 22, 1958
https://www.genealogybank.com/doc/newspapers/image/v2%3A114175180414EFE8%40GB
3NEWS-121212B13A510420%402436499-120FF9DD184FD8B0%409-120FF9DD184FD8B
0%40?h=21&fname=&mname=&lname=eisenberg&kwinc=&kwexc=&sort=old&rgfrom
Date=1957&rgtoDate=1975&formDate=&formDateFlex=exact&dateType=range&process
ingtime=&addedFrom=&addedTo=&page=1&sid=ipamvzjquchlyqxodjaxcwlteqypnhcu_
wma-gateway006_1643169975866

460. "Afternoon Group Has Picnic," *Aberdeen Daily News*, August 17, 1958
https://www.genealogybank.com/doc/newspapers/image/v2%3A114175180414EFE8%40GB
3NEWS-1212118FC8CB3C68%402436433-12115B2C851CCEB0%4018-12115B2C851CCEB
0%40?h=12&fname=&mname=&lname=eisenberg&kwinc=&kwexc=&sort=old&rgfrom
Date=1957&rgtoDate=1975&formDate=&formDateFlex=exact&dateType=range&process
ingtime=&addedFrom=&addedTo=&sid=ipamvzjquchlyqxodjaxcwlteqypnhcu_wma-gate
way006_1643169975866

461. "Church Services," *Aberdeen Daily News*, November 22, 1958 file:///C:/Users/histo/
Downloads/Aberdeen_Daily_News_1958-11-22_5.pdf

462. "Children's Program Held at Synagogue," *Aberdeen Daily News*,
December 13, 1958 https://www.genealogybank.com/doc/newspapers/image/
v2%3A114175180414EFE8%40GB3NEWS-1212156E4739D698%402436551-121166A

45DCC9210%402-121166A45DCC9210%40?h=31&fname=&mname=&lname=eisen
berg&kwinc=&kwexc=&sort=old&rgfromDate=1957&rgtoDate=1975&formDate=&
formDateFlex=exact&dateType=range&processingtime=&addedFrom=&added
To=&page=2&sid=ipamvzjquchlyqxodjaxcwlteqypnhcu_wma-gateway006_1643169975866

463. "Holiday Observance Marks Jewish Victory," *Aberdeen Daily News*, December 6, 1958
https://www.genealogybank.com/doc/newspapers/image/v2%3A114175180414EFE8%40GB
3NEWS-1212155617BDE950%402436544-12116654DFBC2928%404-12116654DFBC2928
%40?h=28&fname=&mname=&lname=eisenberg&kwinc=&kwexc=&sort=old&rgfrom
Date=1957&rgtoDate=1975&formDate=&formDateFlex=exact&dateType=range&process
ingtime=&addedFrom=&addedTo=&page=1&sid=ipamvzjquchlyqxodjaxcwlteqypnhcu_
wma-gateway006_1643169975866

464. "Local Rabbi Announces Resignation," *Aberdeen Daily News*, March 9, 1959
https://www.genealogybank.com/doc/newspapers/image/v2%3A114175180414EFE8%40GB
3NEWS-121216A8CD4F49A0%402436637-1211A7F059250AD0%404-1211A7F059250AD
0%40?h=32&fname=&mname=&lname=eisenberg&kwinc=&kwexc=&sort=old&rgfrom
Date=1957&rgtoDate=1975&formDate=&formDateFlex=exact&dateType=range&process
ingtime=&addedFrom=&addedTo=&page=2&sid=ipamvzjquchlyqxodjaxcwlteqypnhcu_
wma-gateway006_1643169975866

465. "Farewell Luncheon for Mrs. Eisenberg," *Aberdeen Daily News*, June 17, 1959
https://www.genealogybank.com/doc/newspapers/image/v2%3A114175180414EFE8%40GB
3NEWS-121217BE520BEB38%402436737-120FF9FD43B11D38%4015-120FF9FD43B11D3
8%40?h=40&fname=&mname=&lname=eisenberg&kwinc=&kwexc=&sort=old&rgfrom
Date=1957&rgtoDate=1975&formDate=&formDateFlex=exact&dateType=range&process
ingtime=&addedFrom=&addedTo=&page=2&sid=ipamvzjquchlyqxodjaxcwlteqypnhcu_
wma-gateway006_1643169975866

466. "Dr. Kertes Returns to Aberdeen," *Aberdeen Daily News*, July 10, 1959
https://www.genealogybank.com/doc/newspapers/image/v2%3A114175180414EFE8%40GB
3NEWS-121217F5DD1C6480%402436760-1211FB0C6022C2C8%402-1211FB0C6022C2C
8%40?h=1&fname=&mname=&lname=kertes&rgfromDate=1959&rgtoDate=1965&form
Date=&formDateFlex=exact&dateType=range&kwinc=&kwexc=&sort=old&sid=rymcvygt
ftcfyugmcykrlqvzsotkqvtp_wma-gateway003_1644442545551

467. "Rabbi Talks at Meeting," *Aberdeen Daily News*, July 22, 1959
https://www.genealogybank.com/doc/newspapers/image/v2%3A114175180414EFE8%40GB
3NEWS-1212181076DE5B30%402436772-1211FB8F0CA3F258%405-1211FB8F0CA3F258%40
?h=2&fname=&mname=&lname=kertes&rgfromDate=1959&rgtoDate=1965&formDate=&
formDateFlex=exact&dateType=range&kwinc=&kwexc=&sort=old&sid=rymcvygtftcfyug
mcykrlqvzsotkqvtp_wma-gateway003_1644442545551

468. "Aid Plans Brunch, Bake Sale, *Aberdeen Daily News*, September 11, 1959
https://www.genealogybank.com/doc/newspapers/image/v2%3A114175180414EFE8%40GB
3NEWS-1215B0E510B0C420%402436823-121258F09182B250%406-121258F09182B250%4
0?h=3&fname=&mname=&lname=kertes&rgfromDate=1959&rgtoDate=1965&formDate=&
formDateFlex=exact&dateType=range&kwinc=&kwexc=&sort=old&sid=rymcvygtftcfyug
mcykrlqvzsotkqvtp_wma-gateway003_1644442545551

469. "The Judeo-Christian Meanings of Passover and Easter," *Aberdeen Daily News*, April
10, 1960
https://www.genealogybank.com/doc/newspapers/image/v2%3A114175180414EFE8%40GB
3NEWS-1216048A5EEBE8A8%402437035-1213B35ABB6A6748%4022-1213B35ABB6A6748%
40?h=13&fname=&mname=&lname=kertes&rgfromDate=1959&rgtoDate=1965&formDate

=&formDateFlex=exact&dateType=range&kwinc=&kwexc=&sort=old&sid=rymcvygtftcf
yugmcykrlqvzsotkqvtp_wma-gateway003_1644442545551

470. "A History of the Jewish Community of Aberdeen, South Dakota, 1887-1964," by Bernice Premack.

471. Dr. Kertes Leaving for Medical Reasons," *Aberdeen Daily News*, September 27, 1964
https://www.genealogybank.com/doc/newspapers/image/v2%3A114175180414EFE8%40GB
3NEWS-1215A321CB6E6828%402438666-1213A925167D04E0%4016-1213A925167D0
4E0%40?h=2&fname=abraham&mname=&lname=kertes&kwinc=&kwexc=&rgfrom
Date=1964&rgtoDate=1964&formDate=&formDateFlex=exact&dateType=range&pro
cessingtime=&addedFrom=&addedTo=&sid=rchtmrzeuftqhwhcjyvdnodcjwduhmzl_
wma-gateway003_1648662312529

472. "Dr. Kertes Dies in California, *Aberdeen Daily News*, October 21, 1965
https://www.genealogybank.com/doc/newspapers/image/v2%3A114175180414EFE8%40GB
3NEWS-1215F760F6739728%402439055-1214A3EE13B0BDB0%402-1214A3EE13B0BD
B0%40?h=2&fname=&mname=&lname=kertes&rgfromDate=1959&rgtoDate=1965&form
Date=&formDateFlex=exact&dateType=range&kwinc=&kwexc=&sort=bst&sid=rymcvygt
ftcfyugmcykrlqvzsotkqvtp_wma-gateway003_1644442545551

473. Gail Pickus, Bea and Herschel Premack interview recorded by author, May 18, 2018.

474. "Sale Set by Jewish Ladies Aid, *Aberdeen Daily News*, September 19, 1965
https://www.genealogybank.com/doc/newspapers/image/v2%3A114175180414EFE8%40GB
3NEWS-1215F5FF92FAE300%402439023-12107639B4A37AA8%4011-12107639B4A37AA8
%40?h=3&fname=&mname=&lname=finkel&rgfromDate=&rgtoDate=&formDate=&form
DateFlex=exact&dateType=range&kwinc=Rabbi&kwexc=&sid=ygqeckaxlqbvuzlhzgsvnd
jakdxdfbel_wma-gateway009_1643300616252

475. Gail Pickus, Bea and Herschel Premack interview recorded by author, May 18, 2018.

476. Esther Mazor telephone interviews with the author, Feb 16, 2022 and Feb 20, 2022.

477. Ibid.

478. Ibid.

479. Ibid.

480. "Holocaust Encyclopedia: Tehran Children," United States Holocaust Memorial and Museum, https://encyclopedia.ushmm.org/content/en/article/tehran-children (accessed March 15, 2022).

481. Gail Pickus, Bea and Herschel Premack interview recorded by author, May 18, 2018.

482. "Their Roots in Poland and Israel," *Aberdeen Daily News*, March 5, 1967
&formDate=&formDateFlex=exact&dateType=range&kwinc=&kwexc=&-
sort=old&sid=btlfjkggffxjpylixuirnljmzahyfetv_s074_1644445075315

483. Esther Mazor telephone interviews with the author, Feb 16, 2022 and Feb 20, 2022.

484. Ibid.

485. Ibid.

486. Ibid.

487. Ibid.

488. Ibid.

489. Ibid.

490. Ibid.

491. Dr. James Strosberg, written recollection sent to to Bea Premack, 1987.

492. Esther Mazor telephone interviews with the author, Feb 16, 2022 and Feb 20, 2022.

493. Ibid.

494. Ibid.

495. Ibid.

496. Ibid.

497. Ibid.

498. Ibid.

499. Ibid.

500. Ibid.

501. Ibid.

502. Ibid.

503. "Their Roots in Poland and Israel," March 5, 1967.

504. Ibid.

505. "The God and Country Ner Tamid Award," *Aberdeen Daily News*, February 11, 1968 https://www.genealogybank.com/doc/newspapers/image/v2%3A114175180414EFE8%40GB 3NEWS-121167A9C4B87348%402439898-12111E277AE1B718%4029-12111E277AE1B718%4 0?h=20&fname=&mname=&lname=Mazor&rgfromDate=&rgtoDate=&formDate=&form DateFlex=exact&dateType=range&kwinc=&kwexc=&sort=old&page=1&sid=btlfjkggffxj pylixuirnljmzahyfetv_s074_1644445075315

506. "First to Earn Award in Nyoda," *Aberdeen Daily News*, April 7, 1968 https://www.genealogybank.com/doc/newspapers/image/v2%3A114175180414EFE8%40GB 3NEWS-12116F6E5CC6AB30%402439954-12116D160A4D7768%4018-12116D160A4D7768% 40?h=28&fname=&mname=&lname=Mazor&rgfromDate=&rgtoDate=&formDate=&form DateFlex=exact&dateType=range&kwinc=&kwexc=&sort=old&page=1&sid=btlfjkggffxj pylixuirnljmzahyfetv_s074_1644445075315

507. "Feinstein's Fashion Forecast," *Aberdeen Daily News*, March 27, 1967 https://www.genealogybank.com/doc/newspapers/image/v2%3A114175180414EFE8%40GB 3NEWS-1216A44CA3C61C90%402439577-121116B894FA1A18%401-121116B894FA1A18%4 0?h=8&fname=&mname=&lname=Mazor&rgfromDate=&rgtoDate=&formDate=&form DateFlex=exact&dateType=range&kwinc=&kwexc=&sort=old&sid=btlfjkggffxjpylixuirnl jmzahyfetv_s074_1644445075315

508. "Models for Style Show Announced," *Aberdeen Daily News*, February 16, 1968, https://www.genealogybank.com/doc/newspapers/image/v2%3A114175180414EFE8%40GB 3NEWS-121167B2923F5748%402439903-12111E27DA33DAF0%4013-12111E27DA33DA F0%40?h=22&fname=&mname=&lname=Mazor&rgfromDate=&rgtoDate=&formDate=& formDateFlex=exact&dateType=range&kwinc=&kwexc=&sort=old&page=1&sid=btlfjkg gffxjpylixuirnljmzahyfetv_s074_1644445075315

509. "Mrs. Mazor Tells About Med. Center, *Aberdeen Daily News*, April 13, 1967 https:// www.genealogybank.com/doc/newspapers/image/v2%3A114175180414EFE8%40GB 3NEWS-1216A6AEF428E3D8%402439594-1214A8DA1EC3BF68%408-1214A8DA1EC3BF68 %40?h=9&fname=&mname=&lname=Mazor&rgfromDate=&rgtoDate=&formDate=&form DateFlex=exact&dateType=range&kwinc=&kwexc=&sort=old&sid=btlfjkggffxjpylixuirnl jmzahyfetv_s074_1644445075315

510. "Ancestry.com," relational database, *https://www.ancestry.com/* (https://www.ancestry.com/discoveryui-content/view/197670668:2238?tid=&pid=&query Id=a16d81ec87b0cb98d5ba61a8f07afa4a&_phsrc=PWt721&_phstart=successSource: April 3, 2022) U.S. World War II Draft Cards, 1940-47.

511. Judge Moses Lindau written recollections sent to Bea Premack, 1987.

512. Ibid.

513. Ibid.

514. Ibid.

515. Ibid.

516. "Birth of Daughter," *Aberdeen Daily News*, June 25, 1969 https://www.genealogybank. com/doc/newspapers/image/v2%3A114175180414EFE8%40GB3NEWS-12116EF7A13A1 2B0%402440428-12110B39D1071D98%4013-12110B39D1071D98%40?h=32&fname=&m

name=&lname=Mazor&rgfromDate=&rgtoDate=&formDate=&formDateFlex=exact&dateType=range&kwinc=&kwexc=&sort=old&page=2&sid=btlfjkggffxjpylixuirnljmzahyfetv_s074_1644445075315

517. "Jewish Ladies Aid Notes Holiday Plans," *Aberdeen Daily News*, September 24, 1967 https://www.genealogybank.com/doc/newspapers/image/v2%3A114175180414EFE8%40GB3NEWS-1211BE434DAC7918%402439758-1211183A4AD1FD30%4017-1211183A4AD1FD30%40?h=11&fname=&mname=&lname=Mazor&rgfromDate=&rgtoDate=&formDate=&formDateFlex=exact&dateType=range&kwinc=&kwexc=&sort=old&sid=btlfjkggffxjpylixuirnljmzahyfetv_s074_1644445075315

518. Ibid.

519. Bea and Herschel Premack interview recorded by author, May 19, 2018.

520. "Practically the Whole Megillah" May 1980.

521. Author notes from May 2018.

522. "This Day in History," *Brown County South Dakota*, https://brown.sd.us/dacotah-prairie-museum/news/this-week-in-history/mar24-31

523. "SDPB Supporter Spotlight: Charter Member, Bea Premack," *South Dakota Public Broadcasting*, June 4, 2021 https://www.sdpb.org/blogs/news-and-information/sdpb-supporter-spotlight-charter-member-bea-premack/

524. Bea and Herschel Premack interview recorded by author, May 19, 2018.

525. Dr. James Strosberg, written recollection sent to to Bea Premack, 1987.

526. Ibid.

527. Ibid.

528. Ibid.

529. Ibid.

530. Ibid.

531. Ibid.

532. Ibid.

533. "They Feel at Home in the Hub," *Aberdeen Daily News*, September 28, 1969 https://www.genealogybank.com/doc/newspapers/image/v2%3A114175180414EFE8%40GB3NEWS-12145E065FD78128%402440493-1211AB02519D1438%4011-1211AB02519D1438%40?h=4&fname=rABBI&mname=&lname=BERGLAS&kwinc=&kwexc=&sort=old&rgfromDate=&rgtoDate=&formDate=&formDateFlex=exact&dateType=range&processingtime=&addedFrom=&addedTo=&sid=bikbhutnzjrayatzepuucyjrkhihigyy_wma-gateway005_1644790311773

534. "ALCW has Program by Rabbi," *Aberdeen Daily News*, October 8, 1969 https://www.genealogybank.com/doc/newspapers/image/v2%3A114175180414EFE8%40GB3NEWS-12145E2726235DE0%402440503-1211AD8A60018AE0%4018-1211AD8A60018AE0%40?h=5&fname=rABBI&mname=&lname=BERGLAS&kwinc=&kwexc=&sort=old&rgfromDate=&rgtoDate=&formDate=&formDateFlex=exact&dateType=range&processingtime=&addedFrom=&addedTo=&sid=bikbhutnzjrayatzepuucyjrkhihigyy_wma-gateway005_1644790311773

535. "They Feel at Home in the Hub," September 28, 1969

536. "Bat Mitzvah for Wendy Feinstein," *Aberdeen Daily News*, September 7, 1969 https://www.genealogybank.com/doc/newspapers/image/v2%3A114175180414EFE8%40GB3NEWS-12145DA19AF5B3F0%402440472-12110DC4E678C528%4021-12110DC4E678C528%40?h=1&fname=rABBI&mname=&lname=BERGLAS&kwinc=&kwexc=&sort=old&rgfromDate=&rgtoDate=&formDate=&formDateFlex=exact&dateType=range&processingtime=&addedFrom=&addedTo=&sid=bikbhutnzjrayatzepuucyjrkhihigyy_wma-gateway005_1644790311773

537. "New Year Service Set," *Aberdeen Daily News*, September 11, 1969 https://aberdeennews.newsbank.com/doc/image/v2:114175180414EFE8@NGPA-SDAN-12145DC3C33A4F28@2440476-1211A72717B79438@2-1211A72717B79438@?search_terms

ABERDEEN: A JEWISH HISTORY

538. "Synagogue Youth to Meet Here," *Aberdeen Daily News*, May 2, 1971
https://www.genealogybank.com/doc/newspapers/image/v2%3A114175180414EFE8%40GB
3NEWS-1216A1BFFA0C8110%402441074-12164DD58177EA60%4010-12164DD58177EA6
0%40?h=9&fname=rABBI&mname=&lname=BERGLAS&kwinc=&kwexc=&sort=old&rg
fromDate=&rgtoDate=&formDate=&formDateFlex=exact&dateType=range&process
ingtime=&addedFrom=&addedTo=&sid=bikbhutnzjrayatzepuucyjrkhihigyy_wma-gate
way005_1644790311773

539. Manfred "Fred" Haeusler and his older sister, Debbie, children of Holocaust surivors, came from Minot, North Dakota, to this regional convention. Years later, Fred would marry Leslie Martin, who edited this book.

540. "Synagogue Youth to Meet Here," May 2, 1971.

541. Ibid.

542. "Tzedakah Maven: Danny Siegel," *issuu, Inc.*, https://issuu.com/torahaura/docs/
eizehu_gibor_ebook_2b5513f2a22099/s/10754455

543. Ibid.

544. Bea and Herschel Premack interview recorded by author, May 19, 2018.

545. https://www.findagrave.com/memorial/21974638/josef-berglas.

546. Bea and Herschel Premack interview recorded by author,, May 19, 2018.

547. Oral History Interview of Herschel and Bea Premack, taken by author, May 19, 2018, Aberdeen.

548. Ibid.

549. Ibid.

550. Adam Altman interview taken by author, June 25, 2021, Aberdeen.

551. Ibid.

552. Ibid.

553. "Hadassah's 60th Anniversary Being Observed Here This Week," *Aberdeen Daily News*, February 7, 1972
https://aberdeennews.newsbank.com/doc/image/v2:114175180414EFE8@NGPA-SDAN-
121A450BEC140AD8@2441355-121A419E48A85EA0@10-121A419E48A85EA0@?search_
terms

554. "Hadassah Chairmen Announced, *Aberdeen Daily News*, August 30, 1972 https://aber-
deennews.newsbank.com/doc/image/v2:114175180414EFE8@NGPA-SDAN-123DEAFC
9C0825C0@2441560-123D9B09D71CCF20@17-123D9B09D71CCF20@?search_terms

555. https://aberdeennews.newsbank.com/doc/image/v2:114175180414EFE8@NGPA-SDAN-
1214659984BA5F78@2442313-1211CA2FF7325348@14-1211CA2FF7325348@?search_terms

556. https://aberdeennews.newsbank.com/doc/image/v2:114175180414EFE8@NGPA-
SDAN-1217F2696D0F7A08@2443419-12159AF8C1A38A58@47-12159AF8C1A38A58@?
search_terms

557. "Contests Close," Aberdeen Daily News," June 5, 1974
https://aberdeennews.newsbank.com/doc/image/v2:114175180414EFE8@NGPA-SDAN-
1214613462178A00@2442204-1213FCE1A37773D8@2-1213FCE1A37773D8@?search_terms

558. "AFS Endeavors Bring Honor to Aberdonian," *Aberdeen Daily News*, October 26, 1975
https://aberdeennews.newsbank.com/doc/image/v2:114175180414EFE8@NGPA-SDAN-
1749D5C6C985450E@2442712-121164012C47E830@5-121164012C47E830@?search_terms

559. Conversation with Wendy Feinstein, January, 2022.

560. Ibid.

561. https://ballotpedia.org/Marc_Feinstein.

562. Practically the Whole Megillah May 1980.

563. "Aberdeen's Jewish Community Began Nearly a Century Ago," January 29, 1984.
https://www.genealogybank.com/doc/newspapers/image/v2%3A114175180414EFE8%40GB
3NEWS-1215FC8D5CC6BAD0%402445729-121413A7B8375B80%4077-121413A7B8375B80%
40?h=36&fname=&mname=&lname=Mazor&rgfromDate=&rgtoDate=&formDate=&form

DateFlex=exact&dateType=range&kwinc=&kwexc=&sort=old&page=2&sid=btlfjkggffxj
pylixuirnljmzahyfetv_s074_1644445075315

564. Ben Victor, "phone conversation with author," February 16, 2022.

565. https://benjaminvictor.com/2011/11/gallery/monuments-large-works/aberdeen-
war-memorial/

566. https://www.onlinenevada.org/articles/sarah-winnemucca

567. https://www.aoc.gov/explore-capitol-campus/art/sarah-winnemucca-statue

568. https://benjaminvictor.com/2012/01/gallery/monuments-large-works/sarah-
winnemucca-2/

569. https://benjaminvictor.com/biography/

570. Ardis, Kelly, "Bakersfield native breaks the mold with third statue at US capitol,"
Bakersfield.com, August 23, 2019
https://www.bakersfield.com/entertainment/bakersfield-native-breaks-the-mold-with-
third-statue-at-us/article_db88bdd0-c052-11e9-9a92-d352280efc06.html

571. Ben Victor, "phone conversation with author," February 16, 2022.

572. Ibid.

573. https://www.aberdeennews.com/obituaries/story-obituaries-2021-02-18-nathan-
green-43724661

574. https://www.aberdeenfuneralhome.com/obituary/Theresa-Green

575. Liz Sills and Matt Perreault interview taken by author, June 26, 2021.

576. Ibid.

577. Ibid.

578. Ibid.

579. Jerry Taylor "emails to author, December 2020."

580. Hubbard, Kaia, "The 10 States With the Least Racial Diversity," *U.S. News and World
Report*, August 23, 2021
https://www.usnews.com/news/best-states/slideshows/the-10-least-racially-diverse-
states-in-the-us?slide=2 (accessed August 31, 2021)

581. "State Register of Historic Places," https://history.sd.gov/preservation/docs/SRHP.pdf

CPSIA information can be obtained
at www.ICGtesting.com
Printed in the USA
BVHW012022231022
650107BV00004B/12

9 780999 310632